LONDON'S AMERICAN PAST

LONDON'S AMERICAN PAST

A Guided Tour

Fran Hazelton

Illustrations by Elizabeth Harbour

PAPERMAC

First published in 1991 by
PAPERMAC
a division of Macmillan Publishers Limited
4 Little Essex Street, London WC2R 3LF
and Basingstoke

Associated companies in Auckland, Delhi, Dublin, Gaborone,
Hamburg, Harare, Hong Kong, Johannesburg, Kuala Lumpur,
Lagos, Manzini, Melbourne, Mexico City, Nairobi, New York,
Singapore and Tokyo

ISBN 0-333-47451-1

A CIP catalogue record for this book is available
from the British Library

Typeset by Macmillan Production Limited, 4 Little Essex Street, London WC2

Printed in Hong Kong

To the memory of Mil Fleming (1946–88)
and John Horne Tooke, the Londoner who
was fined £1200 and imprisoned for a year
after he set up a relief fund for the widows and
orphans of American men killed by British
troops at Lexington and Concord in 1775

As an avid runner, I find London provides a unique benefit in the bits and pieces of history waiting around virtually every corner. When I recently passed a stately townhouse and noticed a plaque announcing that 'American patriot Benedict Arnold' had lived there, I did a classic double-take. Americans for centuries have had their own wide-ranging reactions to the abundant Americana they encounter in London, as the fascinating material unearthed by Fran Hazelton illustrates. Her London guide to America's past forms part of this unbroken chain of testimony to the enduring bonds between Britain and America.

Henry E. Catto
United States Ambassador to the United Kingdom

Contents

List of Maps

Acknowledgements

I would like to thank Joyce and Peter Hazelton for their expertise and example over the past twenty-five years in the business of presenting London and history to the public for enjoyment and entertainment as well as education; John Shirley and John Slater for encouragement at the initial stages of *London's American Past*; Andrew Davies for his vital role in getting the idea accepted and the research off the ground; the many American friends in London who helped along the way, particularly Coleen Rogers, Karmen Butler, Diane Evasick and Ariel Oaks; and my husband, Laith Hayali, for his electronic wizardry, etc.

Fran Hazelton
September 1990

Introduction

This book describes a twelve-mile guided walk linking more than a hundred places of American historical interest in London, from the Tower of London to Grosvenor Square.

The walk takes the reader down the highways and byways of London on a voyage of discovery through British and American history. At the well-known tourist sights such as St Paul's Cathedral, Covent Garden, Buckingham Palace, Trafalgar Square and Westminster Abbey is blazed a treasure-trail of little-known items which are a must for Americans in search of historical roots and a sense of the past.

Famous personalities encountered on the way include Sir Walter Ralegh, Virginia Dare, Princess Pocahontas, William Penn, Benjamin Franklin, Thomas Paine, George Washington, Benedict Arnold, Mrs Abigail Adams, Abraham Lincoln, Buffalo Bill, George Peabody, Mark Twain, Henry James, Scott Fitzgerald, Gordon Selfridge, Lady Nancy Astor, Harry Houdini and Franklin D. Roosevelt.

London's American Past covers the transatlantic explorations of the late fifteenth and the sixteenth centuries, the English colonisation of North America in the the seventeenth century, the birth of the independent United States of America in the eighteenth century and the changing economic, social, political and cultural relationship between London and the USA in the nineteenth and twentieth centuries.

The story begins in AD 878, when the church of St Clement Danes was founded in Aldwych. The Danish Norsemen – Vikings – living in London were a part of the great movement of people from Scandinavia which also led to European settlements being briefly established in North America at the end of the tenth century.

In 1489 Bartholomew Columbus – Christopher Columbus's brother – met King Henry VII in London and gave him a copy of Columbus's map of the world. According to Columbus's son, Ferdinando, his uncle had travelled to London 'to entreat of an agreement with the King of England for the discovery of the Indies' and when Henry 'had seen the map, and that which my father Christopher Columbus offered unto him, he accepted the offer with joyful countenance, and sent to call him into England.'[1]

So said Ferdinando Columbus. But according to a sixteenth-century Spanish historian, 'the king laughed at the idea, considering all that

Columbus had said to be nonsense.'² Whatever the truth of the matter, when Columbus landed on the Caribbean island of Hispaniola – now Haiti and the Dominican Republic – on 6 December 1492 he was sponsored not by King Henry of England but by King Ferdinand and Queen Isabella of Spain.

Four years later, at Westminster, Henry VII signed the earliest surviving document linking England and America. It was a charter empowering John Cabot, a Genoese explorer, to cross the Atlantic under the English flag, which he did, discovering Newfoundland. Copies of Cabot's map of Newfoundland were displayed in merchants' houses in the City of London and in the Palace of Westminster, where two Eskimos from Newfoundland were received at the royal court in 1502.

Amerigo Vespucci gave the continent of America its name and tales of his voyages inspired Sir Thomas More – who lived in London – to write *Utopia*. This was the classic vision of an ideal society possible in the New World. More's brother-in-law, John Rastell, a London printer, made an attempt to reach America which ended in fiasco off the coast of Ireland. His play based on the experience, *An Interlude of the Four Elements*, put forward the case for English colonisation of America. In 1536 a shipload of young lawyers from the Inns of Court successfully crossed the Atlantic but ran out of supplies and resorted to eating each other.

The great sea-dog Francis Drake was dubbed *Sir* Francis Drake by Queen Elizabeth I at Greenwich in 1580 after he had circumnavigated the globe and claimed New Albion (California) for England. A magnificent banquet in his honour was held in the Middle Temple Hall. This was built in 1571 and is still used for dining by members of the Middle Temple – one of the four Inns of Court – as it was in Drake's day.

Land discovered by English explorers on the east coast of America was named Virginia after the Virgin Queen. From 1585 to 1590 Sir Walter Ralegh spent a fortune trying to establish an English settlement there, at Roanoke. Among the Roanoke settlers were two parishioners of St Bride's church in Fleet Street. Their daughter, Virginia Dare, was the first recorded European child born in America. The Roanoke settlement disappeared almost without trace, but America continued to fire the imagination of Londoners.

The poet John Donne – who preached in Lincoln's Inn Chapel and became Dean of St Paul's – likened one of his mistresses to the unexplored continent of America. Ben Jonson, the playwright, created the character of Captain Seagull telling tall tales about America in a tavern at Billingsgate. 'Come boys,' he urged his eager listeners, 'Virginia longs till we share the rest of her maidenhead.' ³

In 1606 the Virginia Company of London sent from Blackwall on the River Thames three ships loaded with the settlers who would establish the first permanent English colony of Jamestown in Virginia. These three ships

– *Discovery, Susan Constant* and *Godspeed* – are pictured in a stained-glass window in the church of St Sepulchre at Newgate. The window overlooks the tomb of Captain John Smith, the man who introduced work-discipline into early Virginia and was saved from execution by the Amerindian chief's young daughter, Princess Pocahontas. John Smith lived to become the first Governor of Virginia but returned to London and was buried here.

In 1607 Henry Hudson attended a service at the church of St Ethelburga-the-Virgin in Bishopsgate before setting off on the first of the sea voyages in which he discovered and explored the Hudson River. In 1609 the Virginia Company distributed handbills around London advertising for 'labouring men and women' willing to 'adventure' to Virginia. Those interested had to sign up in Philpot Lane. The two or three hundred men, women and children who sailed for Virginia from the Thames were shipwrecked in Bermuda before they reached Jamestown; their experience gave William Shakespeare the idea for his fantasy play *The Tempest*.

In 1614 London received the first cargo of Virginia tobacco made 'sweet-scented' by John Rolfe, a settler who helped secure an eight-year peace with the Amerindians by marrying Princess Pocahontas. The Virginia Company brought Pocahontas and her young son to London as a public relations exercise in 1616. She made a big impact but became ill and died at Gravesend on her way back to Virginia.

One of the Virginia Company subcontractors, a London merchant called Thomas Weston, in 1620 chartered the *Mayflower* for the English Separatists living in Holland who wanted to go to Virginia. He made up the numbers on the ship with people recruited in and around London. The *Mayflower* was fitted out on the Thames and its captain, Christopher Jones, was later buried at St Mary's church, Rotherhithe.

In 1621 the Virginia Company effectively granted Virginia constitutional independence when it ruled that the colony was bound by Company orders only if its own House of Burgesses ratified them. This was a blow in the battle being waged in Britain against royal absolutism. King James I hit back by disbanding the Virginia Company and taking over the running of Virginia as a Crown colony from 1624.

Twenty years later William Penn was born at Tower Hill in London. He was baptised at the church of All-Hallows-by-the-Tower and went to school there. The Penn family lived in Seething Lane, next door to Samuel Pepys, the diarist, who worked at the nearby Navy Office with William Penn's father, Admiral Sir William Penn, after whom Pennsylvania was named.

In 1662 Pepys and Admiral Sir William Penn watched the execution on Tower Hill of a former Governor of Massachusetts, Sir Henry Vane. Two years later Pepys recorded in his diary the capture by the British of New Netherlands, which became New York. During the Great Fire of London in 1666 Admiral Sir William Penn and Pepys ordered dockyard workmen to pull down houses to create a fire-break, thus saving the Navy Office and two churches which can be still be visited – All-Hallows-by-the-Tower and St Olave, Hart Street.

Soon after the Great Fire young William Penn, now a Quaker, published without license a book called *Sandy Foundation Shaken*. For this he was imprisoned in the Tower for a year before his father secured his release though the intervention of James, Duke of York, brother of King Charles II. In 1670 William Penn was arrested in Gracechurch Street for preaching to an unlawful assembly outside the Quaker Meeting House. The jury at the Old Bailey refused to convict him and the jurymen were locked up without food until a judge ruled that they had the right to reach their own verdict. Penn was later granted land to set up a colony in America as payment for a royal debt to his father. He planned to call the colony Sylvania because of its beautiful forests, but in the document which granted him the land Charles II described it as Pennsylvania, to keep alive the memory of his old friend, Admiral Sir William Penn.

No. 10 Downing Street was built in 1681 by George Downing, an unpleasant and slippery character who grew up in New England and was one of the first nine graduates of Harvard College. In 1694 the Bank of England was founded by the Scottish merchant William Paterson when he returned from doing business in the American colonies.

In 1711, after defeating the Dutch, Britain became the leading slave-trading nation in the world. The establishment of a black population in the American colonies was largely organised and financed by City of London merchants. Trade flourished between Britain and the colonies in North America, much of it conducted in City of London coffee houses such as the New England Coffee House, the New York Coffee House, the Pennsylvania Coffee House, the Carolina Coffee House and the Maryland Coffee House. Some of the American merchants lived in America Square, near the Tower of London.

The most famous American to live in London was Benjamin Franklin, who arrived in London for the first time in 1725 when he was eighteen years old. His intention was to buy printing equipment but he ended up having to work in London for a year or so before he could return to Philadelphia, employed first at Palmer's Printing House in the converted Lady Chapel of the church of St Bartholomew-the-Great in Smithfield and later at Watt's Printing House in Lincoln's Inn Fields. Young Benjamin Franklin lived in the street called Little Britain, where, coincidentally, the evangelist John Wesley was converted to God in 1738 after returning from a mission preaching Christianity to Amerindians in Georgia. Wesley had left Georgia in a hurry because his relationship with the niece of the Chief Magistrate of Savannah led her newly wed husband to threaten him with prosecution.

The 1758–63 French and Indian War – known in Britain as the Seven Years' War – secured the territorial integrity of the British colonies in North

America. In Westminster Abbey monuments to those who fell in the war include one for the brother of Charles Townshend, the British politician whose taxes were later to provoke the Boston Tea Party. The British government's policy of imposing taxes on the American colonies was strongly opposed by City of London merchants. Their town hall – the Guildhall – was the centre of English support for the American colonists. In 1775 letters of thanks seeking further support were read out in Guildhall from the New York Committee and the Congress at Philadelphia.

The main spokesman for the American colonists was Benjamin Franklin, who had returned to London in 1757, aged fifty-one, as a representative of the Pennsylvania Assembly. By 1770 he was also representing Georgia, New Jersey and Massachusetts, and acting as an advisor on American affairs to opposition MPs such as William Pitt, the Earl of Chatham. Franklin lived for thirteen years in a house in Craven Street, which is still standing, where he was looked after by his landlady, Margaret Stevenson, and her daughter 'Polly'. When his attempt to prevent a breach between Britain and the American colonies proved unsuccessful, Franklin left London for good on the eve of the War of Independence.

Monuments in London from the days of the American Revolution include a plaque in Westminster Abbey to the Loyalist who drowned off the coast of Holland before he could reach England. The statue of General Cornwallis in St Paul's Cathedral is imposing but does not mention his role as Commander of the British Forces in North America. John Burgoyne, who became a successful comedy writer after his decisive surrender at Saratoga in 1777, is buried under a modest tombstone in the cloister of Westminster Abbey. The monument in the Abbey to Major John André – 'that amiable spy' – has several times had its head removed and is known to have been visited by Benedict Arnold and his young second wife, Peggy.

Many of the men who signed the American Declaration of Independence and drafted the Constitution of the newly independent United States of America were trained as lawyers in London's Inns of Court, particularly the Middle Temple. Their legal thinking was greatly influenced by Judge Blackstone's *Commentaries on the English Law*. The statue of Judge Blackstone in the Royal Courts of Justice in the Strand is a gift from the American Bar Association.

In 1785 John Adams was received by King George III at the Court of St James as the first US Minister (Ambassador). His wife Abigail found a house she liked in Grosvenor Square; it is still standing. This was the beginning of London's 'Little America'. The Adamses' daughter, Nabby, was married from the house to a former officer in the American Revolutionary Army. In 1797 the wedding took place in London of Nabby's brother, the future sixth President, John Quincy Adams. His bride was the daughter of the American consul in London and they were wed at the church of All-Hallows-by-the-Tower.

The war between the USA and Britain which was fought from 1812 to 1815 is commemorated in St Paul's by a monument to General Ross, the British commander who led an arson attack on President Madison's house. The scorch marks were later painted white and it became known as the White House. General Ross was killed attacking American forces outside Baltimore; it was during the siege of Baltimore that 'The Star-Spangled Banner' was composed.

In 1824 the Queen of Hawaii and her husband were buried in the church of St Martin-in-the-Fields after they died of measles during an official visit to London. At the first World Anti-Slavery Convention, held in 1840 in Great Queen Street, the American representatives Elizabeth Cady Stanton and Lucretia Mott were made to sit in silence in the gallery with other women delegates and their male supporters. When they returned to the USA they organised the first American women's rights convention.

From 1842 to 1845 the Republic of Texas had its own diplomatic legation at the Court of St James, with offices in Pickering Place. In 1855 the American writer Nathaniel Hawthorne was tricked by the Lord Mayor of London into giving a speech on Anglo-American relations in the Egyptian Hall of the Mansion House.

Henry James, the American novelist, made his first visit to London from Boston in 1869 and 'eventually attached myself by a hundred human links to the dreadful, delightful city'. George Peabody, the Danvers-born merchant-banker, set up the Peabody Trust which pioneered the building of low-rent flats in London. There is a statue of him in Threadneedle Street, close to the Bank of England. In 1882 Astor House was built near the Temple for American-born Nancy Astor, the first woman MP in the House of Commons.

Since the beginning of the nineteenth century American entertainers of all kinds have left their mark on London. The New York actor Howard Payne was a great success at the Theatre Royal Drury Lane but fell into debt, for which he was imprisoned. He later composed 'Home Sweet Home'. Edwin Forrest began a rivalry in 1836 with the London actor William Macready which resulted in people being shot dead by police on the streets of New York. The American tragedienne Charlotte Cushman made her début as Romeo at London's Theatre Royal Haymarket. Ethel Barrymore was performing in London when she received telegrams from her father in the USA congratulating her first for getting engaged and then for breaking off the engagement. She was one of many American stars promoted by the Ohio-born impresario Charles Frohman, who revolutionised London's West End theatre before he died in the sinking of the *Lusitania* in 1915. The escape-artist Harry Houdini was taken to Scotland Yard to test his skills, but the London police chief who chained him up had not left the room before Houdini was at his side. When Fred and Adèle Astaire made their London début at the Shaftesbury Theatre in 1923 they were described by *The Times* as 'lithe as blades of grass, as light as gossamer'.

Things did not always go smoothly for American performers in London. In 1920 Douglas Fairbanks and Mary Pickford planned to honeymoon at the Ritz Hotel but were forced to leave when English fans invaded the dining room looking for them. In 1929 the black American singer and actor Paul Robeson was refused admission to the Grill Room at the Savoy Hotel during a party given in his honour.

In 1918 President Wilson became the first non-royal head of state to stay as a guest at Buckingham Palace. His wife recorded that her room was unheated but she had a high-backed chair beside the marble bathtub 'as big as a throne'. The romance between King Edward VIII and Wallis Simpson led in 1936 to speculation that there would be an American Queen of England. Selfridge's department store, founded by Chicago-born Gordon Selfridge in 1909, was lavishly decorated for the Coronation, but Wallis Simpson was unacceptable to the British Establishment and to marry her the King had to give up the throne.

There are many American memorials in London dating from the First and Second World Wars. During the First World War the Savoy Hotel was the headquarters for Herbert Hoover's American Relief Committee, formed to help stranded Americans return home from Europe. American troops were briefly billeted at the Tower of London and took part in the ancient Ceremony of the Keys. In 1921 the American Congressional Medal was awarded to the Unknown Soldier buried at Westminster Abbey.

One of those killed in the Battle of Britain in 1941 was the American Pilot Officer William Fiske, whose RAF wings are displayed with his memorial in the crypt of St Paul's. American servicemen and women who died during the Second World War while based in the UK are commemorated in rolls of honour in the American Memorial Chapel behind the altar at St Paul's and at St Clement Danes in the Strand. American writers who recorded their impressions of London during the Second World War included John Steinbeck, Edmund Wilson and William Saroyan.

In 1948 a statue of Franklin D. Roosevelt was unveiled in Grosvenor Square by Eleanor Roosevelt, accompanied by King George VI. There are also statues of George Washington in Trafalgar Square, Abraham Lincoln in Parliament Square and Dwight Eisenhower in Grosvenor Square. A bust of John F. Kennedy can be seen in Marylebone Road.

Two major items have been removed from London to the USA since the Second World War. One is the Wren church of St Mary Aldermanbury, which is now at Westminster College in Fulton, Missouri. The other is the nineteenth-century London Bridge, which now spans Lake Havasu in Arizona.

The spirit of exploration and enterprise which led to the foundation of the USA is nowadays expressed by journeys into space. Miniature UK and US flags that flew on board the space-shuttle *Columbia* in 1981 are on display in the public gallery at Lloyd's of London.

Even in a twelve-mile walk it is impossible to include all the places related to London's American past. Off this route is Southwark Cathedral, south of London Bridge, where John Harvard's baptism record can be seen. There are American historical connections in Greenwich, Hampstead, Regent's Park and scattered throughout London. But you will find plenty here to get stuck into. Whether you are walking or travelling in your armchair, have a good journey!

ONE

The Tower of London

'The Tower is the worst argument in the world. . . . My prison shall be my grave before I will budge a jot: for I owe my conscience to no man.'

William Penn, imprisoned at the Tower 1668–9

AMERICA SQUARE

CROSSWALL

CRUTCHED FRIARS

COOPERS ROW

Roman Wall

William Penn born 1644 station

TOWER HILL

Ex-Govenor of Massachusetts beheaded 1662

muel pys

OVY ST

U.S Troops 1917

Sir Walter Ralegh 1605

All-Hallow's by-the-Tower

Buffalo Bill 1887

Tower Bridge

The Tower is London's most popular tourist attraction, with three million visitors a year coming to see the Beefeaters, the Bloody Tower, the Crown Jewels, the block and axe, the medieval torture instruments and the legendary ravens hopping about Tower Green execution site. Nine hundred years of British history are embodied in the Tower, but American visitors who look a little more closely and take the time to venture off the usual tourist track will also find echoes of their own country's past.

On arrival at Tower Hill underground station, instead of heading straight for the Tower, turn right from the station exit to find, on the right, the birthplace of William Penn, the founder of Pennsylvania. The house where he was born has long since disappeared, but it stood roughly on the site of 43 Trinity Square, in what used to be called George Court. Most of George Court was demolished in 1833 to make way for Tower Hill station. A section of London's old city wall – first built by the Romans in AD 200 – formed part of George Court and can be seen by taking a pedestrian turning to the right immediately beyond 43 Trinity Square. Most of the city wall was pulled down in 1760, but it survived here because a warehouse had been built on to it.

A gap through the wall leads into Vine Street and to the left, under a railway bridge, lies America Square. Although the square's architecture is now all modern, it was originally laid out in the style of Grosvenor Square between 1768 and 1774 and was inhabited by wealthy sea captains and merchants trading with America. They would have been among the first to hear the news of the surrender of Cornwallis from ships sailing up the Thames into London. In 1836 the London and Blackwall Railway encroached upon America Square, and several more of its eighteenth-century houses on the west side were demolished in 1880 when the railway was extended. Excavations revealed remains of the Roman city wall under the surviving houses. When the square was bombed in 1941 the last of the original houses were destroyed. But the name remains, and in our era of global markets in commodities and finance the present occupants seem to appreciate having America Square as their address.

From America Square, turn left into Crosswall and Crutched Friars – the street named after the Friars of the Holy Cross who lived here from 1298 to 1539 – and continue to Seething Lane. Here, on the corner with Hart Street, stands the church of St Olave, where in 1884 the American Minister (Ambassador) James Russell Lowell delivered a speech at the unveiling of a monument to Samuel Pepys, London's seventeenth-century diarist and naval administrator. Lowell, born in Cambridge, Massachusetts, represented the USA in London from 1880 to 1885. He was a poet and essayist as well as a diplomat and used his diplomatic skills when describing English weather, including London's yellow fog. This, he wrote,

> always enlivens me, it has such a knack of disfiguring things. It flatters one's self-esteem in a recondite way, promoting one for the

moment to that exclusive class which can afford to wrap itself in a golden seclusion. It is very picturesque also. Even the cabs are rimmed with yellow, and people across the way have all that possibility of suggestion which piques the fancy so in the figures of fading frescoes. Even the grey, even the black fogs, make a new and unexplored world, not unpleasing to one who is getting palled without familiar landscapes. [1]

St Olave's church 'lies at the heart of the City and the Blackwall Railway shrieks at it daily,' wrote Charles Dickens. 'It is a small, small churchyard with a ferocious strong spiked iron gate, like a jail. The gate is ornamented with skulls and crossbones larger than the life, wrought in stone.' The church is dedicated to Olave, a Norse pirate who rose to be King of Denmark. In 1014 he collaborated with Ethelred the Unready of England to win the Battle of London Bridge. Although he was made a Christian saint after his death in 1025, his London Bridge victory was credited to the pagan god of war, Odin, in the earliest surviving version of the London Bridge rhyme:

> London bridge is broken down
> Gold is won, and bright renown
> Shields resounding
> War-horns sounding
> Hildur shouting in the din
> Arrows singing
> Mailcoats ringing
> Odin makes our Olave win.

Soon after St Olave's death, a wooden church in his honour was built on this site. In the thirteenth century it was replaced by a stone church, the remains of which form the crypt of the present building, which was commissioned in 1450 by Robert and Richard Cely, two local fellmongers (sellers of animal hides). The list of priests at St Olave's goes back to 1319 and its parish register contains an entry for 'Mother Goose', buried on 14 September 1586. During the Great Plague of 1665, St Olave's parishioners died at the rate of one a day; Samuel Pepys recorded in his diary, 'it frighted me . . . to see so [many] graves lie so high upon the churchyard, where people have been buried of the plague.'[2] Overlooking the churchyard today is a plaque on the church wall showing where there

used to be a special door for staff at the nearby Navy Office. Those who entered St Olave's through it included Samuel Pepys and his colleague Admiral Sir William Penn, William Penn's father and the man after whom Pennsylvania was named.

The memorials inside St Olave's include one to John Hyland, a skinner who died in 1619 aged eighty-seven, leaving forty shillings a year to be spent on 'Newcastle cole for the relief of the poor of this parish'. A stained-glass window beside the altar honours four illustrious women: Elizabeth Fry (1780–1845), the prison reformer; Florence Nightingale (1820–1910), the pioneer of nursing; Josephine Butler (1828–1906), the health campaigner; and Edith Cavell (1865–1915), the First World War heroine. A fine white marble bust of Elizabeth Pepys, wife of the great diarist, gazes down from the niche near the altar where her husband had it installed after she died, aged only twenty-nine, in 1669.

Shortly before she died Elizabeth read aloud to Samuel the book young William Penn had written against the doctrine of the Trinity: *Sandy Foundation Shaken*. William Penn had returned from his travels 'a Quaker again,' wrote Pepys, 'or some very melancholy thing; that he cares for no company; which is not a pleasant thing after his being abroad so long, and his father such a hypocritical rogue, and at this time an atheist.'[3] Pepys thought Penn's book was 'too good for him ever to have writ it – and it is a serious sort of book, and not fit for everybody to read. And so to supper and to bed.'[4]

Samuel Pepys' diary was written using shorthand and some non-English words between 1660 and 1669, when he was aged twenty-eight to thirty-seven. He stopped writing the diary before going on holiday with his wife, Elizabeth, to try to salvage their marriage. Elizabeth had found Samuel having his hair combed by their maid and 'embracing the girl [with] my hand sub su coats; and indeed, I was with my main in her cunny.'[5] Elizabeth became ill abroad and died soon after their return to London. By then Samuel had abandoned his diary, fearing for his sight. He never kept one again. Nor did he remarry, although he lived to be seventy. He became an MP, Secretary to the Admiralty Commission and President of the Royal Society. In 1679 he was imprisoned at the Tower with his friend Anthony Deane – a shipbuilder – accused by their enemies of involvement in the Popish Plot. King Charles II sent them a fat buck deer from his forest at Enfield and they were soon released with all charges dropped.

Pepys was buried at St Olave's in 1703. His memorial in the church occupies the site of the old Navy Office door to the right of the altar. At its unveiling, the US Ambassador (Minister) James Russell Lowell told the congregation:

We have no word in English which is equivalent to the French word *bourgeois*, but at all events Samuel Pepys is the most perfect type that ever existed of the class of people whom this word describes. He had all its merits as well as many of its defects. With all those defects Pepys wrote one of the most delightful books that it is man's privilege to read in the English language or in any other. . . . The book is certainly unique in one respect, and that is the absolute sincerity of the author with himself. . . . There is probably more involuntary humour in Pepys' *Diary* than there is in any other book extant.[6]

During his service as a naval administrator, Pepys recorded one important event in American history: the capture by the English in 1664 – with a force of three ships and three hundred men – of the Dutch enclave on Long Island and Manhattan which was to become New York. 'Fresh news', he wrote, 'came of our beating the Dutch . . . which will make them quite mad. . . . the King doth joy mightily at it. . . . they say that we have beat them out of the New Netherlands . . . we have been doing them a mischief a great while in several parts of the world, without public knowledge or reason.'[7]

During the diary years Samuel and Elizabeth Pepys lived next door to the Penn family in the Navy Gardens, Seething Lane. In 1662, when William Penn was seventeen, he and his sister celebrated New Year's Day in the Pepys's house. A barrel of oysters was consumed, then Samuel, Elizabeth and the young Penns went together by coach to see a play. 'From thence home,' wrote Pepys, 'and they sat with us till late at night at cards, very merry, but the jest was Mr. W. Penn had left his sword in the coach and so my boy and he ran out after the coach and by very great chance did at the Exchange meet with the coach and get his sword again.'[8]

On one occasion when it was very hot, Pepys recorded how 'Sir W. Penn came out in his shirt into his leads [flat areas on the house roofs] and there we stayed talking and singing and drinking great draughts of Claret and eating botargo [dried fish roe] and bread and butter till 12 at night, it being moonshine. And so to bed – very near fuddled.'[9] Another time Samuel and Elizabeth came home from a jolly day out and went 'up to the leads; but were, contrary to expectation, driven down again with a stink, by Sir W. Penn's emptying of a shitten pot in their house of office [toilet] close by; which doth trouble me, for fear it do hereafter annoy me. So down to sing a little, and then to bed.'[10]

When Pepys had his hair cropped, 'Sir W. Penn observed mightily and discoursed much upon my cutting off my hair, as he doth of everything that concerns me.' On his wedding anniversary Sir William gave a dinner including 'eighteen mince-pies in a dish, the number of the years that he hath been married.'[11] When Pepys kicked his cookmaid for leaving the door open he

was seen doing so by Sir W. Penn's footboy, which did vex me to the heart because I know he will be telling their family of it, though I did put on presently a very pleasant face to the boy and spoke kindly to him as one without passion, so as it may be he might not think I was angry; but yet I was troubled at it.[12]

It was from the Penn family home in Seething Lane that twenty-one-year-old William Penn set off each day in 1665 to study law in Lincoln's Inn. His journey through plague-ridden London took him past the church of All-Hallows-by-the-Tower at the bottom of Seething Lane where he had been baptised and received some early schooling. All-Hallows-by-the-Tower was known as Barking Church because it was founded in the seventh century by the nuns of Barking Abbey. It survived the Great Fire of London in 1666 – as did St Olave's – thanks to the efforts of Admiral Sir William Penn, Samuel Pepys and the royal dockyard workmen they had at their command.

When the Fire broke out on 2 September 1666, after a long, dry summer, Pepys took a boat across the Thames to Bankside. From an alehouse he

> saw the fire grow . . . in Corners and upon steeples and between churches and houses . . . in a most horrid malicious bloody flame, not like the fine flame of an ordinary fire . . . in a bow up the hill, for an arch of above a mile long. It made me weep to see it.

Then on 4 September he described

> sitting melancholy with Sir W. Penn in our garden and thinking of the certain burning of this office without extraordinary means, I did propose for the sending up of all our workmen from Woolwich and Deptford yards . . . to pull down houses rather than lose this office, which would much hinder the King's business. So Sir W. Penn he went down this night, in order to the sending them up tomorrow morning.

On 5 September

> About 2 in the morning my wife calls me up and tells me of new cries of 'Fire!' – it being come to Barking Church, which is the bottom of our lane. . . . But going to the fire, I find, by the blowing up of houses and the great help given by the workmen out of the King's yards sent up by Sir W. Penn, there is good stop given to it. . . . I up to the top of Barking steeple, and there saw the saddest sight of desolation that I ever saw. Everywhere great fires. Oil cellars and brimstone and other things burning. I became afeared to stay there long; and therefore down again as fast as I could, the fire being

spread as far as I could see it, and to Sir W. Penn's and there eat a piece of cold meat, having eaten nothing since Sunday but the remains of Sunday's dinner.[13]

The Navy Office in Seething Lane where Samuel Pepys and Admiral Sir William Penn were colleagues survived the Great Fire but burned down in 1673. Its visitors had included Tsar Peter the Great when he was building up the Russian Navy. Muscovy Street, so named after the Tsar's visit, links Seething Lane with the Tower Hill execution site. Here – in what is now Trinity Square Gardens – stood the public gallows where, from 1381 to 1747, great and mighty men were put to death for crimes against the state.

Among those executed was Sir Henry Vane, a former Governor of Massachusetts, beheaded on Tower Hill in 1662. Sir Henry had been twenty-four when he went to America in 1635.

Despite his youth he was elected Governor of Massachusetts within a year and, 'as son and heir of a Privy Councillor in England the ships congratulated his election with a volley of great shot.'[14] He supported Ann Hutchinson, one of the first women to speak in public in America, and was not re-elected. He returned to England in high dudgeon, but took a deep interest in the welfare of the American colonies for the rest of his life; Governor Winthrop, the Puritan first Governor of the Massachusetts Bay colony, called him 'a true friend of New England'.

Vane became one of the most influential supporters of Oliver Cromwell, Lord Protector of England's Puritan Commonwealth during the interregnum of 1649-60. In 1653, however, Cromwell and Vane quarrelled. 'Oh, Sir Henry Vane, Sir Henry Vane,' cried Cromwell, 'the Lord deliver me from Sir Henry Vane!',[15] and the turbulent Sir Henry was locked up in Carisbrooke Castle, on the Isle of Wight.

Although he was not one of the regicides who signed King Charles I's death warrant in 1649, Vane was an anti-royalist and those who came to power with the Restoration of the Monarchy in 1660 considered him too dangerous to live. He was tried on a charge of high treason and found guilty. The large crowd that gathered to watch his execution on Tower Hill included Samuel Pepys, who recorded that the condemned man 'changed not his colour to the last, but died justifying himself and the cause he had stood for; and spoke very confidently of his being presently at the right hand of Christ'. Sir Henry made 'a long speech many times interrupted by the Sheriff and others there; and they would have taken his paper out of his hand, but he would not let it go.' The notes his friends took of his speech were seized and 'trumpets were brought under the scaffold that he might not be heard.'

Sir Henry Vane spoke first of the irregularities of his trial for high treason against King Charles I. When the Sheriff stopped him, 'He began to tell them . . . he was born a gentleman . . . and had the qualities of a gentleman, and . . . had been, till he was seventeen year old, a goodfellow. But then it pleased God to lay a foundation of grace in his heart, by which he was persuaded against his worldly interest to leave all preferment and go abroad, where he might serve God with more freedom. Then he was called home and made a member of the Long Parliament; where he never did, to this day, anything against his conscience, but all for the glory of God.'

Sir Henry Vane tried to give an account of the Long Parliament but was silenced by interruptions. So he said prayers for England, the English churches and the City of London. When asked why he did not pray for the King he answered, 'Nay, you shall see I can pray for the King: I pray, God bless him.'

King Charles II had said that Vane's friends could keep his body, so he told those in charge of his execution that 'he hoped they would be civil to his body when dead; and . . . let him die like a gentleman and a Christian and not crowded and pressed as he was . . .', then he prepared himself for the block. 'He had a blister . . . upon his neck, which he desired them not to hurt.'[16]

The executioner put the fatal question: 'Shall you raise your head again?'

Sir Henry Vane spoke his last words: 'Not till the final resurrection.'

Close to the spot on Tower Hill where Sir Henry Vane was executed is Trinity House, headquarters of the lighthouse authority for England and Wales. The organisation is said to derive from a corporation established in the Middle Ages. Trinity House itself was built in 1795 and is decorated with the stone heads of the last king of America, George III, and his wife, Queen Charlotte, who had fifteen children.

The path from Tower Hill to the Tower of London has been trod by many famous American visitors. In 1805 Benjamin Silliman – the Conneticut-born Professor of Chemistry and Natural History at Yale – was particularly interested in the Tower menagerie housed in the Lion Tower, remains of which can still be seen near the ticket office at the Tower entrance.

The menagerie was started in the thirteenth century by King Henry III with an elephant from the King of France, a polar bear from the King of Norway and three leopards – like those on the royal arms of England – from Emperor Frederick II. The Sheriffs of London were ordered to pay the Keeper of the King's Leopard sixpence a day to feed the leopard and three and a half pence a day to feed himself. The leopard in the menagerie during the 1690s used to stare at visitors who came too close and to urinate on them with 'a stink worse than a pole cat's'.

When Benjamin Silliman visited the Lion Tower 'a beautiful black leopardess attracted my particular attention. Her form was exceedingly delicate and elegant, and although black her skin was distinguished by spots of a still deeper black. She was from the coast of Malabar.' He also saw 'a white polar bear of astonishing size and untameable ferocity. When the keeper pointed a stick at him he flew at the bars with incredible fierceness, rose upon his hind legs, and threw open his mouth as made me shudder. He had very large and strong teeth and might have embraced the body of a middle sized man with his fangs.'

It was possible, at that time, to gain admission to the menagerie by bringing a live cat or dog to supplement the animal's rations. One such dog had a charmed life. According to Silliman, the tiger, rather than eat the dog, 'contracted an intimate friendship with it'. Silliman also noted that the two lionesses which were reared in the Lion Tower were the fiercest animals there, whilst the lions taken in the wild were quite tame.[17] In 1835, after a lion attacked some of the soldiers garrisoned at the Tower, the menagerie animals were moved to the zoo in Regent's Park.

In 1855 the Tower was visited by Nathaniel Hawthorne, the American author of *The Scarlet Letter* and *The House of the Seven Gables*. Hawthorne was sent to England as the US Consul in Liverpool but became a great lover of London. He was one of the first Americans well versed in the history and literary associations of London who took to getting lost in it. 'He rejoiced', wrote his son, Julian,

> in the human ocean that flooded its thoroughfares, and eddied through its squares and courts; he greeted as old friends its cathedrals, its river, its bridges, its Tower, its inns, its Temple, its alleys and chop-houses – so strange were they, and yet so familiar; so old, and so full of novelty.
>
> He cast himself adrift upon the great city, and cruised wheresoever the current took him; and when he could keep his feet no longer he would hail a hansom and trundle homeward in happy weariness, to begin his explorations afresh the next morning.
>
> His appetite for London, which had been growing during his lifetime, was almost as big as London itself; he could not gratify it enough. He enjoyed the vague and irresponsible wandering even more than the deliberate and premeditated sight-seeing; but he was always ready for either. London seemed to fulfil his expectations better than any other city – better than Paris, or even Rome.[18]

It cost Hawthorne sixpence a head to take his family into the Tower; the tickets included entrance to the armoury and the Crown Jewels. In particular he liked the Yeoman Warders ('beefeaters'), 'dressed in scarlet coats of antique fashion, richly embroidered with golden crowns, both on the breast and the back, and other royal devices and insignia: so that they looked very much like the kings on a pack of cards, or regular trumps.'[19] Nowadays the beefeaters wear their scarlet coats only on ceremonial occasions. But, in their everyday outfits designed by Queen Victoria's husband Prince Albert, they still greet visitors at the entrance to the Tower.

The first figure in American history to be imprisoned in the Tower was Sir Walter Ralegh, rightly famed as the founder of Virginia. Although he never set foot in America himself, in the 1580s he spent £40,000 trying to establish an English colony there. 'All kingdoms', he wrote, 'are maintained by rents and traffic [trade], but especially by the latter, which in marine places must flourish by means of navigation.'[20]

Described by the poet Edmund Spenser as 'the shepherd of the ocean', Ralegh began his career as a seaman, coloniser and courtier with the help of his older half-brother, Sir Humphrey Gilbert, who in 1578 set sail from England to explore and colonise the coast of North America. He had a charter from Queen Elizabeth I empowering him to seize such 'heathen and barbarous lands . . . not actually possessed by any Christian Prince or people.' The twenty-five-year-old Walter Ralegh captained one of Gilbert's ships and when bad weather drove the others back he remained at sea for a further six months.

In 1580 Ralegh was given command of a company of troops sent to Ireland to put down a Spanish-backed rebellion, and he proved himself both by his reckless courage in action and by his cogent criticism of current policies on Ireland. When he was introduced at Court, his dark good looks, sumptuous dress and spirited conversation quickly admitted him to the innermost circle of courtiers. He became known as 'the Queen's dear minion', and expressed in poetry the expected homage to her beauty and majesty:

> Those eyes which set my fancy on a fire,
> Those crispèd hairs which hold my heart in chains,
> Those dainty hands which conquered my desire,
> That wit which of my thought doth hold the reins.

> Eyes that pierce our hearts without remorse.
> Hairs of right that wears a royal crown,
> Hands that conquer more than Caesar's force,
> Wit that turns huge kingdoms upside down.

The Queen gave Ralegh the 'farm of wines' (a fee of £1 a year payable to him by all vintners); the 'gift of the cloths' (a licence to export undyed woollen broadcloths); and the splendid Durham House on the Strand (demolished in 1769–70) for his London residence. These royal favours made him one of the richest men in England, but he was soon spending lavishly to serve the Queen. When Sir Humphrey Gilbert was lost at sea in 1583 – reading Thomas More's *Utopia*, so it was said – Ralegh took over his leading role in the attempt to set up an English colony in America.

In 1584 he financed and organised a small expedition to explore the coast-line of what is now North Carolina. The captains of the expedition brought back glowing accounts of a land flowing with milk and honey, waters swimming with fish, and soil so fertile that seeds planted by sailors grew to a height of fourteen inches in little over a week. The people were 'most loving, gentle, and faithful, void of all guile and treason, and such as live after the manner of the golden age.' When Ralegh presented these accounts to the Virgin Queen she agreed that the new land should be called Virginia in her honour, and she made him a knight. (Ralegh has been credited with introducing tobacco and potatoes into England from America, but in fact both were already known through the Spanish.)

In 1585 Ralegh sent an expedition to establish a colony in Virginia. Seven ships took 108 would-be settlers to Roanoke Island, but they were dogged by misfortune and after the hardships of their first winter they returned to England in the company of Sir Francis Drake, whose ships had been harrying the Spanish in the Caribbean.

Ralegh sent a second set of settlers to Roanoke in 1587. Owing to the threat of attack on England by the Spanish Armada, there was a delay before a relief expedition carrying much-needed supplies of food and equipment could be sent. When it finally arrived, the Roanoke settlement had completely and mysteriously disappeared, leaving only the incomprehensible work 'CROATAN' carved on a tree.

Not until the early seventeenth century was an English colony successfully established in Virginia, but these brave false starts sponsored by Ralegh established American colonisation as a major concern in England. When the English defeated the Spanish Armada in 1588 – as much by good luck as good management – they ended the threat of Spanish invasion and secured control of the Atlantic. Had the sea-battle gone the other way, modern America might be a very different place.

Sir Walter Ralegh was appointed to a select council-of-war to advise on national defence and looked forward to becoming a statesman by admission to the Privy Council – but it was not to be. Dissatisfied with public courtship of the aging Queen and casual sexual intrigues, he had begun a relationship with twenty-six-year-old Bess Throgmorton, one of the Queen's ladies-in-waiting and twelve years his junior. It was for Bess that he wrote the lines:

> Now Serena be not coy;
> Since we freely may enjoy
> Sweet embraces: such delights
> As will shorten tedious nights.

When the Queen heard that Ralegh and Bess Throgmorton had married secretly, she sent them both to the Tower and had them kept apart. They were freed in 1592, but only after Ralegh had forfeited to the Queen his share of booty from a raid on Panama. Banished to domestic life, in 1595 he tried to regain royal favour by laying the foundations of an English empire in South America. 'The shining glory of this conquest', he wrote, 'will eclipse all those so far extended beams of the Spanish nation . . . whatsoever prince shall possess it shall be the greatest.' The Queen was not inspired by his book *The Large, Rich and Beautiful Empire of Guiana*, but she received him back into her favour during the last years of her reign.

Her successor, King James I, was less well disposed towards Ralegh; according to tradition the Scottish monarch greeted him with the ominous pun, 'I have heard rawly of thee.' In 1603 he was again arrested and sent to the Tower of London, this time on suspicion of high treason. He tried to stab himself with a table knife but hit a rib and his wound soon healed. Accused of encouraging a Spanish plot to dethrone the King in favour of his English cousin, Arabella Stuart, Ralegh was unable to prove his innocence. He was sentenced to death as a traitor, but the King chose to keep him prisoner in the Tower for the next twelve years.

Ralegh lived in the Bloody Tower, administered to by three servants and attended regularly by a physician and clergyman. His wife and his son Wat visited him every day, sometimes staying with him, and a second son, Carew, was born in 1605 and baptised within the precincts of the Tower at the church of St Peter ad Vincula. In a converted henhouse in the Constable's garden Ralegh carried out scientific experiments and distilled medicinal cordials from the herbs and shrubs that he grew. When James I's wife, Anne of Denmark, visited Ralegh to collect some of his Balsam of Guiana – a strawberry-water cordial – she was impressed and charmed by his conversation but could do nothing to assist his release: the King was influenced only by his favourites. The Queen brought her eldest son, Prince Henry – then aged thirteen – to meet Ralegh, who became in effect tutor to the heir to the throne. It was to prepare the boy for kingship that he began his masterpiece, *The History of the World*. When Prince Henry fell ill and died in 1613, Ralegh abandoned the second and third volumes of his book. The first volume was published in 1614, but King James banned it as being 'too saucy in censuring princes'.

Sir Walter Ralegh was released from the Tower in 1616 to take part in a gold-search expedition to Guiana, on condition that he did not clash with the Spanish. His son Wat was killed and his second-in-command stabbed himself to death when he realised that he had broken the King's command by attacking a Spanish fort. King Philip III of Spain now demanded Ralegh's death as a test of King James's friendship, and he was imprisoned in the Tower of London again for six weeks, in 'one of the most cold and direful dungeons'. The death sentence passed fifteen years earlier was carried out in Old Palace Yard, Westminster, on 29 October 1618. In his speech from the scaffold Ralegh thanked God that he died in the light rather than 'in the dark prison in the Tower'.

The upper chamber of the Bloody Tower has been restored as Sir Walter

Ralegh's bedroom. It was originally created for him by inserting a floor, raising the walls and putting in a window. Its small annexe contains a display of paintings and drawings by John White, one of the 1585 Roanoke settlers, including his map of the American coast from Florida to Chesapeake Bay which shows – in the words of John Hariot, another would-be settler – that 'the sea coasts of Virginia are full of islands whereby the entrance into the main land is hard to find.' White's watercolours illustrate the hoopoe bird and a fish called the blue-striped grunt; he also painted two types of Indian village: *pomeiooc*, an enclosed village, and *secoton*, which was unenclosed. 'Their towns that are not enclosed with poles', he noted, 'are commonly fairer than such as are enclosed. The houses are scattered here and there, and they have gardens wherein groweth tobacco, which the inhabitants call *uppowoc*'.

Most of the Bloody Tower dates from the reigns of Edward III and Richard II in the fourteenth century. Initially it was called the Garden Tower, as its upper storey overlooked the Constable's garden; it earned the name 'Bloody Tower' because of the belief that it was here that the uncrowned thirteen-year-old King Edward V and his brother the Duke of York – the 'Princes in the Tower' – were imprisoned and murdered in 1483 by Richard, Duke of Gloucester, the future Richard III. Excavations at the foot of the stairs in 1674 uncovered two small skeletons, which King Charles II accepted as the remains of the little Princes. They were re-interred at Westminster Abbey in 'Innocents' Corner'.

After Sir Walter Ralegh, the next Tower of London prisoner to become part of American history was the twenty-four-year-old William Penn. From December 1668 to July 1669 Penn suffered 'close imprisonment' in the Tower, locked up in his cell with a keeper and given very little fuel throughout a memorably bad winter, permitted to write no letters and receive no presents, and eating only prison food. His crime was having published his book *Sandy Foundation Shaken* without a proper licence. While captive here he wrote another book, *No Cross No Crown* – a dissertation on the Christian duty of self-sacrifice. The King's chaplain called on the prisoner to teach him the error of his ways, but without success. Penn convinced him, however, that *Sandy Foundation Shaken* did not deny the divinity of Christ but argued there was nothing in the Scripture saying that Christ suffered eternal death and infinite vengeance. For Penn, Christ was a God of remission, forgiveness, love and gentleness. He put his view in a second book written in the Tower, *Innocency with her Open Face Presented by way of Apology for the Book Entitled The Sandy Foundation Shaken*. Charles II accepted Penn's explanation and ordered his release.

The Tower's last American prisoner was Henry Laurens of South Carolina, imprisoned from October 1780 to December 1781 under 'suspicion of treason committed at Philadelphia and on the high seas'. Laurens was a former President of the Continental Congress, chosen in 1779 to negotiate a treaty of friendship and commerce with Holland on behalf of the American colonies and to arrange a loan of $10 million. When the ship on which Laurens was sailing, the *Mercury*, was captured by a British man-of-war, he threw his official papers overboard in a sack. The sack floated, the papers were retrieved and Laurens was arrested.

In London the Privy Council refused to accept his claim of diplomatic immunity and sent him to the Tower, where he was accommodated in the house of warden James Futerell and his family. They did all they could to make his imprisonment bearable and he left them a legacy in gratitude. Despite their care, the fifty-six-year-old Laurens was rarely allowed to walk in the Tower grounds and his health deteriorated through lack of exercise. His few permitted visitors found him very ill, emaciated and bitterly invective about his harsh treatment.

Strict British censorship kept Henry Laurens ignorant of Benjamin Franklin's efforts in Paris to secure his release, and he was deeply troubled by what he felt was Congress's indifference to his imprisonment. However, when the surrender of General Cornwallis at Yorktown in October 1781 brought the American War of Independence to a successful conclusion, Henry Laurens was released on bail. 'Thus terminated', he wrote, 'a long, and to me an expensive and painful farce.'[21]

The first foreign soldiers to be welcomed to the Tower of London were sixty-seven Americans headed by Captain George Patton. In June 1917, applauded by British troops, the band of the Honorable Artillery Company led them on a march under the Byward Tower and around the White Tower to Tower Green. They were part of the vanguard of the American Expeditionary Force under General John Pershing and had been assigned quarters in the Tower. During their brief stay the American soldiers took part in the Tower's nine-hundred-year-old locking-up Ceremony of the Keys. On the eve of their departure for France, the toasts and songs at their farewell dinner went on until 4.30 a.m.

The exit from the Tower of London on to Tower Wharf – alongside the Thames – provides a fine view of Tower Bridge and the Pool of London. Here, on 22 April 1887, the steamship *State of Nebraska* dropped anchor close to Traitors' Gate and a crowd of Londoners watched excitedly as the great American showman William Cody – 'Buffalo Bill' – strode down the gangplank, giving a wide wave and a big smile. Behind him came Annie Oakley, accompanied by nine other women, including five Amerindian squaws. They were followed by Big Chief Red Shirt at the head of ninety-two Amerindian braves drawn from the Sioux, Cheyenne, Kiowa, Pawnee and Ogalallas tribes. Then came Sweeney's Cowboy Band – thirty-six musicians wearing grey shirts, slouch hats and moccasins. Last off the ship were the rest of the hundred or so cowboys who made up Buffalo Bill's Wild West Show. They had to unload 180 horses, 18 buffalo, 10 mules, 10 elks, 5 wild Texas steers, 4 donkeys and 2 deer. Although some of the entertainers had

Tower Bridge

actually arrived in London by train a few days earlier, Buffalo Bill had decided that they should return to Gravesend so his entire entourage could steam up the river and disembark together at the Tower. Three special trains took the show on to Earl's Court.

American visitors leaving the Tower should take the steps just beyond the exit up to the church of All-Hallows-by-the-Tower (Barking Church). A telephone call a day or two in advance usually secures a guided tour of the church undercroft. Refurbished with the generous help of the people of Philadelphia and the National Society of the Daughters of the American Revolution, this undercroft contains many treasures. Here – among Roman tiles, tombs and household wares, Saxon stone crosses and seventeenth-century gold and silver church goblets, plates and spoons – are the original parish records of both William Penn's baptism in 1644 and the marriage in 1797 of the future American President John Quincy Adams.

On 26 July Adams wrote in his diary:

> At nine this morning I went, accompanied by my brother, to Mr Johnson's, and thence to the church of the parish of All-Hallows, Barking, where I was married to Louisa Catherine Johnson, second daughter of Joshua and Catherine Johnson, by Mr Hewlett. Mr Johnson's family, Mr Brooks, my brother, and Mr J. Hall were present. We were married before eleven in the morning, and immediately went out to see Tilney House, one of the splendid country seats for which the country is distinguished.[22]

The Church of All-Hallows-by-the-Tower

Adams was thirty years old at the time of his marriage and was in London for the first time as a US consular official accredited to the Navy Office. He returned to London in 1815 on a mission to improve relations between Britain and the USA. Independence movements were pushing Spain out of South America and Britain had begun to develop profitable trade with the former Spanish colonies. By 1823 there were fears that Spain – with French and Russian support – might attempt to regain its colonies, and the British Foreign Secretary, George Canning, suggested to President James Monroe the formation of an Anglo-American alliance against France and Russia.

American foreign policy had been defined in 1801 by President Jefferson as 'peace, commerce, and honest friendship with all nations – entangling alliances with none.' Now, as an elder statesman, Jefferson argued that 'Great Britain is the nation which can do us the most harm of any one, or all on earth, and with her on our side we need not fear the whole world'.[23] John

Quincy Adams, then Secretary of State, urged a different, independent course. 'It would be more candid, as well as more dignified', he told President Monroe's Cabinet, 'to avow our principles explicitly to Russia and France, than to come in as a cock-boat in the wake of the British man-of-war.'[24] Adams's advice was accepted: the USA retained the principle of no entangling alliances, of acting alone. Known as the Monroe Doctrine, the policy was of immense importance for future diplomacy. Any interference with a country which the USA had recognised as independent, warned Monroe, would be regarded as 'the manifestation of an unfriendly disposition toward the United States'. John Quincy Adams became the sixth President in 1825.

From the church of All-Hallows-by-the-Tower, Byward Street leads downhill towards the River Thames and Billingsgate, leaving behind the Tower of London built nine hundred years ago by the Normans and entering the City of London founded two thousand years ago by the Romans. Four hundred years ago the City was the launch-pad for English colonisation of America.

Billingsgate

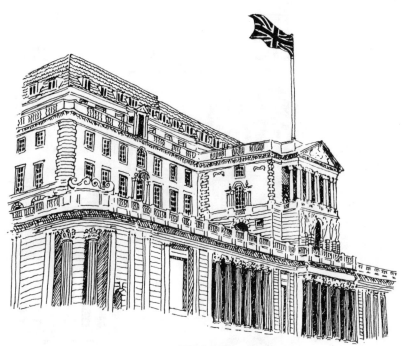

TWO

The City

'Which said country was first discovered in the year 1584
... and Queen Elizabeth called it Virginia; and assigned
the same to Sir Walter Ralegh, as being the chief dis-
coverer thereof. And in the year 1587 there were sent
thither above one hundred men, women and children, and
until the third year of King James all yearly sending thither for plantation ceased; and then upon more exact discoveries there were yearly supplies of men, women and
children sent thither with all necessaries under the conduct of Captain Newport.'

John Stow, Chronicle, *edited by Edmund Howes, 1615*

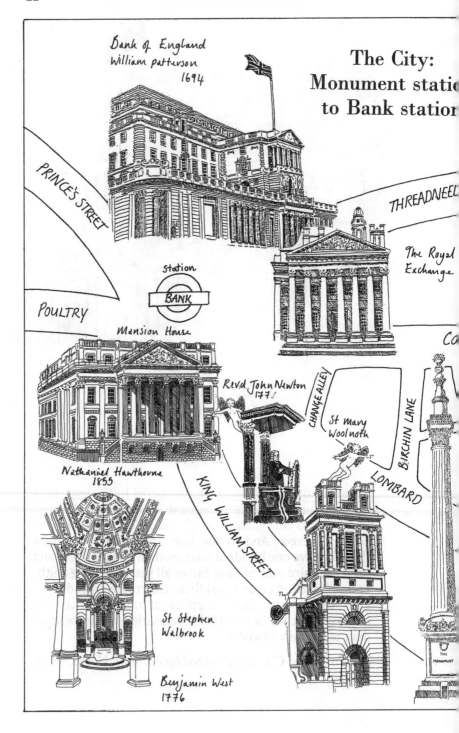

The City:
Monument station
to Bank station

Bank of England
William Patterson
1694

PRINCE'S STREET

THREADNEEDLE

The Royal
Exchange

POULTRY

Station
BANK

Mansion House

Revd. John Newton
1775

CHANGE ALLEY

St Mary
Woolnoth

BIRCHIN LANE

LOMBARD

Nathaniel Hawthorne
1855

KING WILLIAM STREET

St Stephen
Walbrook

Benjamin West
1776

THE MONUMENT

Columbia Space Shuttle 1981

Lloyds of London

ST MARY AXE

Boston Tea party 1773

TEA
TEA TEA

DUKES PLACE

BURY ST

CREECHURCH LN

Pilgrim Fathers 1620

LEADENHALL STREET

ALDGATE

Geoffrey Chaucer 1380

William Penn arrested

FENCHURCH STREET

GRACECHURCH STREET

BELL INN YD

PHILPOT LANE

Signing up for Virginia 1609

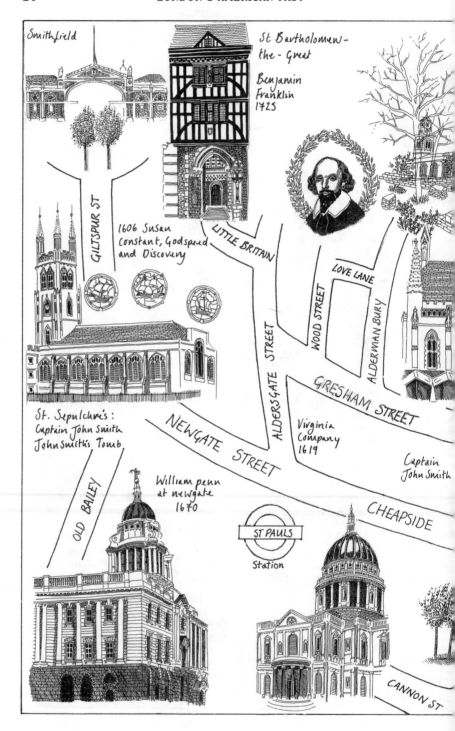

Smithfield

St Bartholomew-
the-Great

Benjamin
Franklin
1725

GILTSPUR ST

1606 Susan
Constant, Godspeed
and Discovery

LITTLE BRITAIN

LOVE LANE

WOOD STREET

ALDERMAN BURY

ALDERSGATE STREET

GRESHAM STREET

St. Sepulchre's:
Captain John Smith
John Smith's Tomb

NEWGATE STREET

Virginia
Company
1619

Captain
John Smith

OLD BAILEY

William penn
at newgate
1670

CHEAPSIDE

ST PAULS
Station

CANNON ST

The City: Bank station to t Paul's station

Mary dermanbury: ow in Fulton, lissouri

Guildhall: Congress letter 1775

LONDON WALL

Abigail Adams 1784

BISHOPSGATE

St Ethelburga: Henry Hudson 1607

THROGMORTON AVENUE

UNTO GOD ONLY BE HONOUR AND GLORY

Drapers Hall

THREADNEEDLE ST

George Peabody 1860

Bank of England

station

BANK

Bi-Centennial garden 1976

Royal Exchange

After Sir Walter Ralegh's doomed attempt to found a settlement at Roanoke in 1585–7 there were no more English settlement expeditions to Virginia for nearly twenty years, but poets, preachers and pamphleteers were none the less busy creating enthusiasm for American colonisation. Ben Jonson, George Chapman and John Marston, in their co-authored play *Eastward Hoe*, first performed at the Blackfriars Theatre in 1605, showed how Virginia had caught the imagination of Londoners. At Billingsgate, in the Blue Anchor Tavern down by the Thames, the silver-tongued Captain Seagull mesmerised his drinking pals Spendall and Scapethrift with tales of the life awaiting them in Virginia:

SEAGULL: Come boys, Virginia longs till we share the rest of her maidenhead.

SPENDALL: Why, is she inhabited already with any English?

SEAGULL: A whole country of English is there man. . . .They have married with the Indians and make 'hem bring forth as beautiful faces as any we have in England: and therefore the Indians are so in love with 'hem, that all the treasure they have, they lay it at their feet.

SCAPETHRIFT: But is there such treasure there Captain, as I have heard?

SEAGULL: I tell thee, gold is more plentiful there than copper is with us: and as much red copper as I can bring, I'll have twice the weight in gold. Why, man, all their dripping pans, and their chamber-pots are pure gold; and all the chains with which they chain up their streets are gold; all the prisoners they take are fettered in gold; and for rubies and diamonds, they go forth on holidays and gather 'hem by the seashore, to hang on their children's coats, and stick in their caps, as commonly as our children wear saffron gilt broaches, and groats with holes in 'hem.

SCAPETHRIFT: And is it a pleasant country with all?

SEAGULL: As ever the sun shined on: temperate and full of all sorts of excellent viands; wild boar is as common there as our tamest bacon is here; venison, as mutton. And you shall live freely there, without sergeants or courtiers or lawyers or intelligencers. Only a few industrious Scots perhaps, who are indeed dispersed over the face of the whole earth. But as for them there are no greater friends to English men and England, when they are out of it, in the world, than they are. And for my part, I would a hundred thousand of 'hem were there, for we are all one countrymen now, yee know; and we should find ten times more comfort of them there than we do here.

Then for your means to advancement, there it is simple, and not preposterously mixed. You may be an alderman there, and

never be a scavinger; you
may be a nobleman, and
never be a slave; you may
come to preferment enough,
and never be a pandar: to
riches and fortune enough
and never have the more vil-
lainy, nor the less in it.

SPENDALL: Gods me! and how far is
it thither?

SEAGULL: Some six weeks sail, no
more, with an indifferent
good wind. And if I get to
any part of the coast of
Africa I'll sail thither with
any wind. Or when I come to
Cape Finnister there's a fore
right wind continually wafts
us till we come to Virginia
... There we shall have no
more law than conscience,
and not too much of either;
serve God enough, eat and
drink enough, and enough
is as good as a feast.'[1]

Billingsgate was London's great
fishmarket from the eleventh century
until 1982, when the site was bought
for £22 million by the London and
Edinburgh Investment Trust. The
Victorian market building was preserved with the interior converted
into a financial dealing room. From
Billingsgate, Monument Street leads
up to Pudding Lane, where the Great
Fire of London began. It raged for
four days in early September 1666,
destroying most of medieval London.

Near Pudding Lane is the 202-foot
column with a gilded ball of flames on
top which commemorates the Great
Fire and is known simply as The
Monument. Sir Christopher Wren

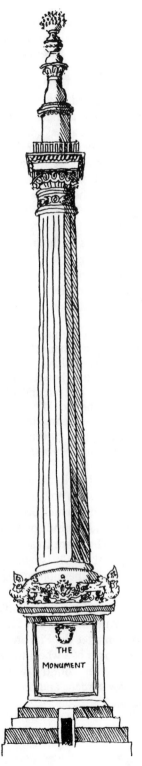

THE
MONUMENT

helped design The Monument but would have preferred it topped with a statue of King Charles II, who appears on the plinth in an allegorical frieze.

The frieze shows a woman representing London languishing in ruins, her head hanging down, her hair dishevelled and her left hand carelessly upon her sword. Time, with wings and a bald head, tries to lift her up, while Londoners behind raise their arms in encouragement. Architecture, Liberty and Science are going to London's rescue. Architecture holds a drawing, square and compasses; Liberty waves a cap in the air; Science has a circle of naked boys dancing on her winged head and carries an image of Nature with numerous breasts, ready to succour all. These figures are commanded by the baton of Charles II, who sports a laurel wreath over his full-bottomed wig and wears the uniform of a Roman army officer. With him is his brother James, Duke of York, holding a garland to crown the rising city and an uplifted sword for her defence.

It was Charles II who invented the name Pennsylvania when, for a rent of two beaver skins and a fifth of any gold or silver discovered, he granted William Penn the land to pay off a £16,000 Crown debt to his father, Admiral Sir William Penn. As William Penn explained in a letter to a friend on 5 March 1681,

> this day my country was confirmed to me . . . by the name of Pennsylvania, a name the King would give it in honour of my father. . . I proposed to have it called New Wales, Sylvania, and they added Penn to it; and though I have much opposed it, and went to the King to have it struck out and altered, he said it was past, and would take it upon him; nor could twenty guineas move the under-secretary to vary the name; for I feared lest it should be looked on as a vanity in me, and not as a respect in the King, as it truly was, to my father, whom he often mentions with praise.[2]

The Duke of York had promised Admiral Sir William Penn that he would take care of his son and granted him territory to the south of Pennsylvania – at a higher rent – which became the State of Delaware. Penn's famous meeting with local Amerindians took place on the banks of the Delaware River. In October 1681 a peace treaty, which was to last for seventy years, was signed affirming that 'all Christians and all Indians should be brothers, as the children of one Father, joined together as with one heart, one head and one body.'

The design of the city of Philadelphia was influenced by the Great Fire of London. William Penn saw Sir Christopher Wren's unused plan for rebuilding London after the Fire and adopted from it the idea of streets radiating like the spokes of a wheel to provide distant vistas. Philadelphia was to be, he said 'a green country town' with plenty of breathing space around the houses 'for gardens and orchards, so that it will never burn and always be wholesome.'[3]

The Monument to the Great Fire stands at the junction of Monument Street and Fish Street Hill, formerly the approach road to the Old London Bridge. That was the London Bridge lined with shops and houses which spanned the Thames from the signing of the Magna Carta in 1215 until the passing of the Great Reform Act in 1832. The Victorian five-arched London Bridge which replaced it was exported to America in 1970 as 'a genuine large antique' and now stands over Lake Havasu in Arizona.

Fish Street Hill leads up to Gracechurch Street. 'Gracechurch' is a corruption of 'Grass Church' and refers to St Benet's Grass Church, which was so called because a hay market was held nearby in the Middle Ages.

Off Gracechurch Street, in White Hart Court, stood London's first Quaker Meeting House. From the 1650s, in England and America, Quakers adopted and preached the 'Principle' that each soul had a spark of divine light within it. The spark, they believed, if responded to, obeyed and accepted 'as a guiding star', would lead to all truth. Such theology was alarming. 'Where all are equals,' warned an English colonel in 1657, 'I expect little obedience in government.'[4] Many Quakers, including unaccompanied women such as Elizabeth Harris of London, made the transatlantic crossing to spread their message in America.

Quakers shared with Puritans a dislike of Church of England hierarchy and ceremony, but unlike Puritans they believed in separation of Church and State and in religious tolerance. The Puritan authorities in America subjected the Quaker missionaries to whippings, ear-croppings, fines and imprisonment. In 1658 the General Court of Massachusetts introduced a law banishing Quakers under penalty of death. Said one Puritan pastor, the Reverend John Wilson, 'I would carry fire in one hand, and faggots in the other to burn all the Quakers in the world.'[5]

In England all public worship outside the Church of England was prohibited by the Conventicle Act of 1665. When William Penn arrived at the London Quaker Meeting House in August 1670 and found it closed, he addressed a crowd in the open air. For this he and William Mead, another Quaker leader, were committed to Newgate Prison and brought before a jury at the Old Bailey. The charge against them was that they, 'with other divers persons to the number of three hundred, did with force and arms in Grace Church Street, preach and speak to the great terror to the King's liege people.'

Penn arrested

George Fox, founder of the Quaker Society of Friends, was seized in 1671 in Gracechurch Street and taken to the Lord Mayor of London for questioning. That year Fox sailed to America for the first time, journeying through Maryland to arrive in Baltimore for the annual assembly of Quakers. When introduced to 'the Indian Emperor, his kings and their cockarooses', he told them 'God was raising up a tabernacle of witness in their wilderness'. Fox spent the final years of his life in London. Among his last words were, 'Mind poor Friends in America.'[6] His grave is in the London Nonconformist burial ground at Bunhill Fields.

John Woolman – the American Quaker and anti-slavery campaigner born in West Jersey – came to Gracechurch Street in 1772 to take part in the annual assembly of English Quakers. He arrived straight from the steerage quarters of a transatlantic sailing ship wearing 'a grey-white beaver hat, a coarse raw linen shirt, without anything about the neck, his coat, waistcoat and breeches of white coarse linen cloth, with wool buttons on . . . without cuffs, white yarn stockings, and shoes of uncured leather, with bands instead of buckles, so that he was all white.' The English Quaker John Fothergill – 'neat in cravat and curled white wig' – wrote to his brother: 'The affairs of the meeting go well. The Americans help us much. John Woolman is solid and weighty in his remarks. I wish he could be cured of some singularities. But his real worth outweighs all the trash.' In America many Quakers had been convinced that slavery was incompatible with Christianity by the anti-slavery campaign that Woolman had pursued from the age of twenty-two. He had begun campaigning after having to prepare a bill of sale for a slave-woman. He objected to sugar because it was produced by slave labour and also advised Friends not to send letters by post because of the harsh conditions imposed on stagecoach horses and postboys. He observed in the journal he kept while in England that

Great numbers of poor people live chiefly on bread and water in the southern parts of England, as well as in the northern parts; and there are many poor children not even taught to read. May those in abundance lay these things to heart! Stage-coaches frequently go upwards of one hundred miles in twenty-four hours; and I have heard Friends say in several places that it is common for horses to be killed with hard driving, and that many others were driven till they grew blind. Postboys pursue their business, each on to his stage, all night through the winter. Some boys who ride long stages suffer greatly in winter nights, and at several places I have heard of their being frozen to death. So great is the hurry in the spirit of the world, that in aiming to do business quickly and to gain wealth, the creation at this day doth loudly groan.[7]

Woolman was in England for only four months before he caught smallpox and died, at the age of fifty-two. He was buried at York.

From Gracechurch Street the equally ancient Fenchurch Street leads towards Aldgate. Fenchurch Street probably gets its name from the old hay market – *faenum* being Latin for hay – or possibly from the fenny banks of a long-lost river, the Langbourne. A turning off Fenchurch Street to the right is Philpot Lane, where in 1609 people had to go if they wanted to put down their names to 'adventure' to Virginia. As a handbill distributed around London at the time explained:

for the better settling of the colony and plantation of Virginia, there is a voyage intended thither by many noblemen, knights, merchants and others. . . . This is . . . to give notice to all artificers, smiths, carpenters, coopers, shipwrights, turners, planters, fowlers, weavers, shoemakers, sawyers, spinsters and all other labouring men and women that are willing to go to said plantation to inhabit there, that *if they repair to Philpot Lane, to the house of Sir Thomas Smith*, Treasurer to the said colony, their names shall be registered and their persons shall be esteemed at a single share, which is twelve pounds ten shillings, and they shall be admitted to go as adventurers in the said voyage to Virginia, where they shall have houses to dwell in, with gardens and orchards, and also food and clothing at the common charge of the joint stock. They shall have their dividend also in all goods and merchandises arising thence by their labours and likewise their dividend in lands to them and to their heirs for ever; and if they shall also bring in money to adventure in the joint stock their shares both in goods and lands shall be augmented accordingly. And likewise all others that will bring twenty-five pounds or more by the last of March though they go not in their persons shall be accepted for freemen of the company, and shall have their bills of adventure as all other adventurers have in the same action.

People attracted by the promotional literature were to be sorely disappointed with the reality of life in early Virginia. A petition by thirty colonists to the House of Burgesses, their elected body established on the instructions of the Virginia Company in 1619, complained that

In those 12 years of Sir Thomas Smith, his government, we aver that the colony for the most part remained in great want and misery under most severe and cruel laws. . . . The allowance in those times for a man was only eight ounces of meal and half a pint of peas for a day . . . mouldy, rotten, full of cobwebs and maggots, loathsome to man and not fit for beasts, which forced many to flee for relief to the savage enemy, who being taken again were put to sundry deaths as by hanging, shooting and breaking upon the wheel . . . of whom one for stealing two or three pints of oatmeal had a bodkin thrust through his tongue and was tied with a chain to a tree until he starved.[8]

Beyond Philpot Lane – at the end of Fenchurch Street – is the Aldgate Pump, erected in 1861 with a brass spout in the shape of a dog's head. It stands on the site of a drinking-well first mentioned in the reign of King John (1199–1216). In 1550 a man was hanged beside the well for spreading news of rural unrest against enclosure of common land. 'There was a commotion of the commons in Norfolk, Suffolk, Essex and other shires,' recorded John Stow, the London historian, writing a generation later,

> by means whereof, straight orders being taken for the suppression of rumours, divers persons were apprehended and executed by martial law; amongst the which the bailiff of Romford in Essex was one, a man very well beloved. He was early in the morning of Mary Magdalen's day, then kept a holiday, brought by the sherrifs of London and the knight-marshal to the well within Aldgate, there to be executed upon a gibbet set up that morning, where, being on the ladder, he had words to this effect: 'Good people, I am come hither to die, but know not for what offence, except for words by me spoken yesternight . . .'. I heard the words of the prisoner, for he was executed upon the pavement of my door where I then kept house.[9]

Aldgate was one of the gates in London's city wall first built by the Romans in AD 200 and finally demolished in 1760. Geoffrey Chaucer, author of *The Canterbury Tales* and the best-known of early writers of English, lived in rooms above the Aldgate from 1374 to 1386 while he held the post of Comptroller of Customs and Subsidies on Wools, Skins and Hides in the Port of London. Aldgate was closed at dusk and people had to hurry back into the City if they were not to be 'benighted in the fields'. As Chaucer put it:

> The wardeyne of the yates gan to calle
> The folk which that withoute the yates were,
> And bad hem dryven in hire bestes alle,
> Or al the nyght they moste bleven there. . . .[10]

The Aldgate where Chaucer lived consisted of a single entrance flanked by two large semi-circular towers. It had been repaired in 1215 – on the orders of the barons at war with King John – using stones from the vandalised homes of London's Jewish community. A new Aldgate was built in 1607 with 'a fair golden sphere with a goodly vane on it'. Two model soldiers, 'denying entrance to any bold enemies', stood in the battlements of the gate above a statue of King James I wearing a gilded suit of armour.

These figures were familiar sights
to Thomas Weston, the ironmonger
from Aldgate who chartered the
Mayflower and organised financial
backing for the Pilgrim Fathers.
Weston was an Elizabethan 'mer-
chant-adventurer', an entrepreneur
whose business interests included
illicit cloth-trading in Holland. When
his contacts among the English
Separatists in Holland began contem-
plating resettlement in America, he
advised them not to rely on the New
Netherlands Company or the Virginia

Company. They should 'neither fear want of shipping or money,' he said, for
he and other London merchants would finance their venture.

Weston drew up an agreement with the leaders of the English Separatist
community in the Dutch town of Leyden and formed a joint-stock company
in London of about seventy 'merchant-adventurers'. Most of these invested
small sums in the company, but some committed as much as £500. They
expected a good return on their investment, because the would-be settlers
were 'industrious and frugal', not men 'whom small things can discourage
or small discontents cause to wish themselves at home again.'

The articles of Weston's company stipulated that all profits from 'trade,
traffic, trucking, working, fishing or any means' were to be put into its
account. Out of the company account the settlers were 'to have their meat,
drink, apparel and all provisions'. At the end of seven years, 'all capital and
profits, viz. the houses, lands, goods and chattels' were to be divided
between the settlers and company adventurers on the basis of the number of
shares held. Shares rated at £10 were given to anyone who contributed £10
in money or provisions. In addition, every male settler was to receive in the
final division a share for himself and for each person in his household over
sixteen years of age – wife, servants and older children. Children aged
between ten and sixteen were rated at half a share and those under ten at
'fifty acres of unmanured land'.

The English Separatists had no objection to these conditions, but they
were bitterly annoyed by the deletion of two clauses from Weston's original
contract. One had exempted their houses, 'gardens and home lots' from the
final division. The other allowed them to work two days a week not for the
the company but 'for ye more comfort of themselves and their families'.
Without a 'day's freedom from task', they complained, the contract was
more for 'thieves and bondslaves than honest men'.

Many of the English Separatists thus withdrew from the project, each
man wishing he 'had again his money in his purse'. Undeterred, Thomas
Weston recruited in and around London about seventy potential settlers,

regardless of their religious beliefs. He chartered the 180-ton *Mayflower* from an adventurer called Thomas Goffe and engaged as its pilot 'one Mr Clarke, who went last year to Virginia' and as its skipper Captain Christopher Jones. In July 1620 the *Mayflower* sailed down the Thames with Mr Christopher Martin as the appointed governor and treasurer of the passengers on board, heading for Southampton where it was to meet up with the *Speedwell*.

The 60-ton *Speedwell* had been bought by the English Separatists in Leyden – despite Weston's scornful laughter – so that they would have a ship they could keep in the New World for 'fishing and such other affairs as might be for the good and benefit of the colony'. It arrived at Southampton a week after the *Mayflower* with about fifty men, women and children on board. They were all from the English Separatist community in Holland, though only some were from Leyden. Four had lived in Scrooby, the English town from which twelve years earlier the congregation led by William Brewster and John Robinson had fled to Holland in search of religious freedom.

The passengers from Holland and the people from in and around London had little in common apart from the fact that there was not a drop of blue blood among them. After 'mutual congratulations, with other friendly entertainments, they fell to parley about their business.' Christopher Martin had already spent £700 at Southampton, 'upon what I know not', complained Deacon Cushman, one of the leaders of the Leyden group. When asked for accounts, Martin 'crieth out of unthankfulness for his pains and care, that we are suspicious of him, and flings away and will end nothing.' He condemned Weston's amended contract for reducing the future colonists to the status of slaves and denounced the merchant-adventurers as 'bloodsuckers'.

Weston, in London, was annoyed. He feared the voyage would never get under way while the leaders were 'going up and down, wrangling and expostulating'. He arrived in person at Southampton to have the contract signed by the English Separatist leaders. They refused, and Weston returned to London in a huff. Before the ships could sail, the passengers were forced to give up some of their provisions for harbour fees, and in desperation they wrote to Weston pleading for money, withdrawing their objection to houses being included in the final share-out and offering to extend the contract beyond seven years if the company had not made a substantial profit by then. Thomas Weston ignored their pleas.

A letter then arrived in Southampton from Pastor Robinson in Leyden. He was sorry, he said, he was not with them to help shoulder 'this first brunt'. He urged them to be patient 'against ye evil day', and not to 'shake the house of God . . . with unnecessary novelties'. The settlers were to avoid the pursuit of private profit 'as a deadly plague', direct their efforts to 'ye general convenience', and put down self-interested men 'as so many rebels against ye common good'.

After two more weeks of anxious delay, the *Mayflower* and the *Speedwell* finally sailed out of Southampton harbour on 5 August. Christopher Martin was in charge of the ninety passengers on board the *Mayflower*, Deacon Cushman of the thirty on the *Speedwell*. As governors they were to 'order ye people by ye way, and to see to ye disposing of their provisions and such like affairs'. After a few days at sea the *Speedwell* was leaking so badly that its Captain Reynolds decided, in consultation with Captain Christopher Jones of the *Mayflower*, that they must turn back. If the *Speedwell* had stayed at sea three or four hours longer, wrote Deacon Cushman, 'she would have sunk right down.' When the two ships docked at Dartmouth tempers were understandably frayed.

The sailors were so incensed by Christopher Martin's 'ignorant boldness' that they threatened to 'mischief him'. He behaved towards the people from Holland 'as if they were not good enough to wipe his shoes,' wrote Deacon Cushman. 'They complain to me and alas I can do nothing for them. If I speak to him he flies in my face as mutinous and saith no complaints shall be heard or received but by himself.' Martin told Cushman that those who complained were

> forward and waspish, discontented people and I do ill to hear them. . . . Where is ye meek and humble spirit of Moses? Is not the sound of Rehoboam's brags daily heard amongst us? If ever we make a plantation God works a miracle, especially considering how scant we shall be of victuals, and most of all ununited amongst ourselves and devoid of good tutors and regiment. Violence will break all.

When the two ships set sail again they passed Land's End and reached well into the Atlantic, but then had to turn back yet again because the *Speedwell* was leaking so badly it could not possibly complete the crossing. This time they put into Plymouth, England, and there twenty people – including Deacon Cushman and his friend William Ring – stayed behind after 'another sad parting'.

On 10 November 1620 the *Mayflower* finally reached the east coast of North America and the remaining 102 passengers were able to disembark. Less than half of them – sixteen children, sixteen women and nine men – were from the English Separatist community in Holland. All, however, were under the rule, of the 'Mayflower Compact', which had been drafted while they were still at sea in the face of 'discontents and murmurings amongst some and mutinous speeches and carriages in others.' Forty-one men had signed the compact, half of them 'saints' from Holland and half 'strangers' recruited by Thomas Weston in London. They included a few servants and hired hands. The signatories to the Mayflower Compact committed themselves 'solemnly and mutually in ye presence of God and one of another [to] combine ourselves together into a civil body politic.' They elected Deacon John Carver, 'a man godly and well approved amongst them', as their governor.

When the *Mayflower* returned to London empty of any cargo and without Thomas Weston's contract duly signed, he was furious. On the *Fortune*, which sailed to New England a few months after the *Mayflower*, he sent the Pilgrims, now settled in New Plymouth, a stinging letter:

> If you mean, bona fide, to perform the conditions agreed upon, do us ye favour to copy them out fair, and subscribe them with ye principal of your names. . . . That you sent no lading in the ship is wonderful, and worthily distated. I know your weakness was the cause of it, and I believe more weakness of judgment than weakness of hands. A quarter of the time you spent in discoursing, arguing and consulting would have done much more, but that is past.

Faced with the threat of Weston's company spending not another penny on their settlement, the Pilgrim Fathers signed the contract they so hated. Many of the settlers were arguing that the cornfields and common lands should be divided into equal shares and permanently allotted to individuals as private property, but they were told that the contract must be honoured as a matter of moral obligation and practical expediency. Their ideas were condemned in a sermon entitled 'The Dangers of Self-Love' preached by Deacon Cushman.

The *Fortune* was loaded with hardwood timber, wainscoting, 'good clapboard' and several hogsheads of beaver and otter pelts. The cargo was worth £500, almost half the amount the merchant-adventurers had advanced. With it went a letter to Weston answering his sarcasm. 'To be greatly blamed for not freighting the ship', wrote the Pilgrim Fathers, 'doth indeed go near us and much discourage us. But you say you know we will pretend weakness; and so you think we had not cause? Many of our arms and legs can tell us to this day we were not negligent.' Unfortunately, the *Fortune* was attacked by French pirates and sailed up the Thames stripped of anything of value. The merchant-adventurers began to quarrel. Weston wrote to inform the New Plymouth settlers that the principal stockholders of his company had decided 'to break it off, and do pray you to ratify and confirm the same on your parts. . . . I fear you must stand on your legs and trust (as they say) to God and yourselves.'

The New Plymouth settlers began to achieve economic viability through trade in beaver pelts. Thomas Weston threatened their prospects when he sent men to set up a rival colony in Wessagusset, on the site of the modern city of Weymouth. In 1623 Captain Myles Standish, the Pilgrims' military leader, took a group of heavily armed men from New Plymouth to Wessagusset and killed some of the Massachusetts braves who lived there. One of them, Wituwamat, had insulted Standish in an earlier incident. His head was brought triumphantly back to New Plymouth and put on a pole on the roof of the fort, where it remained for several years. After this violent 'huggery' at Wessagusset it was too dangerous for Weston's men to remain in Massachusetts territory. They turned down the offer of going to New Plymouth and returned to England.

Thomas Weston himself then arrived in New Plymouth in the 'disguise of a blacksmith', with little more than the clothes he stood up in. He had been shipwrecked on the coast and robbed of everything he owned by Amerindians. He persuaded some of the Pilgrim Fathers secretly to loan him two hundred pounds of beaver, then he travelled on to Virginia, where he became a member of the House of Burgesses in 1628. He moved to Maryland and served in the Assembly in 1642, but soon after returned to England, where he died in Bristol.[11]

Beyond Thomas Weston's home-ground at Aldgate is the church of St Botolph-without-Aldgate. Its list of rectors goes back to 1108; one of them, Thomas Bray, who died in 1730, established eighty parochial libraries in England and thirty-nine in America. Today the church houses the Council for Christian–Jewish Understanding and provides facilities for homeless people. Some of these, sitting with their backs against the church wall, inspired a statue entitled *Sanctuary* by Naomi Blake, an Auschwitz survivor. This was installed in the churchyard in 1985 and is dedicated to all victims of oppression.

Buried in the churchyard is William Symington, builder of the *Charlotte Dundas* Britain's first steamship successfully constructed for practical use (1802); he died 'in want' in 1831. From the 1840s steamships cut the transatlantic journey from two months to two weeks. In 1903 a plaque commemorating Symington was placed in St Botolph-without-Aldgate by the Lord Mayor of London, Sir Marcus Samuel. As a reporter remarked of William Symington at the time, 'Little did he dream of the large numbers of steamships which later on would unload their freights near his last resting-place' – or of the imposing shipping offices which would be built close by.

Following the line of the Roman city wall from St Botolph-without-Aldgate, the road which continues from Old Jewry – Duke's Place – has a plaque on the site of the Great Synagogue built here in 1691. To the left is Creechurch Lane. It was from here, near Sugar Baker Court, that the cargo of tea was dispatched which ended up in Boston Harbor during the Tea Party of 1773. On the corner of Creechurch Lane and Bury Street stood the first Synagogue built in London after the laws excluding the Jewish community from the City were relaxed by Oliver Cromwell in 1657.

Off Bury Street, to the left, is Cunard Place, formerly the home of Cunard, the major British transatlantic shipping company. In 1902, when Cunard was threatened with a takeover by the American businessman and financier J. P. Morgan, the government loaded it £2.4 million for new vessels and to subsidise its operations. Although anathema to many, such support was considered essential to preserve British control of the North Atlantic.

Bury Street and Bury Court wind around the 1903 building of the Baltic Mercantile and Shipping Exchange, known as the Baltic Exchange. Here most of the world's freight-chartering is arranged and half the world's ships are sold. The two thousand members who can go on to the floor of the Baltic Exchange are historical descendants of London's eighteenth-century traders in American goods, who used to meet at the Maryland Coffee House in Newman's Court, off Cornhill. On 24 May 1744 the *Daily Post* announced that

> the Maryland Coffee House . . . is now opened by the name of the Virginia and Baltic Coffee House where all foreign and domestic news are taken in and all letters or parcels directed to merchants or captains in the Virginia or Baltic trade will be carefully delivered according as directed.

The Virginia and Baltic Coffee House became the Baltic Club, with members trading under agreed rules. Later the Baltic Club amalgamated with the London Shipping Exchange to become the Baltic Mercantile and Shipping Exchange.

The front of the Baltic Exchange is in a street called St Mary Axe – the strange name derives from the fact that an axe once preserved here – in the church of St Mary the Virgin and St Ursula and the Eleven Thousand Virgins – was believed to be one of three axes used in the massacre of St Ursula and her friends, carried out by Wannius, Chief of the Huns, and Melga, Chief of the Picts, somewhere near Cologne in AD 393. The church was converted into a warehouse in 1565.

At the corner of St Mary Axe and Leadenhall Street is the pre-Fire church of St Andrew Undershaft, where John Stow (?1525–1605), London's first major historian, is buried. During the Second World War, when Stow's monument had to be bricked up to protect it from bombing, the bill was paid by an American lawyer from Cleveland called Grover Higgins. Explaining the origin of 'Undershaft' in the church's name, Stow tells that

> every year on May day in the morning . . . an high or long shaft or maypole was set up there, in the midst of the street, before the south side of said church; which shaft when it was set on end and fixed in the ground, was higher than the church steeple.[12]

An anonymous poem which Stow mistakenly attributed to Chaucer refers to the maypole in describing a cheerful Londoner:

Right well aloft, and high ye beare your heade,
The weather cocke, with flying, as ye would kill,
When ye be stuffed, bet of wine, then brede,
Then looke ye, when your wombe doth fill,
As ye would beare the great shaft of Cornehill.

The last time the Cornhill maypole was erected outside the church of St
Andrew Undershaft, in 1517, the revelries turned into 'Evil May Day', an
apprentice riot against foreign merchants. Thereafter, John Stow recorded,

the said shaft was laid along over the doors, and under the pentises of
one row of houses and an alley gate, called . . . Shaft Alley. . . . It was
there . . . hung on iron hooks many years, till . . . one Sir Stephen,
curate of St Katharine Christ's Church [St Katharine Cree], preaching
at Paul's cross, said there that this shaft was made an idol, by naming
the church of St Andrew with the addition 'under that shaft' . . . and I
saw the effect that followed; for in the afternoon of that present
Sunday, the neighbours and tenants . . . over whose doors the said
shaft had lain, after they had well dined, to make themselves strong,
gathered more help, and with great labour raising the shaft from the
hooks, whereon it had rested two-and-thirty years, they sawed it in
pieces, every man taking for his share so much as had lain over his
door and stall, the length of his house; and they of the alley divided
among them so much as had lain over their alley gate. Thus was this
idol (as he termed it) mangled, and after burned.[13]

Seventy-five years later, on the other side of the Atlantic, a straight, thin
pine, eighty feet tall, cut down and trimmed for use as a maypole, was
hauled to the top of an oceanside hill to the sound of drums, pistols, guns
and 'other fitting instruments' in 'a solemn manner, with revels and merri-
ment after the old English custom'. The settlement on Mount Woollaston
was being renamed Mare Mount. This meant 'Mountain by the Sea' but the
Pilgrim Fathers called it 'Merry Mount'. It was to be 'a unique settlement,
one of the gayest that ever graced America'. The pole erected for the ceremonial renaming had a pair of antlers fixed to the top as a 'fair sea mark for
directions how to find out the way to mine host of Mare Mount'. A barrel of
beer was laid on to be consumed 'with all good cheer' by those invited to the
festivity, men and women, whites and Amerindians alike. The host was
Thomas Morton, a scholarly aristocrat and distinguished soldier who had
practised law in London, and enjoyed many an evening at the Mermaid
Tavern with the playwright Ben Jonson. Morton had married an elderly
widow, but her sons called on him to give account of the estate, and in 1625
he sailed to America on the *Unity* under Captain Woollaston with thirty
indentured servants 'and provisions of all sorts fit for a plantation'.

The Woollaston settlement on the site of the modern city of Quincy – just
beyond Wessagusset, Massachusetts – was considered by the Pilgrim

Fathers in nearby Plymouth to be a brazen trespass on their domain. But Captain Woollaston and his partners were sponsored by the powerful Sir Ferdinando Gorges, who spent his life trying to acquire New England as a vast feudal estate with himself as overlord. When Captain Woollaston left for Virginia – where indentured servants were being sold into slavery – Thomas Morton invited those who remained to a feast. After 'strong drink and other junkets', according to the Pilgrim Fathers, Morton proposed driving out the men Woollaston had left in charge. 'I, having a part in the plantation,' he promised, 'will receive you as my partners and consociats so you may be free from service, and we will converse, trade, plant, and live together as equals, and support and protect one another.' This proposal was readily received and soon implemented.

Morton tacked a poem he had written on to the maypole and, as his men danced around hand in hand with laughing Amerindian maids, 'one of the company sang and filled out the good liquor, like Gammedes and Jupiter':

> Drink and be merry, merry, merry boys;
> Let all your delight be in Hymen's joys;
> Io to Hymen, now the day is come,
> About the merry maypole take a room.

> Make green garlons, bring bottles out,
> And fill sweet nectar freely about.
> Uncover thy head and fear no harm,
> For here's good liquor to keep it warm.

> Give to the nymph that's free from scorn
> No Irish stuff nor Scotch over-worn.
> Lasses in beaver coats, come away,
> Ye shall be welcome to us night and day.

The Pilgrim Fathers in New Plymouth were incensed by Thomas Morton's 'idle or idol Maypole' and 'lascivious rhymes'. The settlement led by this 'lord of misrule' was nothing but a 'school of atheism' where Thomas Morton and his men were 'pouring themselves into all profaneness . . . inviting Indian women for their consorts, dancing and frisking together (like so many fairies, or furies rather) . . . as if this jollity would have lasted ever.' The Pilgrim Fathers could not hope to keep their servants while Thomas Morton 'would entertain any, how vile soever, and all the scum of the country or any discontents would flock to him from all places.' Worse still, the youth of New Plymouth might be tempted to slip away through the woods to spend time with 'mine host of Mare Mount'. Above all, Merry Mount was a serious competitor in the beaver trade. Morton taught Amerindians to use firearms then employed them to hunt for him, very profitably since they were much better at it than the white settlers, who were mainly townsfolk.

Eventually Morton was captured by Captain Myles Standish and brought

before Governor William Bradford and his council in New Plymouth. He did
not suffer the fate of Chief Wituwamat and, against the wishes of Standish,
was not executed. Instead he was returned to London, condemned as the

> head of a turbulent and seditious crew [living] without all fear of God
> or common honesty, some of them abusing the Indian women most
> filthily, as is notorious . . . maintaining drunkenness, riot and other
> evils among them: yea, and inveigling of men's servants away from
> them, so as the mischief began to grow intolerable, and if it had been
> suffered a while longer, would have been incurable.

Morton, by giving guns to the Amerindians, the Pilgrim Fathers argued,
had 'spoiled the trade in all other things'. He had compelled them 'for the
safety of ourselves, our wives, and innocent children, to apprehend him by
force (though with some peril)'. They insisted steps be taken to protect
them from the 'cankered covetousness of these licentious men'.

Sir Ferdinando Gorges ignored these complaints and within a year
Morton was back at Merry Mount, doing well in the beaver trade. Before
long, however, Captain John Endecott of the Salem Puritans, encouraged by
the Pilgrim Fathers at New Plymouth, marched to Merry Mount, cut down
the maypole and rebuked the inhabitants for their 'profaneness'. Morton's
house was burned to the ground, his goods were confiscated and the name
of the place was changed to Mount Dragon.[14] Maypoles were to reappear as
'liberty poles' during the American Revolution and May Day was taken up by
American trade unions in 1886.

Opposite St Andrew Undershaft – where once the Cornhill maypole stood
higher than the church tower – is the controversial Lloyds of London building, opened in 1986. It was designed by architect Richard Rogers to be added
to with the expansion of the world insurance market. Lloyds is a society of
individual insurers liable to the full extent of their private fortunes for the
risks they underwrite. Membership of Lloyds is open to men and women
who meet the society's financial requirements, regardless of nationality. Of
the 33,500 members, 2800 are US Citizens. Forty per cent of Lloyds' business comes from the United States.

The public exhibition at Lloyds illustrates the development and
importance of insurance. In the words of an Act of Parliament passed in the
reign of Queen Elizabeth I, 'it cometh to pass that on loss or perishing of
any ship there followeth not the undoing of any man, but the loss lighteth
rather easily upon many than heavily upon few.' The San Francisco earth-
quake and fire of 1906 severely tested Lloyds' underwriters, but they
emerged with credit. While other insurers defaulted on commitments they
paid their claims promptly and in full.

Today only about two per cent of the world volume of insurance is
handled at Lloyds but it is the leading market for new and different types of
insurance. On display in the visitors' gallery are the miniature US and UK

flags flown aboard the space-shuttle
Columbia in 1981; they were presented to Lloyds 'in recognition of the
contribution of the Society to the uti-
lization of space for peaceful purposes
for the benefit of mankind by providing insurance coverage for commercial space activities.'

The attendants at Lloyds are called
'waiters' because the Society originated in the 1680s at Edward Lloyd's
coffee house on the corner of Lombard Street. Patrons not only drank
coffee and met business contacts
there but also participated in auc-
tions of ships and listened to mari-
time news read from 'the pulpit' by a
boy called 'the Kidney'.

From Lloyds a pleasant stroll
through Leadenhall Market, which is
on the site of the Roman forum and
basilica, then across Gracechurch
Street and down Bell Inn Yard, leads
to the birthplace of London's coffee-
house culture.

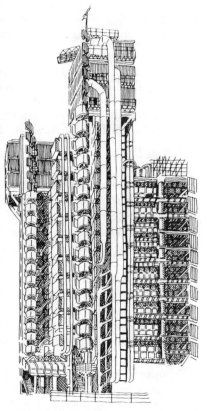

Coffee was first served in London
in 1652 in St Michael's Alley, where
the Jamaica Wine House now stands. An English merchant called Daniel
Edwards brought back from Smyrna, as his servant, a Greek youth called
Pasqua Rosee. The coffee which Pasqua Rosee prepared for his master each
morning attracted so many visitors that a shop was set up 'at the sign of
Pasqua Rosee's head'. Coffee, it was announced, 'is a very good help to diges-
tion, quickens the spirits, and is good against sore eyes'. Coffee houses soon
proliferated. In 1676 King Charles II tried to close them down as places
'where the disaffected meet and spread scandalous reports', but by the end
of the seventeenth century there were hundreds of coffee houses in the City,
Covent Garden and Westminster. As a Swiss visitor observed:

> These houses are extremely convenient. You have all Manner of News
> there: you have a good Fire which you may sit by as long as you please;
> you have a Dish of Coffee, you meet your friends for the Transaction of
> Business, and all for a Penny, if you don't care to spend more.

The French eighteenth-century author, l'Abbe de Prevost, hailed the
London coffee houses 'where you have the right to read all the papers for

and against the government' as 'the seats of English liberty'. American merchants and colonial agents congregated at the American Coffee House in St Michael's Alley, the American and Continental Coffee House in Ludgate Hill, the American and New England Coffee House at 60 Threadneedle Street and later in Lombard Street, the New York Coffee House in Lombard Street, opposite the Post Office, the Carolina Coffee House at 25 Birchin Lane, the Pennsylvania Coffee House in Birchin Lane and the Virginia and Maryland Coffee House in Newman's Court off Cornhill. On 28 September 1728 the *Daily Journal* advertised the sale of 'a negro boy, aged eleven years' at the Virginia Coffee House. On 1 January 1734 it announced that 'at the Virginia Coffee House behind the Royal Exchange is to be seen the largest rattle snake ever seen in England. Just arrived from Virginia.'[15]

From the site of London's first coffee house, Castle Court leads to Birchin Lane where the Pennsylvania Coffee House stood from 1702 to 1822, rebuilt after a fire in 1748. Benjamin Franklin often visited it, particularly to play chess. Across Birchin Lane, to the left, is Change Alley, where the Stock Exchange originated in Johnathan's Coffee House and Garraway's Coffee House in the late seventeenth century, and where the South Sea Bubble burst in 1720.

Change Alley, bearing left, leads to Lombard Street, named after the bankers of Lombardy, in northern Italy, who arrived in London in the twelfth century. At the corner of Lombard Street and King William Street – above entrances to Bank underground station – is the church of St Mary Woolnoth, designed by Sir Christopher Wren's pupil Nicholas Hawksmoor. The present church, completed in 1727, replaced the medieval St Mary Woolnoth which was the burial place in 1695 of Sir William Phips, a Governor of Massachusetts. Phips, 'by a series of fortunate incidents, rather than by any uncommon talents . . . rose from the lowest conditions of life to be the first man in his country.' He was born in 1651 in Panaquid, 'a despicable plantation . . . almost the furthest village of the Eastern Settlement of New England', the son of a gunsmith, and he had twenty brothers and five sisters. He worked first as a shepherd, but abandoned that to serve an apprenticeship as a ship's carpenter. In Boston he learned to read and write, and married a wealthy young widow.

Obsessed by the idea of salvaging sunken Spanish treasure, in 1683 Phips went to England and there won the backing of Christopher Monck, second Duke of Albemarle and Lord of Trade and Plantations. At sea Phips's sceptical crew threatened mutiny, but 'with a most undaunted fortitude he rushed in upon them and with the blows of his bare hands fell'd many of them and quell'd all the rest.'[16] Off the coast of Hispaniola, in a reef of rocks a few leagues to the north of Port de la Plata, with the aid of an ancient Spaniard and some local divers he found a shipwrecked galleon loaded with a cargo of gold and silver ingots, precious stones and coins. It was worth £300,000. He received only £16,000 for his find but in England was made a knight.

In 1691 Sir William Phips persuaded King William III to grant a new charter to Massachusetts and was sworn in as Governor. One of his first acts was to order the women of Salem accused of witchcraft to be put into irons. This was apparently only a gesture of severity to satisfy the witch-hunter Increase Mather. The officers who carried out the order almost at once removed the irons. Increase Mather then admitted that it was better for a guilty witch to escape than for an innocent person to die and Phips brought the persecution to an abrupt end. His last act as Governor of Massachusetts was to issue a general pardon to all who had been convicted or accused of witchcraft. In 1694 he was ordered to London and arrested for customs irregularities. Soon after he arrived, he caught a cold, died and was buried in St Mary Woolnoth. His first biographer, Cotton Mather, wrote of him in 1697:

> Phips our great Friend, our wonder, and our Glory,
> The Terror of our Foes, the world's rare Story.
> England will Boast him too, whose Noble Mind
> Impell'd by Angels, did those Treasures find,
> Long in the Bottom of the Ocean laid,
> Which her Three Hundred Thousand Richer made.
> By Silver yet ne'er Cankered nor defil'd
> By Honour, nor Betray'd when Fortune smiled.
> Since this bright Phoebus visited our Shoar
> We saw no Fogs but what were raised before.

Phips's burial place disappeared in the post-Fire rebuilding of St Mary Woolnoth, but the vaults still contain the remains of the Reverend John Newton, the slave-trade abolitionist who served as rector of the church from 1780 until his death in 1807 at the age of eighty-two. In his own words, inscribed on a white marble plaque in the church, he was 'once an infidel and libertine, a servant of slaves in Africa . . . appointed to preach the faith he had long laboured to destroy.'

Newton's denunciation of the slave trade from the beautifully carved pulpit in St Mary Woolnoth inspired William Wilberforce, one of his parishioners, to campaign in the House of Commons for abolition. 'That unhappy branch of commerce,' wrote Newton in *Thoughts upon the African Slave Trade* (1778), maintained on the Coast of Africa . . . to supply our West Indian islands and the American colonies, when they were ours, with slaves . . . contradicts the feelings of humanity. . . . It is hoped this stain of our national character will soon be wiped out. . . . I know of no method of getting money, not even that of robbery, for it, upon the highway, which has a more direct tendency to efface the moral sense, to rob the heart of every gentle and humane disposition, and to harden it, like steel, against all impressions of sensibility.

Newton – whose father was Governor of York Fort in Hudson Bay from 1748 to 1750 – was able to give evidence against the slave trade from his own experience as a slave trader:

The ship in which I was mate left the Coast with 218 slaves on board; and though we were not much affected by epidemical disorders I find, by my journal of that voyage (now before me) that we buried 62 on our passage to South Carolina, exclusive of those which died before we left the Coast, of which I have no account. . . . It is not easy to write altogether with coolness upon this business, and especially not easy to me, who have formerly been deeply engaged in it.

Recalling one particular incident, Newton described how

a mate of a ship, in a longboat, purchased a young woman, with a fine child, of about a year old, in her arms. In the night the child cried much, and disturbed his sleep. He rose up in great anger and swore, that if the child did not cease making such a noise he would presently silence it. The child continued to cry. At length he rose up a second time, tore the child from the mother and threw it into the sea. The child was soon silenced indeed, but it was not so easy to pacify the woman: she was too valuable to be thrown overboard, and he was obliged to bear the sound of her lamentations till he could put her on board his ship. . . .
When women and girls are taken on board ship, naked, trembling, terrified, perhaps almost exhausted with cold, fatigue and hunger, they are often exposed to the wanton rudeness of white savages. The poor creatures cannot understand the language they hear, but the looks and manner of the speakers are sufficiently intelligible. In imagination the prey is divided, upon the spot, and only reserved till opportunity offers. Where resistance, or refusal, would be utterly in vain, even the solicitation of consent is seldom thought of. But I forbear – this is not a subject for declamation.[17]

The transatlantic slave trade began in 1503 when Africans were brought to Hispaniola and the Spanish Governor complained that runaways were teaching disobedience to the Caribbean Indians. English merchants entered the trade with John Hawkins's delivery of a cargo of slaves to San Domingo in 1562. A million had been transported from Africa to the Portuguese and

Spanish colonies in South America and the Caribbean by 1619, when the first twenty were brought to Jamestown, Virginia, by Dutch traders. Americans in New England became involved when the slave-ship *Desire* sailed from Marblehead in 1637, its holds partitioned into two-foot by six-foot racks fitted with leg-irons and bars.

Dutch control of the trade in slaves – as well as in tobacco, sugar, furs and cod – was broken by wars between England and Holland which began in 1652. The capture of Jamaica in 1655 provided England with a base for expansion in the slave trade as great fortunes began to be made from sugar and tobacco plantations. The Royal African Company, founded soon after the Restoration of the Monarchy in 1660 under the patronage of James, Duke of York, sought to oust the Dutch from their slave-trading dominance. Over the next forty years the company sent five hundred ships to Africa carrying goods worth £500,000. It transported one hundred thousand slaves, imported thirty thousand tons of sugar and made a profit of 500,000 guineas. Between 1660 and 1689 fifteen Lord Mayors and twenty-five Sheriffs of the City of London were shareholders of the Royal African Company. The ending of the company's monopoly in 1698 led to further expansion of English slave trading. In 1711, after the War of the Spanish Succession, England won the coveted *asiento* – the exclusive right to supply slaves to the Spanish Empire – and replaced Holland as the greatest slave-trading nation in the world.

Despite losses of up to twenty per cent in transit, the slave trade was probably the most profitable of all branches of English commerce. Ships left London loaded with textiles, muskets, brass rods, cutlery, copper rods, gunpowder, felt hats, silk pieces, sailcloth, green glass, beads, spirits, tobacco and beer. On the African coast these commodities were bartered for slaves, who were shipped across the Atlantic in the notorious middle passage. In the Caribbean the slaves were exchanged for sugar, spices, molasses, rum and tobacco, which were carried back to Britain.

This system – in which the ships never sailed empty – was enormously profitable for the planters whose slaves produced the sugar and tobacco, for the merchants who sold the slaves, for the industrialists who supplied the manufactured goods, and for the bankers and commission agents who lent them all money. As the merchant Joshua Gee wrote in 1729, 'All this great increase in our treasure proceeds chiefly from the labour of negroes in the plantations.'[18] Or in the words of the mercantilist Malachy Postlewayt, writing in 1749:

> The extensive employment of our shipping in, to, and from America .. . and the daily bread of the most considerable part of our British manufacturers, are owing primarily to the labour of negroes. . . . The negroe-trade . . . may be justly esteemed an inexhaustible fund of wealth and naval power to this nation.[19]

English slave traders were responsible for about a quarter of the trans-atlantic trade up to 1791, and for more than half between 1791 and 1806. They netted a profit of approximately £12 million on the two and a half million Africans they bought and sold between about 1630 and 1807, perhaps half being accrued between 1750 and 1790.[20] A committee of the Company of Merchants Trading to Africa declared in 1788 that 'the effects of this trade to Great Britain are beneficial to an infinite extent . . . there is hardly any branch of commerce in which this nation is concerned that does not derive some advantage from it.'[21] Colonial assemblies in America were not allowed to prohibit or restrict the activities of English slave traders, and a proposal to teach American slaves to spin and weave cotton was stopped by the British Prime Minister William Pitt, the Earl of Chatham.

The black population of the American colonies rose from eight per cent of the total in 1690 to twenty-one per cent in 1770. In the northern states the highest proportion was in New York, where it was ten per cent. After a rebellion in New York in 1712, the Governor reported to London that 'some were burnt, others were hanged, one broke on the wheel and one hung alive in chains in the town.' In 1720 a letter from South Carolina to London reported that

we have had a very wicked and barbarous plot of the design of the negroes rising with a design to destroy all the white people in the country and then to take Charles Town in full body but it pleased God it was discovered and many of them taken prisoners and some burnt and some hang'd and some banish'd.[22]

By the 1750s the population in the Carolinas was made up of twenty-five thousand whites, forty thousand blacks and sixty thousand Creek, Cherokee, Choctaw and Chickasaw Indians. Children of black–white parentage were born throughout the colonial period, despite laws prohibiting inter-racial marriage in Virginia, Massachusetts, Maryland, Delaware, Pennsylvania, the Carolinas and Georgia.

In 1780, seven black Americans in Dartmouth, Massachusetts, petitioned the legislature for the right to vote.

We apprehend ourselves to be aggrieved, in that while we are not allowed the privilege of freemen of the state having no vote or influence in the election of those that tax us yet many of our color (as is well known) have cheerfully entered the field of battle in the defense of the common cause and that (as we conceive) against a similar exertion of power (in regard to taxation) too well known to need a recital in this place.[23]

In England, John Newton's friend, the poet William Cowper – with whom Newton wrote hymns such as 'Amazing Grace' and 'How Sweet the Name of Jesus Sounds' – published a verse in 1788 summing up the moral dilemma posed for him by the slave trade:

I own I am shock'd at the purchase of slaves,
And fear those who buy them and sell them are knaves;
What I hear of their hardships, their tortures, and groans,
Is almost enough to drive pity from stones.
I pity them greatly, but I must be mum,
For how could we do without sugar and rum?

A simple solution was proposed in a letter of 1789 to a gentleman's magazine by a defender of the slave trade: 'The vulgar are influenced by names and titles. Instead of SLAVES, let the Negroes be called ASSISTANT-PLANTERS; and we shall not then hear such violent outcries against the slave-trade by pious devines, tender-hearted poetesses, and short-sighted politicians.'

The British Parliament banned slave trading in 1807 and abolished slavery within the British Empire in 1834. This only had the effect of stimulating the slave trade. Production of sugar declined in the West Indies but increased in Cuba and Brazil, where slavery was not outlawed, creating a new demand for slave labour. For more than a generation the British Navy was actively employed on the African coast hunting down the slave-trading ships of weaker nations. It was in the course of these activities that British colonial power in West Africa was established.

John Newton had lived in West Africa as a young man and praised the quality of life there in comparison with the conditions of late eighteenth-century London:

I have lived long and conversed much amongst these supposed savages. I have often slept in their towns, in a house filled with goods for trade, with no person in the house but myself, and with no other door than a mat; in that security which no man in his senses would expect in this civilised nation, especially in this metropolis, without the precaution of having strong doors, strongly locked and bolted.

Nowadays, the church of St Mary Woolnoth provides lunchtime relaxation and meditation sessions for people working in the City of London, acting as 'a spiritual resource point [against] the pressures of modern life, the "rat-race", the ravages of stress, the cumulative effects of demoralisation and strain'. A one-time bank clerk who felt these pressures was the American-born poet T. S. Eliot. Born in St Louis, Missouri, in 1888, Eliot graduated from Harvard in 1910 and, after further study at the Sorbonne and Oxford, returned to the USA to teach philosophy. In 1914 he travelled to Europe and in 1927 became a British subject, because of his interest in the Church of England. His greatest poem, *The Waste Land*, written during a period of despair and published in 1922, contains a reference to St Mary Woolnoth:

Unreal City
Under the brown fog of a winter dawn,
A crowd flowed over London Bridge, so many,
I had not thought death had undone so many.
Sighs, short and infrequent, were exhaled,
And each man fixed his eyes before his feet.
Flowed up the hill and down King William Street,
To where Saint Mary Woolnoth kept the hours
With a dead sound on the final stroke of nine.

On the far side of King William Street stands the Mansion House, the official residence of the Lord Mayor of London during his or her year of office. It was designed by George Dance the Elder and completed in 1752. The Mansion House contains one of the City of London's two magistrate courts and has cells in its basement. The cell for women is known as 'the Birdcage' and here Emmeline Pankhurst (1859–1928), the English suffragette leader, was once confined.

In 1855, during the crisis which led to the American Civil War, Nathaniel Hawthorne received an invitation from the Lord Mayor of London to a banquet at the Mansion House. In his own words, he

gladly accepted it, taking the precaution . . . to inform the City-King . . . that I was no fit representative of American eloquence, and must humbly make it a condition that I should not be expected to open my mouth, except for the reception of his Lordship's bountiful hospitality.

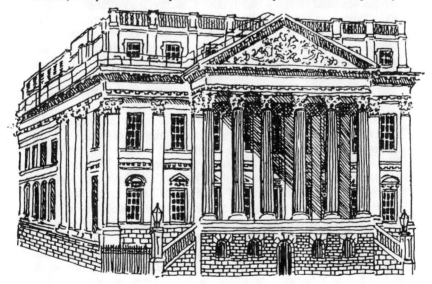

Mansion House

Hawthorne described this visit in *Our Old Home*, published in 1863. The
'real dignity and importance' of the office of Lord Mayor, people had told
him, 'have perished . . . as they do . . . out of all earthly institutions, leaving
only a painted and gilded shell like that of an Easter egg.' This saddened
Hawthorne,

> for the original emigrants of New England had strong sympathies
> with the people of London, who were mostly Puritans in religion and
> Parliamentarians in politics, in the early days of our country; so that
> the Lord Mayor was a potentate of huge dimensions in the estimation
> of our forefathers. . . .
>
> In the entrance-hall I was received by a body of footmen dressed in
> a livery of blue coats and buff breeches, in which they looked wonder-
> fully like American Revolutionary generals, only bedizened with far
> more lace and embroidery. . . . If it were desirable to write an essay on
> the latent aptitude of ordinary people for grandeur, we have an exem-
> plification in our own country, and on a scale incomparably greater
> than that of the Mayoralty, though invested with nothing like the out-
> ward magnificence that gilds and embroiders the latter. If I have been
> correctly informed, the Lord Mayor's salary is exactly double that of
> the President of the United States, and yet is found very inadequate to
> his necessary expenditure.
>
> There were two reception-rooms, thrown into one by the opening of
> wide folding-doors. . . . One very pleasant characteristic . . . was the
> presence of ladies. . . . I saw much reason for modifying certain het-
> erodox opinions which I had imbibed, in my Transatlantic newness
> and rawness, as regarded the delicate character and frequent occur-
> rence of English beauty. . . . My taste, I fear, had long since begun to be
> deteriorated by acquaintance with other models of feminine loveliness
> than it was my happiness to know in America. I often found, or
> seemed to find, if I may dare to confess it, in the persons of such of my
> dear countrywomen as I now occasionally met, a certain meagreness,
> (Heaven forbid that I should call it scrawniness!), a deficiency of phys-
> ical development, a scantiness, so to speak, in the pattern of their
> material make, a paleness of complexion, a thinness of voice. . . . I was
> sometimes driven to a half-acknowledgement that the English ladies,
> looked at from a lower point of view, were perhaps a little finer ani-
> mals than they. The advantages of the latter, if any they could really be
> said to have, were all comprised in a few additional lumps of clay on
> their shoulders and other parts of their figures. It would be a pitiful
> bargain to give up the ethereal charm of American beauty in exchange
> for half a hundredweight of human clay!
>
> At a given signal we all found our way into an immense room, called
> the Egyptian Hall. . . . A powerful band played inspiringly as we
> entered, and a brilliant profusion of light shone down. . . . Glass
> gleamed and silver glistened on an acre or two of snowy damask, over
> which were set out all the accompaniments of a stately feast. We found

our places without much difficulty, and the Lord Mayor's chaplain implored a blessing on the food – a ceremony which the English never omit . . . yet consider, I fear, not so much a religious rite as a sort of preliminary relish before the soup. The soup, of course, on this occasion, was turtle, of which, in accordance with immemorial custom, each guest was allowed two platefuls. . . . After an hour or two of valiant achievement with knife and fork came the dessert. . . . A large silver bowl was then carried round to the guests, containing rose-water, into which we dipped the ends of our napkins and were conscious of a delightful fragrance, instead of that heavy and weary odor, the hateful ghost of a defunct dinner. . . . During the feast . . . there stood a man in armor, with a helmet on his head, behind his Lordship's chair.

When the after-dinner wine was placed on the table, still another official personage appeared behind the chair, and proceeded to make a solemn and sonorous proclamation . . . 'the Lord Mayor drinks to you all in a loving-cup, and sends it round among you!' And forthwith the loving-cup . . . came slowly down with all antique ceremony. . . . Being curious to know all about these important matters, with a view of recommending to my countrymen whatever they might usefully adopt, I drank an honest sip from the loving-cup, and had no occasion for another – ascertaining it to be a Claret of poor original quality, largely mingled with water, and spiced and sweetened. It was good enough, however, for a merely spectral or ceremonial drink. . . .

The toasts now began in the customary order. Hawthorne listened to the Lord Mayor's speech on the relations between Great Britain and the United States, but was then horrified to hear himself invited to respond, despite his earlier request to remain silent. The Lord Mayor's anxiety to have him speak, he decided, arose from Britain's attitude to the political crisis in America at the time:

All England . . . was in one of those singular fits of panic excitement . . . . more sudden, pervasive, and unreasoning than any similar mood of our own public. In truth I have never seen the American public in a state at all similar, and believe that we are incapable of it. Our excitements are not impulsive, like theirs, but, right or wrong, are moral and intellectual. For example, the grand rising of the North, at the commencement of this war, bore the aspect of impulse and passion only because it was so universal, and necessarily done in a moment, just as the quiet and simultaneous getting-up of a thousand people out of their chairs would cause a tumult that might be mistaken for a storm. We were cool then, and have been cool ever since, and shall remain cool to the end, which we shall take coolly, whatever it may be. There is nothing which the English find it so difficult to understand in us as this characteristic. They imagine us, in our collective capacity, a kind of wild beast, whose normal condition is savage fury, and are always looking for the moment when we shall break through the slender barriers of international law and comity, and compel the reasonable part of the world, with themselves at the head, to combine for the purpose of putting us into a stronger cage. . . .

If the English were accustomed to look at the foreign side of any international dispute, they might easily have satisfied themselves that there was very little danger of a war at that particular crisis. . . . It was no such perilous juncture as exists now, when law and right are really controverted on sustainable or plausible grounds, and a naval commander may at any moment fire off the first cannon of a terrible contest. If I remember it correctly, it was a mere diplomatic squabble, in which the British ministers . . . had tried to browbeat us . . . and the American Government . . . had retaliated with staunch courage and exquisite skill, putting inevitably a cruel mortification upon their opponents, but indulging them with no pretence whatever for active resentment.

Now the Lord Mayor, like any other Englishman, probably fancied that War was on the western gale, and was glad to lay hold of even so insignificant an American as myself, who might be made to harp on the rusty old strings of national sympathies, identity of blood and interest, and community of language and literature, and whisper peace where there was no peace, in however weak an utterance. And possibly his Lordship thought, in his wisdom, that the good feeling which was sure to be expressed by a company of well-bred Englishmen, at his august and far-famed dinner-table, might have an appreciable influence on the grand result. Thus when the Lord Mayor invited me to his feast, it was a piece of strategy. He wanted to induce me to fling myself . . . into the chasm of discord between England and America, and, on my ignominious demur, had resolved to shove me in with his own right-honorable hands, in the hope of closing up the horrible pit forever. On the whole, I forgive his Lordship. He meant well by all parties – himself, who would share the glory, and me, who ought to have desired nothing better than such an heroic opportunity – his own country, which would continue to get cotton and breadstuffs, and mine, which would get everything that men work with and wear. . . . I got upon my legs to save both countries, or perish in the attempt. . . .[24]

At the back of the Mansion House is the Lord Mayor's parish church, St Stephen Walbrook. It is considered to be Sir Christopher Wren's masterpiece and its perfect proportions display 'the simplicity of genius'. A rectangular shape is divided by sixteen columns to create six bays east–west and five north–south. The fusion of a Latin cross with a central domed square results in remarkable geometric interplay, and the barrel-vaulted ceiling is breathtaking. At the centre of the church stands the Henry Moore travertine marble altar, described by hostile critics as resembling a Camembert cheese. The altar was installed in 1986, after an Appeal Court comprising three bishops and two Lord Justices of Appeal unanimously overturned the finding

of the Consistory Court of the
Diocese of London, and judged it to
be a 'table' as prescribed by Canon
Law.

In 1776 the Rector of St Stephen
Walbrook, Dr Thomas Wilson, presented the church with a painting of
The Martyrdom of St Stephen by the
American artist Benjamin West.
Born in Springfield, Pennsylvania, in
1738, West travelled to Europe and,
in 1763, moved from Italy to
London. He was appointed President
of the Royal Academy in 1792 and
lived in England until his death in
1820. His most famous painting,
Death of General Wolfe, shows
British soldiers wearing their ordi-
nary uniforms, not the Greek or
Roman costumes in which they were
conventionally painted. The leading

British painter of the day, Sir Joshua Reynolds, saw West's *Death of General
Wolfe* before it was finished and remonstrated with the artist about the costumes; West replied:

> The event to be commemorated happened in the year 1759 in a region
> of the earth unknown to the Greeks or Romans, and at a period of
> time when no warriors who wore such costume existed. The subject I
> have to represent is a great battle fought and won, and the same prin-
> ciple which gives law to the historian should rule the painter.

When the painting was completed, Reynolds apologised. 'West has conquered,' he said. 'He has treated the subject as it ought to be treated. I
retract my objections. I foresee that this picture will become not only one of
the most popular, but will occasion a revolution in art.'[25]

St Stephen Walbrook was built at the edge of the River Walbrook which
used to flow into the Thames close to where Cannon Street station stands
today. London began as a Roman settlement on the banks of the Walbrook
in the first century AD. By the late fourteenth century the stream was
blocked by rubble and debris thrown into it and in 1440 it was in part covered over. By 1598, when Stow was writing his *Survey of London*, it had van-
ished completely. The road called Walbrook goes uphill from the church of
St Stephen Walbrook, past the Mansion House, to the shortest street in the
City – Mansion House Street. This leads to the busy junction at the heart of
the City of London known simply as Bank because the Bank of England has
stood here for more than two and a half centuries.

The Bank of England – now protected by a windowless late eighteenth-century curtain wall – was founded in 1694 by a Scottish merchant called William Paterson after he returned from America, where he had 'a considerable reputation in many places'. In America, according to Paterson, 'one labouring man is of more advantage to England, though out of it, than any thirty of the like kind can be within it.' He attributed the rise of the North American colonies to

> the necessities of many wrought upon by the examples, the wisdom, the success of some few individuals, without any formed design, help or assistance from our State counsels or legislators. In less than one century, they have thrived so well that they are the envy, and might be the terror, of all our neighbouring maritime nations; so that it can be from no cause but want of information that many of our laws, and court manners, and practices run opposite to their encouragement and increase.

William Paterson secured from the Scottish Parliament an Act to set up a company with 'with monopoly in Scotland of trade with Asia, Africa or America for 31 years'. The company was authorised

> to take possession of uninhabited territories in any part of Asia, Africa or America or in any other place, by consent of the inhabitants, provided it was not possessed by any European sovereign; and there to plant colonies . . . all those who might settle in or inhabit any of their plantations to be declared free citizens of Scotland, and to have the privileges thereof. In token of allegiance, the company to pay yearly his Majesty and his successors a hogshead of tobacco.[26]

The Scottish colony of Darien which Paterson established in Panama was shortlived but enthusiastically praised in 'Trade's Release, or Courage to the Scotch-Indian Company', a ballad sung to the tune of 'The Turks are All Confounded':

> To Scotland's just and never-dying fame,
> We'll in Asia, Africa and America proclaim
> Liberty! Liberty! – nay, to the shame
> Of all that went before us.
> Where'er we plant, trade shall be free.
> And in three years' time (I plainly see)
> GOD BLESS THE SCOTTISH COMPANY
> Shall be the Indian chorus.
> No brawls, no murmur, no complaint,
> No cause of any discontent,
> Where *Patersonian* government
> Shall once commence a footing.

William Paterson's scheme for founding the Bank of England as a joint-stock bank was accepted by the British government to fund the war against France which began in 1688. The government was loaned £1,200,000 at eight per cent interest. The 633 subscribers to the loan were allowed to incorporate themselves as the Governor and Company of the Bank of England with the power to print bank notes which could circulate as currency. The Bank became 'the receptacle of the metallic hoard of the country, the centre of gravity of all commercial credit' (Karl Marx) and 'part of the Constitution' (Lord North).[27] It enabled capital to be accumulated and concentrated in Britain throughout the eighteenth century. When Napoleon sold Louisiana to the United States in 1803 to finance his war with Britain, the $11.25 million purchase price was borrowed through the British banking system based in the City of London.

By the mid-nineteenth century, the City was the main source of world investment and the pound sterling was as acceptable as gold. The USA remained a British colony in economic terms, mainly selling raw materials and buying manufactured goods in return. Nearly half the USA's international trade was with Britain, funded by British banking houses. Three-quarters of foreign investment in the USA was British, particularly in ranches, mines and transport. There were calls in the USA for tariffs to keep out British goods and protect infant American industries. American farmers blamed the City of London commodity and money markets for the decline of wheat, cotton and corn prices during the depression of 1873–96.

The expansion of American railroads in the last thirty-five years of the nineteenth century from thirty-five thousand to two hundred thousand miles of track – more than throughout the whole of Europe – was chiefly financed by the City of London, but the railroads stimulated American production of coal, iron and steel and brought remote farming areas within reach of big cities and seaports. The spread of the electric telegraph and the telephone further contributed to the creation of a huge national US market. Mass-production methods were developed, in which parts for products such as clocks, sewing machines and typewriters were standardised and made interchangeable. By 1914 Henry Ford was applying the assembly-line technique to car production in Detroit with dramatic success. Tycoons like John D. Rockefeller in the oil business and Andrew Carnegie in steel ruled their industries, buying out rivals and controlling every stage of production from raw materials to retailing.

The massive demand for cash and credit was met by specialist investment bankers such as J. P. Morgan, chief banker to the giant conglomerate US Steel. He arranged much of Britain's borrowing to finance both the Boer War and the First World War. During the First World War the vast British assets in the USA were sold off and by 1918 the USA was the European allies' main banker. Its international position had changed from that of a net debtor owing $3.7 billion to a net creditor owed $3.7 billion. New York became a major world money market, and banking houses like J. P. Morgan's and National City Bank developed expertise and influence as they mobilised American funds for overseas investment.

After the First World War, the Governor of the Bank of England, Montagu Norman, spearheaded the British attempt to continue to run the world financial system from the City of London without the resources Britain had had before 1914. In April 1925, Chancellor of the Exchequer Winston Churchill announced a return to the gold standard – the parity between gold and the pound sterling – which had been disrupted during the war. But the Wall Street Crash led to a general banking collapse and, in September 1931, Britain went off the gold standard. The following week Douglas Dillon, a future US Treasury Secretary, began his career as a Wall Street banker. He later recalled:

> We'd looked to the pound for years – everything I'd been brought up with – so when I started it was with the realization that we were coming into a new era and a new world. . . . England was no longer commanding the world financial markets. They were just another player in the game.

The changed reality of international finance affected feelings and perceptions on both sides of the Atlantic. In 1921 Britain's Liberal Prime Minister David Lloyd George felt that 'the people who govern America are our own people. They are our kith and kin. The other breeds are not on top'; but in 1932 the Conservative Prime Minister Stanley Baldwin believed 'you will get nothing from Americans but words, big words but only words.' By 1935 many in the USA shared the opinion of radio commentator Raymond Gram Swing: the United States, he said, had gone into the First World War 'in part to save from ruin the bankers who had strained themselves to the utmost to supply Great Britain and France with munitions and credits.' As Ernest Hemingway put it, 'Of the hell broth that is brewing in Europe we have no need to drink. Europe has always fought: the intervals of peace are only armistices. We were fools to be sucked in once in a European war, and we shall never be sucked in again.'[28]

By 1944, however, the USA was producing forty per cent of the world's armaments. A wartime boom laid the foundations of American prosperity for the next quarter of a century. In the post-war currency system, under the supervision of the International Monetary Fund (IMF), the dollar was fixed against gold; other currencies were to remain in a narrow range of par value against the dollar. This reorganisation of world finance was designed in the USA at Bretton Woods by John Maynard Keynes, the British economist, and Harry Dexter White, who was later accused of being a communist agent. The Bretton Woods agreement lasted until the 1970s, when it became clear that the US dollar fixed to gold could no longer underpin the world credit system. The City of London maintained a leading role in international financial operations because it was much less regulated than American money markets. It became a centre for dealings in Eurodollars – dollar deposits held in Europe.

September 1982 saw the launch of the City of London's most modern money market – LIFFE (London International Financial Futures Exchange). LIFFE's time-zone location means its trading hours overlap with those of Japan and the USA, and visitors to LIFFE around lunchtime may notice the flurry of activity caused by the opening of the financial futures markets in Chicago and New York. LIFFE is housed close to the Bank of England in the Royal Exchange, one of the most impressive and historic buildings in the City of London.

The present Royal Exchange, of classical design with Corinthian columns and a pediment frieze showing merchants of many nations engaged in commerce, was opened by Queen Victoria in 1844. It is the third Royal Exchange

on this site. The first, built in the reign of Elizabeth I, was destroyed in the Great Fire of London. The second, built in the reign of Charles II, caught fire in 1838. In 1701 a bookseller trading in the piazza in front of the second Royal Exchange at the sign of the Unicorn published an essay entitled 'The Government of the English Plantations of the Continent of America' written by 'an American'. The author made the point that although the King's officials might look upon privateers and pirates as robbers and thieves, 'the good people of Pennsylvania esteem them very honest men for bringing money into their country and encouraging their trade.' He concluded, however, that

> it is not necessary for the plantations to have more money than just so much as is sufficient to manage their trade; and that they will have in a few years, when trade and the coin is settled upon an equal foot . . . it is not expedient for England to give the plantations opportunities of laying up great banks of treasure among themselves.

Behind the Royal Exchange is a statue of George Peabody, the nineteenth-century American businessman and merchant-banker whose philanthropy provided Londoners with low-cost housing still in use today. Peabody was born in 1795 in the small town of South Danvers, Massachusetts, since

renamed Peabody. When he left school
at the age of eleven he was apprenticed to a grocer and worked with his
older brother in a drapery store. Their
father died when he was fourteen and
he became the main provider for his
mother and six younger brothers and
sisters. At the age of nineteen he was
taken on as a partner by a dry-goods
merchant called Elisha Riggs, who
was impressed by his business sense.
Their company flourished and in 1815
they moved to Baltimore; in the 1820s
they opened branches in Philadelphia
and New York.

From 1827 to 1837 George Peabody made five trips to Europe, particularly to develop trade with the textile industries of Lancashire. His reputation for sound business dealings and personal integrity attracted wealthy
merchants on an ever-increasing scale. In 1837, when Queen Victoria came
to the throne, Peabody, by then aged forty-one, settled in London as a merchant-banker specialising in foreign exchange and American securities. His
company headquarters became a meeting place for eminent Americans
visiting London, renowned for hospitality, although he himself lived in rela-
tively modest circumstances.

In the north of England Peabody had seen how the industrialised population endured great hardship, and in London he found himself surrounded
by poverty and human misery. London had grown dramatically during the
Industrial Revolution and accommodation was desperately needed for the
hundreds of thousands of impoverished people arriving in search of work.
Public hygiene reformers such as Dr Southwood Smith and Lord
Shaftesbury had established, in 1830, the Society for the Improvement of
the Condition of the Labouring Classes; this was later to merge with the
Peabody Trust. At the Great Exhibition of 1851, which displayed the industrial and artistic achievements of the British Empire, the English reformers
exhibited models of slum-replacement housing. The display of American
products was financed by a $15,000 donation from George Peabody. In
March 1862 he made a donation of £150,000 – increased to £500,000 – to
establish the Peabody Trust 'to ameliorate the condition of the poor and
needy of this great metropolis'. The Trust would finance 'the construction of
such improved dwellings for the poor as may combine in the utmost possible degree the essentials of healthfullness, comfort, social enjoyment and
economy.'

As Peabody Dwellings began to go up – first in Spitalfields, then in
Chelsea, Islington and Shadwell – a ballad entitled 'Good George Peabody'

became popular in London's music halls. Queen Victoria offered Peabody a baronetcy or the Grand Cross of the Order of the Bath, but he declined these honours. When asked what gift would be acceptable he replied that what he would most value would be a letter from the Queen of England which he could carry across the Atlantic 'and deposit as a memorial of one of her most faithful sons.' The Queen complied and the letter, which refers to Peabody's 'princely munificence', is now in the Peabody Institute at Danvers (Peabody) together with a portrait of Queen Victoria which she presented to him as a personal gift.

Early in 1869 Peabody was made an honorary Freeman of the City of London. In July of that year, while he was visiting America for the last time, the bronze statue of him by the American sculptor W. W. Story was erected behind the Royal Exchange in Threadneedle Street, paid for by public subscription and unveiled by the Prince of Wales. The Prince said of Peabody that

> England could never adequately repay the debt of gratitude which she owes to him, London especially, where his wonderful charity has been so liberally distributed. For a man not born in this country to give a sum, I believe, more than a quarter of a million pounds sterling for purposes of benevolence, is a fact unexampled.

The Lord Mayor of London praised Peabody's 'simplicity of character, which won the hearts not only of the people of this country, but of that of which he is a native.'

In October George Peabody returned to London, but by then he was a very sick man. Queen Victoria wrote asking him to visit her: 'He was not to worry about dinners but to regard himself as an intimate and honoured guest, as she wished to have many quiet talks with him.' On 4 November 1869 he died at the house of Sir Curtis Lampson in Eaton Square. His last words were, 'Danvers, Danvers, don't forget.'[29] In the USA his fortune founded the Peabody Institute in Baltimore, the Peabody Museums at Harvard and Yale, and the Peabody Education Fund to advance education in the South.

A century before Threadneedle Street was graced with George Peabody's statue, it was well known as an American rendezvous because the New England Coffee House stood here. On 4 July 1775 Samuel Curwen, a merchant from Salem, Massachusetts, went straight to this coffee house when he arrived in London and found there 'an army of New Englanders'. Curwen had left America to escape the Revolution, with which he had no sympathy. Neither was he a convinced Loyalist, but he deplored political controversy as an interruption of useful daily work and settled routine. He remained in England throughout the War of Independence, recording his experiences and thoughts in a journal. He believed that there was too much wealth in London and observed that

The dissipations, self-forgetfulness and vicious indulgences of every kind which characterize the metropolis are not to be wondered at. The temptations are too great . . . the unbounded riches of many afford the means of every species of luxury, which (thank God) our part of America is ignorant of.

While Curwen was in London, he spent most afternoons and evenings at the New England Coffee House, reading the New York newspapers and talking with the American clientele. Most were Loyalists, but not all. 'America furnishes matter for disputes in the coffee houses,' he wrote, but

it is unfashionable and even disreputable to look askew on one another for differences of opinion in political matters; the doctrine of toleration, if not better understood, is, I thank God, better practised here than in America . . . the upper ranks, most of the capital stock-holders, and, I am told, the principal nobility, are forcing supremacy of parliament over the colonies, and from the middle classes down are opposed to it. . . . The opposition in Parliament is too considerable in numbers, weight and measures to hinder the progress of the administration in their plans respecting America.[30]

At the end of Threadneedle Street, in Bishopsgate, stands the church of St Ethelburga-the-Virgin within Bishopsgate, built in 1430. The modern visitor enters St Ethelburga's through a fourteenth-century door beneath a fifteenth-century window. The motto on the floor inside, 'Bonus Intra Melior Exi [Come In Good, Go Out Better]', was added to the church in the early twentieth century along with the screen, organ-case, pulpit and lectern. The oak gallery replaced one built in 1629 'for the daughters and maidservants of the parish to sit in.' St Ethelburga-the-Virgin is the City's smallest church, measuring only sixty feet by thirty feet and less than thirty-one feet high.

On 19 April 1607 'Master Henry Hudson,' a Muscovy Company log-book recorded, 'at St Ethelburga-in-Bishopsgate did communicate with the rest of the parishioners . . . pur-posing to go to sea four days after

for to discover a passage by the North Pole to Japan and China.' Sailing from
Gravesend in the *Hopewell* with ten men and a boy, Hudson reached
Greenland and Spitzbergen. The following year he sailed again, from
London's St Katharine's Dock, although his ship was forced to return before
reaching the other side of the Atlantic. Two of the crew claimed to have seen
a mermaid and gave Hudson a full description of her:

> She was come close to the ship's side, looking earnestly on the men: a
> little after a sea came and overturned her: from the navel upward, her
> back and breasts were like a woman's . . . her body was as big as one of
> us; her skin very white; and long hair dangling down behind of colour
> black; in her going down they saw her tail, which was like the tail of a
> porpoise, and speckled like a mackerel. Their names that saw her were
> Thomas Hilles and Robert Rayner.[31]

In 1609, on his third voyage, in the *Half-Moon*, Hudson entered the great
river that was to take his name and explored it for a month, sailing as far as
the site of the modern city of Albany, New York. This voyage was sponsored
by the Dutch East India Company and established the Dutch claim to the
area, which became known as the New Netherlands.

Henry Hudson's fourth, final and fatal voyage in 1610–11 was sponsored
by three adventurers associated with the Virginia Company. His ship, the
Discovery, sailed into Hudson Strait and Hudson Bay, but it was a difficult
trip in miserable winter conditions and the crew mutinied. They forced
Hudson, his son and seven loyal sailors into a small boat and abandoned
them.

Hudson's story is illustrated in the church of St Ethelburga-the-Virgin by
three 1920s stained-glass windows. They show him taking Holy
Communion in the church; sailing up the Hudson River, met by 'the red
Indians'; and cast adrift in Hudson Bay to 'sleep among the brave who lie
forever still.' The Hudson River window is a gift of US citizens.

From St Ethelburga-the-Virgin the road called Bishopsgate continues
north to cross the line of London's city wall at the site of the old Bishop's
Gate, which was demolished in 1760. It is commemorated by two golden
mitres on nearby office buildings. A fragment of the city wall can be seen in
the garden of All Hallows church in London Wall, which is built on the
remains of a Roman bastion or tower.

London Wall is the road which sweeps west from Bishopsgate, following
the line of the city wall. Running off London Wall to the left is Throgmorton
Avenue, which was visited in July 1784 by Abigail Adams, whose husband
John Adams and son John Quincy Adams were to be the second and sixth
Presidents of the USA. John Adams had been sent to Paris as an American
representative in 1779 and subsequently served as a Minister (Ambassador)
in Holland. He was one of the commissioners who negotiated the peace
treaty with Britain and after it was signed in September 1783 was ordered to
remain in Europe, working with Benjamin Franklin and Thomas Jefferson

on negotiations for commercial treaties. He was a devoted family-man but although his son was with him he had not seen his wife and daughter for five years, so it was agreed that they should travel to Europe for a reunion. An added motive was the fact that a young lawyer was avidly pursuing nineteen-year-old Nabby Adams and her parents thought a cooling-off period desirable.

Abigail and Nabby sailed from Boston in June 1784 and arrived in London a month later. John Quincy Adams joined them there and, after a brief stay, they travelled with him to The Hague to meet John Adams. Abigail sent letters to her sister in Boston and kept a diary describing life in London. She found London pleasanter than she had expected:

> the buildings more regular, the streets much wider, and more sunshine than I thought to have found. . . . At my lodgings I am as quiet as at any place in Boston. . . . You must put a hoop on and have your hair dressed, but a common straw hat, no cap, with only a ribbon upon the crown, is thought dress sufficient to go into company. Muslins are much in taste; no silks but lutestrings worn. . . . The sides of the streets here are laid with flat stone as large as tile. The London ladies walk a vast deal and very fast.

When seventeen-year-old John Quincy Adams arrived his mother was quite taken aback by his appearance, because it was 'that of a Man, and in his countenance the most perfect good humour.' Before leaving to join her husband in The Hague, Abigail spent a few days visiting places of interest in London and felt 'exceedingly matronly with a grown up son on one hand, and daughter upon the other, and were I not their mother, I would say a likelier pair you will seldom see in a summer's day.'

She came to Throgmorton Avenue to view the hall and garden of the Worshipful Company of Drapers. The Drapers' Hall, she wrote to her sister, was

> a magnificent edifice at the end of which is a most beautiful garden surrounded by a very high wall, with four alcoves and rows of trees placed upon each side of the walks: in the middle of the garden is a fountain of circular form in the midst of which is a large swan, out of whose mouth the water pours, and is conveyed ther by means of pipes under ground. Flowers of various sorts ornament this beautiful spot: when you get into these appartments and others which I have seen similar, you are ready to fancy yourself in Fairy Land.[32]

Today the gates at the end of Throgmorton Avenue display the heraldic devices (coats-of-arms) of the Worshipful Company of Drapers, one of the City's richest and most prestigious livery companies. These livery companies began as the 'guilds' which governed London's many trades and crafts – the 'mysteries' – in the Middle Ages. Their monopoly power was destroyed by the development of joint-stock companies and by the

Industrial Revolution of the eighteenth century. Some disappeared completely, but many evolved to become influential social clubs for business people, with much inherited wealth to administer, often for charitable projects. The livery companies still play a key role in selecting the Lord Mayor of London; more than a hundred freemen of the Drapers' Company have been elected Lord Mayor of London.

From the Drapers' gates Throgmorton Street leads along the back of the Stock Exchange and the Bank of England to Gresham Street, to the right of which is Guildhall, the City of London's town hall, built in 1411. Guildhall was the centre of English support for American colonists in the late 1760s and 1770s. The Lord Mayor, Aldermen and Liverymen who met in Guildhall as the Court of Common Council representing the City of London merchants found a shared cause with the American rebels. Guildhall became the place where their views could be expressed and support for them became a major part of the City merchants' battle against encroachment on their liberties by King George III.

George III was a Hanoverian from the royal House of Brunswick, who came to the throne in 1760 on the death of his grandfather, George II, who had succeeded George I, England's first Hanoverian sovereign. The Hanoverians had been invited by Parliament to take over as monarchs of England when Queen Anne died in 1714 without an heir, none of her seventeen children having survived. In 1702 Queen Anne had succeeded her childless sister Mary II, who had reigned as joint monarch with her husband, William III, after the 'Glorious Revolution' of 1688.

The Guildhall

In the Glorious Revolution leading landowners, churchmen, City of London merchants and army commanders turned against the last Stuart – and Catholic – monarch, James II, and made a bloodless revolution which ensured that all future monarchs would be Protestants. They offered the throne to James II's Protestant daughter Mary and her husband William of Orange, subject to conditions laid down in a Bill of Rights. The monarch was in future not to disregard laws or suspend them, and was to give up control of the army and judges. Finance was to be dealt with entirely by Parliament, which was to be called at least every three years and not to sit for longer than three years. By accepting these conditions William secured the wealth and manpower of England for his Dutch kingdom's war against France.

In the reigns of George I and George II – who were more interested in Hanover than in England – Parliament acquired executive power as the Cabinet system developed. Politicians not only made the laws and levied taxes but also took control of the day-to-day running of the country and of policy-making. Unlike George I and George II, their successor George III was determined to have an independent political role. He chose his own Cabinet ministers and packed Parliament with his 'placemen'. As a result his government was strongly opposed by those who considered themselves the true protectors of the Glorious Revolution. Many of these men were City of London merchants who had trading connections and business partners in America.

When George III came to the throne in 1760, Britain was engaged in the Seven Years' War (French and Indian War) with France over territory in North America, India and the Caribbean. The surrender of any territory to France was strongly opposed by the City merchants. They were particularly concerned that 'the sole and exclusive right of our acquisitions in North America, and the fisheries, be preserved to us.'

The war ended with British victory, but to pay for it the King tried to impose a new tax in Britain on wine, cider and perry. The City merchants opposed the tax, complaining that 'meritorious subjects of this country' should not have to 'feel the extension of excise laws among the first fruits of peace.' Such an extension 'into private houses, whereby the subject is made liable to a frequent and arbitrary visitation of officers' would be 'inconsistent with those principles of liberty which have hitherto distinguished this nation from arbitrary governments . . . the precedent is formidable, not to commerce only, but hath a fatal tendency which your petitioners tremble to think of.' The new taxes would be 'a badge of slavery upon your people,' they told the King, beseeching him to 'keep them happy and at ease, free from apprehension of being disturbed in their property.'[33]

The tax on cider in Britain was withdrawn but the Stamp Act under which it had been imposed was extended to the colonies, requiring Americans to buy stamps as a duty on specified commodities. This led to riots. 'The

Boston mob,' reported General Gage, Commander of British Forces in North America,

> raised first by the instigation of many of the principal inhabitants, allured by plunder, rose shortly after of their own accord, attacked, robbed and destroyed several houses, and amongst others that of the Lieutenant Governor. . . . People began to be terrified at the spirit they had raised, to perceive that popular fury was not to be guided and each individual feared he might be the next victim of their rapacity.[34]

In London, the City merchants continued to petition George III against 'the numberless unconstitutional regulations and taxations in our colonies', always linking maladministration in North America with denial of their political rights in Britain. One City merchant who challenged the government and raised mobs in support of his causes was John Wilkes. As well as being popular with the poor of London – who rallied to the slogan 'Wilkes and Liberty!' – he led a daring and determined campaign by City merchants in solidarity with the American colonists against the King. This reached a climax in 1775 when he was Lord Mayor of London.

In January 1775, with Wilkes presiding as Lord Mayor, a letter was read out in Guildhall from the agent of the Protestant settlers in Quebec, seeking support for their demand to have English laws and a provincial assembly. In February the City merchants resolved that 'in consequence of the severe proceedings against the American colonists' it was their duty 'to use every possible endeavour to prevent further oppression'.

The Americans were operating a boycott of British goods through the Continental Association which had been formed by the First Continental Congress assembled in Philadelphia in 1774. When the British government introduced an Act of Parliament to halt trade in Boston and demand billets for British soldiers, the City of London merchants declared that it was 'not only contrary to many of the fundamental principles of the English constitution and most essential rights of the subject, but also apparently inconsistent with natural justice and equity.' They were of the opinion, they declared, that 'our fellow subjects, the Americans, are justified in every constitutional opposition to the Act'.

They set up a committee to examine the Act in detail. It concluded that

> the extensive commerce between Great Britain and her colonies will be greatly injured as a capital source of remittance will be stopped which will not only disconnect the future commercial intercourse between those colonies and this country but will render them incapable of paying large debts already due to merchants of this City.

The King said he was astonished that any of his subjects were 'capable of encouraging the rebellious disposition which unhappily exists in some of my colonies in North America.'

In April 1775 blood was shed at Concord and Lexington and the American Revolution began. In Guildhall in June a letter was read out from the General Committee of Association for the City and County of New York. Accompanied by a copy of the New York Committee's constitution, the letter explained that

> the struggles excited by the detestable Stamp Act have so lately demonstrated to the world that Americans will not be slaves. . . . America is growing irritable by oppression . . . the least shock, in any part, is by the most powerful and sympathetic affection instantaneously felt through the whole continent. . . . This city is as one man in the cause of liberty.

In July the City merchants petitioned George III, 'praying that his Majesty will be pleased to suspend hostilities against our fellow-subjects in North America' and lamenting 'those measures whose destructive principles have driven our American brethren to acts of desperation.' The King replied that 'while the constitutional authority of this kingdom is openly resisted by a part of my American subjects I owe it to the rest of my people . . . to continue and enforce those measures by which alone their rights and interests can be asserted and maintained.'

In September a letter was read out in Guildhall from John Hancock, President of the Second Continental Congress at Philadelphia. This Congress was to go much further than the First Congress, becoming the central government of the colonies in revolt against Britain. 'Permit the delegates of the people of twelve ancient colonies', it wrote to the Lord Mayor, Aldermen and Livery of the City of London,

> to pay your Lordship and the respected body of which you are the head the just tribute of gratitude and thanks for the virtuous and unsolicited resentment you have shown to the violated rights of a free people. North America, my Lord, wishes most ardently for a lasting connection with Great Britain, on terms of just and equal liberty; less than which generous minds will not offer, nor brave ones be willing to receive. A cruel war has, at length, been opened against us, and, whilst we prepare to defend ourselves, like the descendants of Britons, we still hope that the mediation of wise and good citizens will at length prevail over despotism and restore harmony and peace on permanent principles to an oppressed and divided empire.

But the empire could not be kept undivided. War was under way and ten months later the American colonies declared their independence. At first there were profitable government contracts to be had which encouraged support for the war, but within three years the City merchants were urging George III to seek peace. 'A few inconsiderable islands,' they pointed out to him,

> and one deserted town on the continent where your Majesty's army has a perilous and insecure footing are the only fruits of an expense

exceeding twenty millions; of ninety-three ships of war; sixty thousand of the best soldiers which could be procured, either at home or abroad. . . . The general sense of the whole American people is set and determined against the plans of coercion, civil and military which have been hitherto employed against them; an whole united and irritated people cannot be conquered; if the force now employed cannot do it no force within our abilities will do it.[35]

In the two centuries since the Lord Mayor, Aldermen and Livery of the City of London were assembling in Guildhall to formulate their strong opinions on the 'American crisis', the building has changed little apart from the replacement of the roof and the addition of monuments. Alderman William Beckford's statue, erected in 1770, stands close to the Lord Mayor's canopy, under which the Prime Minister nowadays delivers a speech at the annual Lord Mayor's Banquet. At the far end of Guildhall is the dais used for the high table at banquets attended by royal guests, and used by the Lord Mayor and Aldermen during meetings of the Court of Common Council. On the wall behind the dais, and under the Lord Mayor's canopy, are shelves on which the City's gold plate is displayed during special functions. Fluttering above are colourful banners showing the heraldic devices of the City's 'great twelve' livery companies: Mercers, Grocers, Drapers, Fishmongers, Goldsmiths, Merchant Taylors, Skinners, Haberdashers, Salters, Ironmongers, Vintners and Clothworkers. The arms of the eighty or so other livery companies, including the Brewers, Weavers, Apothecaries, Barbers, Coopers, Innholders, Leathersellers, Tallow Chandlers and Fan Makers, decorate the hall in a line along the top of the walls. The Guildhall windows are engraved with the names of the hundreds of men and one woman who have been Lord Mayors of London since the first, Fitzailwyn, who held office from 1192 to 1212. Dick Whittington, Lord Mayor in 1397–8 and 1406–7, takes his place there as well as John Wilkes.

The most recent monument in Guildhall is that of Sir Winston Churchill, who was present at the unveiling of the original statue in 1955. The bronze cast now installed was made in 1958. Nearby is the minstrels' gallery, occasionally used by the Royal Trumpeters, from which look down the larger-than-life models of Gog and Magog, the giants associated in popular legend with the foundation of London. In fact London was founded by the Romans in about AD 50 and the remains of Londinium's amphitheatre were discovered in 1988 outside Guildhall, beneath Guildhall Yard. To the right of Guildhall Yard, in the street called Aldermanbury, is the Guildhall Library. Its collection, dating from the early 1420s, includes the New York Committee letter read out in Guildhall in 1775. A facsimile of the letter was presented to the popular Mayor of New York, 'Jimmy' Walker, when he visited London in 1927.

At the junction of Aldermanbury and Love Lane is a small public garden containing the foundation stones of the church of St Mary Aldermanbury, designed by Sir Christopher Wren after the Great Fire. The church is now in Westminster College, Fulton, Missouri. It was dismantled, transported and rebuilt there, in 1966, as a memorial to Sir Winston Churchill, whose historic phrase 'the Iron Curtain' was first used in Fulton, Missouri.

Rising above the foliage of the garden of St Mary Aldermanbury is a bust of William Shakespeare. It commemorates not the playwright himself but the two St Mary Aldermanbury parishioners without whom his work would not be known today: John Hemminge and Henry Condell. Fellow actors and personal friends of Shakespeare, Hemminge

and Condell worked with him at the Globe Theatre in Southwark and, when he died in 1616, they assembled his manuscripts and published them as the First Folio in 1623. In the Preface addressed 'to the great variety of readers', Hemminge and Condell explained that

> it had been a thing, we confess worthy to have been wished, that the author himself had lived to have set forth and overseen his own writings, but since it hath been ordained otherwise and he by death departed from that right, we pray you do not envy his friends the office of their care and pain to have collected and published them; absolute in numbers as he conceived them, who as he was a happy imitator of nature was a most gentle expresser of it. His mind and hand went together and what he thought he uttered with that easiness that we have scarce received from him a blot in his papers.

Many English turns of phrase were first coined by William Shakespeare and today millions of English-speakers from Calcutta to California use them all the time without realising that they are quoting the great Bard. Such phrases include 'in the mind's eye', 'salad days', 'laid on with a trowel', 'eaten out of house and home', 'it was Greek to me', 'a lean and hungry look', 'the dogs of war', 'the milk of human kindness', 'the world's my oyster', 'the be-all and

end-all', 'a tower of strength', 'all our yesterdays', 'strange bedfellows', 'in a nutshell', 'nearest and dearest', 'what the dickens', 'brave new world' and 'have not slept a wink'.

From the John Hemminge and Henry Condell memorial, Love Lane leads across Wood Street – on the line of the main north–south road through the Roman barracks built in AD 125 – into St Albans Court and Oat Lane. The halls of the Goldsmiths and the Haberdashers stand to the left, while Pewterers' Hall is on the right. At the end of Oat Lane, Noble Street contains important remains of the Roman barracks and city wall. Near the Roman remains, on the corner of Noble Street and Gresham Street, is the red-brick church of St Anne and St Agnes designed by Sir Christopher Wren in 1676–87 and now a Lutheran church popular with Americans living in London.

From Gresham Street turn right into Aldersgate, where in the early seventeenth century one of the houses had furniture made of black walnut from Virginia. It was the home of the English statesman and merchant Sir Edwin Sandys, who has been described as 'the founder-in-chief of representative government in America'.[36] His house in Aldersgate was one of the places where the Virginia Company of London met to conduct its business.

There were two Virginia Companies, one in Plymouth, the other in London. In 1606 each was granted by King James I a tract of land in Virginia covering 10,000 square miles. The Plymouth Company was to establish a colony between the 38th and 45th parallels; the London Company between parallels 34 and 41. The merchants in the London Company had the necessary capital and credit to finance the 'plantation' of Virginia; they had experience of managing distant ventures through the East India Company; and they were close to King James in his palaces at Westminster and Whitehall.

By royal charter of 1606 – which listed eight 'adventurers' – James I granted powers of government to the Virginia Council meeting in London. The Council consisted of City merchants appointed by the King and sworn by special oath to his service. Its aims included the discovery of a route to China through American rivers, but it also sent out the colonists who founded the Jamestown settlement in Chesapeake Bay. These included, in 1606, Captain John Smith, the first Governor of Virginia and, in 1608, the first women sent to the colony, Mrs Forrest and her maid, Anne Burras.

A second charter was granted to the Virginia Company of London in 1609. Drafted by Sir Edwin Sandys and presented to King James by Sir Francis Bacon, this charter differed significantly from the first. The Council hitherto appointed by King James was henceforth to be 'nominated, chosen, continued, displaced, changed, altered, supplied . . . out of the Company of the said Adventurers by the voice of the greater part . . . in their Assembly for that purpose.' More than 650 individual men and 55 City livery companies were incorporated as the 'Treasurer and Company of Adventurers and Planters of the City of London for the first Colony in Virginia'.

Under the 1606 charter land had been granted by the King to men approved by the Council; under the 1609 charter the Council could grant land to anyone who 'adventured' either a minimum of £12.10s or their person. Virginia, which already stretched between what became North Carolina and Maine, was extended a further hundred miles along the coast and a hundred miles inland. The Virginia Company was empowered 'to make all manner of orders, laws, directions, instructions, forms and ceremonies of government and magistry fit and necessary for and concerning the government of the said colony or plantation.'[37]

As soon as the charter was agreed, the Company opened its books for subscriptions to a joint-stock fund. This was not the permanent joint-stock of a modern corporation; it was set up for final division in seven years' time, with profits payable on capital plus a grant of land in Virginia. How much profit and land would be available for distribution depended on the success of the venture. One of the inducements held out to subscribers was the promise of a voice in determining the policies of the Company. In the words of Gondomar, the Spanish Ambassador in London, 'Fourteen counts and barons have given 40,000 ducats, the merchants give much more and there is no poor man or woman who is not willing to subscribe something.'[38] The 'labouring men and women' invited to adventure their persons in Virginia faced a kibbutz-style life. Their 'houses to dwell in, with gardens and orchards, and also food and clothing at the charge of the common stock' would be very much do-it-yourself.

Amid great excitement and enthusiasm, two or three hundred men, women and children sailed down the Thames on 15 May 1609 in nine vessels, heading for Virginia. On the far side of the Atlantic one of the ships, *Sea Adventure*, ran into a fierce storm and was completely wrecked. The 150 crew and passengers did not go down with the ship, but were rescued by another of the expedition's ships, *Providence*, and landed safely on the shores of Bermuda, where they enjoyed an idyll which Shakespeare recreated in *The Tempest*. Some would gladly have stayed in Bermuda, but two small ships, the *Patience* and the *Deliverance*, were built using local cedar wood and all the passengers from the wrecked *Sea Adventure* were eventually transported to Jamestown, Virginia. There they were greeted by the few emaciated survivors of a starvation winter, one of whom was said to have eaten his wife. Everybody was ready to give up and go back to London when 150 new colonists arrived, sent by the Virginia Company with Lord de la Warre as their governor.

Instructions from the Virginia Company explained how Lord de la Warre was to break the power of King Powhatan, the Amerindian leader, and bring his people under English rule.

For Powhaton . . . it is clear even to reason beside our experience that he loved not our neighbourhood and therefore you may in no way trust him. . . . Every lord of a province shall pay you and send you into your fort where you make your chief residence so many measures of corn at every harvest, so many baskets of dye, so many dozens of skins, so many of his people to work weekly . . . by which means you shall quietly draw to yourselves an annual revenue of every commodity growing in that country. . . . This tribute paid to you – for which you shall deliver them from the exactions of Powhaton which are now burdensome, and protect and defend them from their enemies – shall also be a means of clearing much ground of wood and of reducing them to labour and trade. . . . For this rent only they shall enjoy their houses and the rest of their travail quietly and many other commodities and blessings of which they are not yet sensible.[39]

When the Company realised how hard it would be to implement this policy, they considered abandoning the Virginia project. But Sir Thomas Gates – who had sailed as governor with those shipwrecked in Bermuda – convinced them that valuable commodities such as sugar, wine, silk, iron, sturgeon, furs, timber, rice and aniseed could be produced in the colony given time and support. The Company appealed for more subscriptions:

The eyes of all Europe are looking upon our endeavours to spread the Gospel among the heathen people of Virginia, to plant an English nation there and to settle a trade in those parts which may be peculiar to our nation, to the end we may thereby be secured from being eaten out of all profits of trade by our more industrious neighbours.[40]

A total of £18,000 was raised to fund further settlement expeditions. By 1612 the company had despatched twenty-two vessels and nearly fourteen hundred colonists, but in the streets and marketplaces of London, they complained, only God was more profaned than Virginia:

Divers and sundry persons which have been sent and employed there . . . misbehaved themselves by mutinies, sedition and other notorious misdemeanours . . . and by the most vile and slanderous reports made and divulged . . . bring the voyage and plantation into disgrace and contempt.

A third charter empowered the Company to call in such people, bind them over and send them back. It also allowed the Company to finance future colonisation from lotteries run by William Leveson – a trustee of the Globe Theatre – and to admit new members. The Company's General Assembly was granted the right to elect the Council – voting by head rather than share – and to make final decisions.

Black walnut timber was still the main cargo arriving from the colony, but in 1614 London received its first shipment of Virginia tobacco. A tobacco plant could be grown in a few months and the tobacco habit was spreading. This was despite – or maybe because of – its association with tippling and bawdy houses. 'Poor men', one anti-tobacco MP protested, 'spend fourpence of their day's wages in smoke'. Virginia tobacco was bitter, but one of the leading colonists, John Rolfe, experimented successfully with seeds from Trinidad and Venezuela and it was thereafter known as 'sweet-scented'. Rolfe was helped by Pocahontas, the daughter of Powhatan whom he married in 1612 after she had been taken hostage by the colonists. Their marriage sealed a peace treaty between the English and King Powhatan.

The Virginia Company brought Princess Pocahontas to London as a public-relations exercise in 1616, the year those who had subscribed in 1609 were due to receive profits on their investment. In the event there were no profits to be shared out and adventurers returning from Virginia reported that under the harsh regime of Governor Dale it was no better than a penal colony.

The wrath of the Company's small shareholders turned upon its Treasurer, Sir Thomas Smith, a great City merchant who was a staunch supporter of King James I. In spring 1619 they elected in his place Sir Edwin Sandys, who was considered by the King to be 'a crafty man with ambitious designs, our greatest enemy'.[41]

In July, on Company instructions, the first General Assembly of American colonists was convened in Jamestown. Twenty-two men representing the various plantations and boroughs of Virginia deliberated for six days. They imposed a tax of ten pounds of tobacco on every male over the age of sixteen, including 'gentlemen unused to labour'; they agreed a code of local laws to come into effect immediately and they named themselves the House of Burgesses.

In November, easy-going Governor Yeardley, sent to replace the harsh Governor Dale, warned the Company that even colonists who had been in Virginia for years were 'not settled in their minds to make it their place of rest and continuance'. They were still thinking of returning to London as wealthy men. 'For the remedying of that mischief and establishing a perpetuity of the plantation', Governor Yeardley proposed the sending over of 'one hundred young maids to become wives, that wives, children and families might make them less moveable and settle them, together with their posterity, in that soil.'[42]

The Company duly dispatched shiploads of women to Virginia

> to be made into wives, which the planters there did very much desire, by the want of whom have sprung the greatest hindrance of the increase of the plantation. . . . Care has been taken to provide them with young, handsome and honestly educated maids . . . being such as were especially recommended into the Company for their good bringing up by their parents or friends of good worth; which maids are to be disposed in marriage to the most honest and industrious planters, who are to defray and to satisfy to the adventurers the charge of their passages and provisions at such rates as they and the adventurers' agents there shall agree.[43]

In spring 1620 James I ruled that Sir Edwin Sandys was not to be re-elected as Treasurer of the Virginia Company: 'Choose the devil if you will,' he said in a passion, 'but not Sir Edwin Sandys!'[44] Affronted by this interference in their affairs, the Company's General Assembly refused to elect the King's nominee and adjourned without a Treasurer. In June they elected a Sandys supporter, the Earl of Southampton.

A year later, Virginia was effectively granted independence. The Council of the Virginia Company stated its intention to set up in the colony 'by Divine assistance . . . such a form of government . . . as may be to the greatest benefit and comfort of the people'. The General Assembly in Virginia would have

> free power to treat, consult and conclude as well of all emergent occasions concerning the public weal . . . as also to make, ordain and enact such general laws and orders . . . as shall time to time appear necessary and requisite. . . . *No orders of our court afterward shall bind the colony unless they be ratified in like manner in their general assembly.*[45]

The Spanish Ambassador Gondomar warned King James that 'it was time to look to the Virginia courts, which were kept at the Ferrars' house, where too many of these nobility and gentry resorted to accompany the popular Lord Southampton and the dangerous Sandys.'[46] Sir Edwin Sandys' leadership of the Company was vigorously opposed by Sir Thomas Smith, particularly over management of a tobacco-tax contract offered by the King.

In Virginia the English population was now so large and powerful that peaceful opposition by the Amerindians could not deter its growth. Powhatan had been succeeded by his warlike brother Opechancanough and in 1622 he led a massacre of the colonists in which 350 were killed, including John Rolfe. When news of the massacre reached London Sir Thomas Smith called for a royal investigation into the Company. He and Sandys were summoned before the Privy Council and, after 'much heat and bitterness', the King revoked the Company's 1609 and 1612 charters and took over the government of Virginia.

In the eighteen years between the Company's foundation in 1606 and its dissolution in 1624, the colony of Virginia came into being. A settlement originally planned for gold prospecting and exploration of trade routes became a community developing natural and agricultural resources, with private ownership of land, freedom of trade and local government. As Thomas Jefferson was to put it, 'The ball of the Revolution received its first impulse not from the actors in that event, but from the first colonists.'[47] The Virginia Company of London, in the words of the American historian Herbert L. Osgood, 'belongs at once to the romantic period of our own beginnings and to the heroic period of England's great struggle against absolutism.'[48]

Throughout its existence, the Company had no permanent headquarters in London. Its meetings took place mainly at the homes of its leading members: Nicholas Ferrars' house in Seething Lane, Sir Thomas Smith's house in Philpot Lane and Sir Edwin Sandys' house in Aldersgate.

On 24 May 1738, at 28 Aldersgate, John Wesley, the English Methodist leader, experienced the evangelical conversion to God which a missionary trip to America had made him realise he lacked. Shortly before his conversion he wrote:

> It is upward of two years since I left my country, in order to teach the Georgian Indians the nature of Christianity, but what have I learned myself in the meantime? Why (what I least of all suspected), that I, who went to America to convert others, was never converted to God myself. Though thus I speak, I am not mad, but speak the words of truth and soberness.

Wesley had gone to Georgia in 1735 with his brother Charles at the invitation of Governor Oglethorpe. Georgia – named after King George II – had been founded to provide asylum for English debtors and to serve as a barrier against Spanish and French aggression from Florida and Louisiana. Slavery was not allowed in Georgia, and neither was rum, 'only wholesome, homely, English beer'. Soon after he arrived, Wesley became friendly with a young woman named Sophia Hopkey, whose uncle was the chief magistrate of Savannah. He gave her French lessons. She wore white to please him and nursed him through a fever. Then, however, she married William Williamson. When she showed him Wesley's letters, Williamson told her that she must stop attending the preacher's chapel. Wesley retaliated by refusing to give Sophia the Sacrament. Williamson brought an action for defamation of his wife's character and obtained a warrant for the arrest of Wesley, who fled to England. 'The reason for which I left', he wrote in his journal,

> had now no force; there being no possibility as yet of instructing the Indians: neither had I as yet found or heard of any Indians on the continent of America who had the least desire of being instructed. . . . I shook off the dust of my feet and left Georgia, after having preached the Gospel there . . . one year and nine months. I was seized with a violent flux, which I felt came not before I wanted it. Yet I had strength enough to preach once more to this careless people . . . .[49]

After his conversion at Aldersgate, Wesley spent more than fifty years as an evangelist, preaching some forty thousand sermons while the light within him burned brightly. He was the first major religious leader to speak against slavery.

His younger brother, Charles, the author of more than six thousand hymns, was converted in a house in Little Britain, the street which runs alongside the church of St Botoloph-without-Aldersgate. The street derives its name from the Dukes of Britanny, who lived there in the sixteenth century.

It was in Little Britain that the young Benjamin Franklin took lodgings with his Philadelphia friend James Ralph when they found themselves stranded in London in 1725. Their board cost 'three shillings and sixpence a week – as much as we could afford then.'

In America, Franklin 'had made some courtship . . . to Miss Read.' As he later explained in his autobiography,

> I had a great respect and affection for her, and had some reason to believe she had the same for me; but as I was about to take a long voyage, and we were both very young, only a little above eighteen, it was thought most prudent by her mother to prevent our going too far at present, as a marriage, if it was to take place, would be more convenient after my return, when I should be, as I expected, set up in my business. Perhaps, too, she thought my expectations not so well founded as I imagined them to be. . . . Having taken leave of my friends, and interchanged some promises with Miss Read, I left Philadelphia.

During his transatlantic journey, Franklin met a Mr Denham, who 'contracted a friendship for me that continued during his life. The voyage was otherwise not a pleasant one, as we had a great deal of bad weather.' When Franklin's letters of introduction proved useless in London he found Mr Denham and asked him what to do. 'Among the printers here', he was told, 'you will improve yourself, and when you return to America, you will set up to great advantage.'

This Franklin did. He also learned some important lessons from his life with James Ralph. They were inseparable companions and Ralph soon revealed to Franklin that he had never intended to return to the wife and child he had left behind him in Philadelphia. While Franklin started work at Palmer's famous printing house in Bartholomew Close, Ralph found some relations in London, 'but they were poor and unable to assist him'. His attempts to get work as an actor and then as a writer were unsuccessful and the young men's outings to plays and other places of amusement had to be financed from Franklin's earnings. The savings Franklin had brought from America were soon used up and they 'now just rubbed on from hand to mouth'. Ralph, Franklin later wrote, 'seemed quite to forget his wife and child, and I, by degrees, my engagements with Miss Read, to whom I never wrote more than one letter, and that was to let her know I was not likely soon to return. This was another of the great errata of my life, which I should wish to correct if I were to live it over again.'

Lodging in the same house in Little Britain as Franklin and Ralph was a young woman, a milliner, who 'had been genteelly bred, was sensible and lively and of most pleasing conversation'. Ralph read plays to her in the evenings and they 'grew intimate'. She moved to other lodgings but he followed her and they lived together there. Her income was not enough to maintain them with her child and Ralph decided to leave London and try for a job as a teacher in a country school. He did not wish to use his own name because he expected to become a great poet and was 'unwilling to have it known that he once was so meanly employed'. So he gave a false name and 'did me the honour to assume mine', wrote Franklin.

In the meantime the young woman, referred to by Franklin only as Mrs T., having on account of Ralph 'lost her friends and business, was often in distresses, and used to send for me, and borrow what I could spare to help her out'. Franklin grew fond of Mrs T.'s company and, 'being at that time under no religious restraint, and presuming upon my importance to her, I attempted familiarities (another erratum) which she repulsed with a proper resentment'.

Mrs T. told Ralph that Franklin had made a pass at her, and

when he returned again to London, he let me know he thought I had cancelled all the obligations he had been under to me. So I found I was never to expect his repaying me what I lent him, or advanced for him.

This, however, was not then of much consequence, as he was totally unable; and in the loss of his friendship I found myself relieved from a burthen. I now began to think of getting a little money beforehand, and, expecting better work, I left Palmer's to work at Watt's, near Lincoln's Inn Fields, a still greater printing house. Here I continued all the rest of my stay in London. . . . My lodging in Little Britain being too remote, I found another in Duke Street, opposite the Romish Chapel.[50]

While he lived in Little Britain Franklin had a very short walk to work. Palmer's was just around the corner in the disused Lady Chapel of St Bartholomew-the-Great, West Smithfield, London's oldest surviving church. It was built as part of an Augustinian Priory founded in 1123 by Henry I's court jester, Rahere, who became a monk. After Henry VIII's Dissolution of the Monasteries in the 1530s, the nave of St Bartholomew-the-Great remained a place of worship for local people but other parts of the church were put to various light industrial uses. The choir became a factory making wool and silk fringes; wine and coal were stored in the crypt; horses were stabled in the cloisters; and there was a blacksmith's forge in the north transept.

Today visitors enter St Bartholomew-the-Great from the end of Little Britain through a restored Tudor gateway and along a path that leads to the fifteenth-century west door. The fabric of the church has changed little since Benjamin Franklin's day, when it was already six hundred years old. Rahere's skeleton rests in his tomb of 1143 beneath a colourful effigy, topped by a fifteenth-century stone canopy. Overlooking the tomb is an oriel window built in 1517 for Prior Bolton. Its stone casement is decorated with a carved arrow, or 'bolt', passing through a barrel, or 'tun', in a type of visual pun known as a rebus.

A family monument on the wall nearby dates from 1588, the year of the Spanish Armada. It shows Percival and Agnes Smalpace both as a behatted middle-aged Tudor couple and lying naked on their marriage bed. 'Behold yourselves by us,' reads the inscription. 'Such once were we as you, and you in time shall be even dust as we are now.'

Close to the altar is a monument to Edward Cooke – a distinguished philosopher and Doctor of Physick who died in 1652 – holding a book in which he is writing. The inscription reads:

> Unsluice your briny floods, what! can you keep
> Your eyes from tears and see the marble weep,
> Burst out for shame: or if you find no vent
> For tears, yet stay, and see the stones relent.

Cooke's statue is made of a material that attracts condensation in damp weather and therefore has often been seen to weep. Sadly, the effect was lost when radiators were installed in the church.

In the north ambulatory, a tablet commemorates Margaret and John Whiting, who lived near St Bartholomew-the-Great in Long Lane and had twelve children. Margaret died in 1680 and John the following year. 'She first deceased,' their inscription reads, 'he for a little tried to live without her, liked it not and died.'

The Lady Chapel where Benjamin Franklin worked is at the east end of the church, behind the altar. While Franklin was here he wrote *A Dissertation on Liberty and Necessity, Pleasure and Pain*. He printed a hundred copies of the pamphlet, gave a few to friends but burned the rest, 'conceiving it might have an ill tendency'. The Lady Chapel was restored and re-opened for worship in 1897. It now contains the war memorial of the former 600 City of London Squadron, Royal Auxiliary Air Force, which was unveiled by Her Majesty Queen Elizabeth the Queen Mother, Honorary Air Commodore, on 26 July 1950.

Outside St Bartholomew-the-Great is Smithfield, London's famous meat

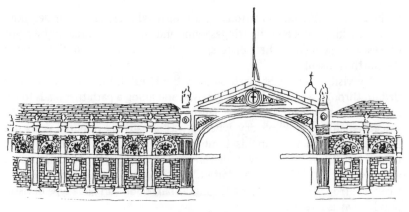

Smithfield

market. There has been a market here since at least the twelfth century, and the spot was also well known for political executions. Those stabbed, hanged or burned at the stake here include: in 1305 William Wallace, leader of the Scots against the English army of Edward I; in 1381 Wat Tyler, leader of the Peasants' Revolt; in the 1400s Lollard men and women who followed the teachings of John Wycliffe and distributed extracts of the Bible in English; in 1546 Agnes Agnew, an early Protestant theoretician who had to be put on the bonfire tied to a chair because she was so crippled by torture at the Tower; and in the 1550s those who fell foul of Queen Mary's attempt to re-Catholicise England. Smithfield was also the site of London's annual Bartholomew Fair, the great cloth fair held for three days around St Bartholomew's Day from 1123 until its suppression for rowdiness in 1855.

From Smithfield there is a fine view of the Old Bailey – the Central Criminal Court – topped by the figure of Justice. Her scales are perforated to stop them filling up with rainwater. The Central Criminal Court stands on the site of Newgate Prison, which was demolished in 1902, having been a notorious feature of London life for more than eight hundred years. Newgate Prison was the birthplace of the fictional heroine of Daniel Defoe's novel *Moll Flanders*, published in 1722. When Moll's mother, a Newgate prisoner, was sentenced to death for stealing fabric from a draper in Cheapside, she

> pleaded her belly, and being found quick with child, she was respited for about seven months, in which time having brought me into the world. . . . She was call'd down, as they term it, to her former judgement, but obtain'd the favour of being transported to the plantations, and left me about half a year old; and in bad hands you may be sure.

Moll, during a life of 'continued variety', was 'twelve year a whore, five times a wife (whereof once to her own brother), twelve year a thief, eight

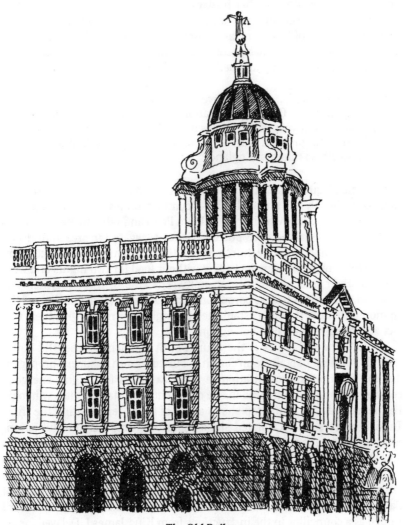

The Old Bailey

year a transported felon in Virginia, at last grew rich, liv'd honest and died a penitent.'

When she was sent to America as a convict, Moll knew that

Maryland, Pensilvania, East and West Jersey, New York and New England all lay north of Virginia, and that they were consequently all colder climates, to which . . . I had an aversion . . . I therefore consider'd of going to Carolina, which is the most southern colony of the English.

On the way there, Moll and her husband were helped by an honest Quaker. They bought 'two servants viz. an English woman-servant just come on shore from a ship of Liverpool, and a Negro man-servant; things absolutely necessary for all people that pretend to settle in that country.' Then Moll discovered, to her surprise and delight, that her mother had left her

> a small plantation . . . on York River . . . with the stock of servants and cattle upon it. . . . Our new plantation grew upon our hands insensibly; and in eight year which we lived upon it, we brought it to such a pitch that the produce was, at least, 300 pounds sterling a year; I mean, worth so much in England.[51]

A marble plaque installed at the Old Bailey in 1907 – at the suggestion of Horace J. Smith of Philadelphia – commemorates the 'courage and endurance' of the jury which tried William Penn and William Mead in 1670. When the two Quakers were put on trial at Newgate for preaching to an unlawful assembly in Gracechurch Street, the jury refused to convict them, although its members were locked up without food for two nights and were fined for their final verdict of not guilty. The case of these jurymen was reviewed on a writ of habeas corpus and Chief Justice Vaughan delivered the opinion of the court which established the right of juries to give their verdict according to their own convictions.

Opposite the Old Bailey is the church of St Sepulchre – the 'Old Bailey Church' – where Captain John Smith is buried. Smith, a superb propagandist for the English colonisation of America and a forthright, energetic coloniser himself, is honoured in one of the church's stained-glass windows. His heraldic device at the top shows a trio of heads representing the three Turkish officers he decapitated single-handed during his youthful adventures as a mercenary in Asia, Europe and Africa. At the bottom of the window are pictures of the three ships which sailed for Virginia from Blackwall in London on 19–20 December 1606. The 20-ton *Discovery*, the 120-ton *Susan Constant* and the 40-ton *Godspeed* were under the command of Captain Thomas Newport. John Smith was one of the seven men aboard named as a councillor in the instructions from King James I. Delayed for six weeks by bad weather, the three ships carrying 105 Englishmen arrived at the James River in May 1607. Forty miles upstream the ships were moored and Jamestown was founded.

When Newport, Smith and twenty other men set out to explore the river, they met

> people in all places kindly entreating us, dancing and feasting with us with strawberries, mulberries, bread, fish. . . . Captain Newport kindly requited their least favour with bells, pins, needles, beads of glass

St Sepulchre

which so contented them that his liberality made them follow us from place to place, and ever kindly to respect us.

They were welcomed by King Powhatan and Queen Apamatecs, who was 'fat and lusty with long black hair'. Every man offered overnight accommodation found 'a woman fresh painted red with *pocones* and oil to be his bedfellow'.

After Captain Newport sailed again for England in June, leaving provisions for thirteen or fourteen weeks, those left behind began to fall ill and to quarrel with each other. They were so plagued 'with famine and sickness that the living were scarce able to bury the dead'. By September, forty-six men had died. Their President, Captain Wingfield, kept the sherry, mineral water and 'other preservatives for our health' to himself. He was generally hated and was eventually deposed, with Captain Radcliffe being elected in his place. The colonists, wrote John Smith, were in 'such despair they would rather starve and rot with idleness than be persuaded to do anything for their own relief.'

In December, Smith set off with a handful of companions to explore the territory further. They were ambushed, brought before a *werowance* (tribal chief) who was King Powhatan's half-brother, and then to King Powhatan. They found the chief

> proudly lying on a bedstead about a foot high upon ten or twelve mats, richly hung with many chains of great pearls about his neck and covered with a great covering. . . . At his head sat a woman, at his feet another, on each side sitting upon a mat upon the ground were ranged his chief men on each side of the fire ten in a rank, and behind them as many young women, each a great charm of white beads over their shoulders, their heads plaited in red and with such a grave and majestical countenance as bore me into admiration to see such state in a naked savage.

Smith described to Powhatan 'the territories of Europe which were subject to our great king whose subject I was, the innumerable multitude of his ships and gave him to understand the noise of trumpets and the terrible manner of fighting.' From their sign-language discussion, Smith gathered that among the Amerindians 'the kings have as many women as they will . . . subjects two and most but one.' After a fortnight he was allowed to return to Jamestown, where he was immediately put on trial and condemned to death for the loss of his two companions. He was saved only by the arrival that night of Captain Newport with a hundred new settlers.

Carrying gifts, John Smith set off once more to visit King Powhatan.

> This proud savage . . . expressed himself as upon a throne . . . with such majesty . . . and with a kind countenance bad me welcome. . . . I presented him with a suit of red cloth, a white greyhound and a hat. As jewels he accepted them . . . with a public confirmation of perpetual league of friendship. After that he commanded the Queen of Apamatecs, a comely young savage, to give me water, a turkey cock and bread to eat. . . . He proclaimed me a *weroance* . . . that all his subjects should so esteem us . . . and that the corn, women and country should be to us as to his own people. . . . With the best languages and figures of thanks I could express I took my leave.

Exchanges continued. A thirteen-year-old Amerindian boy was sent to Jamestown with food and beans. When Powhatan asked 'Why we came armed in that fort, seeing he was our friend?', John Smith told him 'it was the custom of our country, not doubting of his kindness in any way.' Jamestown settlers and Amerindians met on the river bank and spent a day 'in trading, dancing and much mirth'. But when a group of curious young braves arrived at the Jamestown fort Smith decided 'I should terrify them with some torture to know if I could their intent.' The braves were tied to a mast and muskets were fired close to them.

> Powhatan understanding we detained certain savages sent his daughter, a child of ten years old which not only for feature, countenance,

proportion much excelleth any of the rest of his people but for wit, and spirit is the only nonpareil of his country . . . desiring me that the boy might come again which he loved exceedingly, his little daughter he had taught this lesson also: not taking notice at all of the Indians that had been prisoners three days till that morning that they saw their fathers and friends come quietly, and in good terms to entreat their liberty. . . . I gave them to Pocahontas, the King's daughter, in regard of her father's kindness in sending her; after having well fed them, as all the time of their imprisonment, we gave them their bows, arrows and what else they had, and with much content sent them packing. Pocahontas we also requited, with such trifles as contented her. . . . We now remaining being in good health, all our men well contented, free from mutinees, in love with another, as we hope in continual peace with the Indians, where we doubt not but . . . to see our nation to enjoy a country not only exceedingly pleasant for habitation but also very profitable to commerce . . . pleasing to almighty God, honourable to our gracious sovereign and commodious generally to the whole kingdom.

John Smith's account of the first eighteen months of the Jamestown settlement was sent to London and published at the sign of the Greyhound in St Paul's Churchyard in 1608 as *A True Revelation of such occurences and accidents of note as hath happened in Virginia since the first planting of that colony which is now resident in the south part thereof till the last return from thence.* Smith also wrote to the Virginia Company saying

When you send again I entreat you rather send but thirty carpenters, husbandmen, gardeners, fishermen, blacksmiths, masons and diggers up of trees, well-provided, than a thousand such as we have: for except as we be able both to lodge them, and feed them, the most will consume with want of necessaries before they can be made good for anything.[52]

The Virginia Company was to act on John Smith's advice, but in the fledging colony the fragile peace with the Amerindians broke down. Smith was captured by Powhatan, offered wealth to help wipe out the colony and condemned to die when he refused. He was saved from execution only when young Princess Pocahontas intervened.

In September 1608 Smith became President of the Council in Jamestown and during the next year he provided the colony with stern leadership based on the principle 'he that will not work neither shall he eat.' He strengthened defences, enforced discipline and encouraged agriculture.

In September 1609, having suffered serious gunpowder burns, he set sail for England, never to return to Virginia. In London his map of Chesapeake Bay was published in 1612. In 1614 he made a voyage to New England, gave the name Plymouth to the harbour where the *Mayflower* pilgrims would land six years later and returned to London as the Admiral of New England.

In 1620, he advised the *Mayflower* Pilgrims. In 1624 his *General History of Virginia* was published. In 1630, he advised the Puritans who sailed to settle in Salem, Massachusetts, and published his *True Travels*. He died in London in 1631. A brass plaque in St Sepulchre's marks his burial place. Its inscription reads:

> Here lies one conquered that conquered kings,
> Subdued large territories and done things
> Which to the world impossible would seem. . . .
> In Virginia, that large continent,
> He subdued kings unto his yoke
> And made those heathens flee, as wind doth smoke,
> And made their land, being of so large a station,
> An habitation for our Christian nation.

The City of London's statue to John Smith stands outside the church of St Mary-le-Bow, reached from St Sepulchre's by walking along Newgate towards St Paul's Cathedral and turning left into Cheapside. The statue honours Smith as 'first among the leaders of the settlement at Jamestown Virginia from which began the overseas expansion of the English-speaking peoples.' It is a replica of a statue in Jamestown and was presented to the City of London by the citizens of Jamestown to mark their 350th anniversary in 1957.

It was in Cheapside, at the Half-Moon Tavern, that agitated City Liverymen met on 25 September 1775 to draft a petition to the electors of Great Britain conveying the 'alarms and apprehensions' they felt because of the 'unnatural war excited in America'. They blamed George III's ministers and viewed with alarm the prospect of

an expensive and ruinous war with our own colonies, from which so much of our commerce and therefore the sources of our wealth are derived. . . . The people of the colonies have appealed to their fellow-subjects in Great Britain for the justice and necessity of their conduct. We are convinced of their having been injured and oppressed. We sympathise in their griefs and revere their fortitude. Every motive of

humanity, of justice, and of interest calls upon us to condemn the
measures of which they complain and to declare that we will never
willingly contribute to urge their oppressions or abridge their liberties.[53]

The liverymen's petition was presented at the Guildhall a few days later and
won the backing of the Lord Mayor, Aldermen and Court of Common
Council.

From Cheapside, the delightful Bow Lane at the back of St Mary-le-Bow
leads to Watling Street, originally part of the most famous of Britain's roads
built by the Romans, which ran from Dover to St Albans. In Watling Street,
from the Old Watling pub founded in 1666, there is a fine view of the back of
St Paul's Cathedral. No. 1 Watling Street is the Bank of America. The public
path through its precincts follows the line of Friday Street, where fish was
sold in pre-Fire London.

Since before the Great Fire the City of London has had a special relationship with North America. Its most adventurous inhabitants left to become
settlers in early Virginia and New England. Its coffee houses were the homes
of an American business community. Its Guildhall was a bastion of support
for the American cause before the War of Independence.

At the end of the Friday Street path is a garden laid out to mark the bicen-
tenary of the USA. It symbolises the special relationship between the City
and the USA and was accepted by the Lord Mayor as a gift to the City on 20
May 1976. Close by is the back of St Paul's Cathedral and the bicentennial
garden is overlooked by Sir Christopher Wren's great dome.

THREE

St Paul's Cathedral

'License my roving hands and let them go,
Before, behind, between, above, below.
Oh my America! My Newfoundland,
My kingdom, safeliest when with one man manned.
My mine of precious stones, my empery,
How blest am I in this discovering thee!'

*John Donne, Dean of St Paul's Cathedral 1621–31, from his
poem,* To His Mistress Going to Bed, *written circa 1600*

The ancient burial grounds at the back of St Paul's Cathedral were laid out as public gardens in 1878. The railings surrounding the gardens are fine examples of early cast-ironwork and were made in Sussex in 1714, soon after the cathedral itself was completed.

Close to St Paul's underground station is a path beside the public garden known as St Paul's Churchyard. In the seventeenth and eighteenth centuries this was London's publishing centre, and most of the houses in it were occupied by booksellers. One of these, John Newbery (1713–67), published *Goody Two-Shoes* and *Mother Goose* from No. 65, at the sign of the Bible and Sun. His home was not only a publishing house and bookshop but also London's earliest recorded juvenile library. In 1978 the Pennsylvania Library Association installed a plaque on the wall of St Paul's Churchyard 'in sincere tribute to the man who first made the issue of books intended for children an important branch of the publishing business and for whom the John Newbery medal was named.'

No. 72 St Paul's Churchyard was the home of the bookseller Joseph Johnson, who in 1791–2 published Thomas Paine's *The Rights of Man*. Paine was the political scientist, pamphleteer and religious thinker who

issued the first public call for the American colonies to declare their independence from Britain. Born in Thetford, Norfolk, he worked as a corset-maker, schoolmaster and customs inspector before travelling from London to America in September 1774, with a letter of recommendation from Benjamin Franklin.

For six months Paine wrote poems and essays for the *Pennsylvania Magazine*, favouring reconciliation with Britain. His understanding of the situation was dramatically changed by the battles of Lexington and Concord in April 1775. Encouraged by Benjamin Rush, the Philadelphia physician, in January 1776 Paine published his booklet *Common Sense*, expressing the view that 'until an independence is declared, the Continent will feel itself like a man who continues putting off some unpleasant business from day to day, yet knows it must be done, hates to set about it, wishes it were over, and is continually haunted with the thoughts of its necessity.'[1] More than a hundred thousand copies of *Common Sense* were sold within three months. Its effect on Americans, Benjamin Rush noted, was 'sudden and extensive'. It was widely read 'by public men, repeated in clubs, spouted in schools', and everywhere aroused discussion about monarchy, the origin of government, English constitutional ideas and independence.

Paine served in the Continental Army and published a series of propaganda pieces entitled *The American Crisis* which began with the words

'These are the times that try men's souls'. They revived morale among troops and civilians and were credited with having particularly contributed to American victory at the battle of Trenton. In April 1777 he was elected secretary of the congressional Committee of Foreign Affairs but had to resign after releasing to a newspaper privileged information about treaty negotiations with France.

Paine then turned his attention to the problems of bridge-building. Having watched ice-packs moving in the Schuylkill river in Pennsylvania and realising that they would crush the piers of any bridge, he conceived the idea of a single-arch bridge constructed from separate segments like a spider's web. He sent a model of such a bridge on a sled to Benjamin Franklin. When the Pennsylvania Assembly would not agree to fund the building of his bridge, Paine, on the advice of Franklin, submitted the model to the French Academy of Science. It was much appreciated, but the efforts of Thomas Jefferson, then the American Minister (Ambassador) in Paris, to persuade the French government to build the bridge over the River Seine were unsuccessful. Paine travelled to London, hoping to see his bridge built over the Thames. 'Great scenes inspire great ideas,' he wrote in May 1789 to the British scientist Sir Joseph Banks.

> The natural mightiness of America expands the mind . . . the war with all its evils . . . energised invention. At the conclusion of it every man returned home and set himself to repair the ravages it had occasioned. . . . As one among thousands who had borne a part in that memorable Revolution I returned with them to the enjoyment of a quiet life and, that I might not be idle, undertook to construct an arch for this river.[2]

A large model of the bridge, built of iron in Sheffield, was erected in London at Lessom Square, near Paddington, in August 1790. On the first day it was open to the public to view and try out, the foreman, an American named Bull, fell from the scaffold and tore a 7–8 inch flap of flesh from his leg. Paine had to supervise the bridge himself for much of the time that it remained standing. It was dismantled after a year. Paine believed it would 'produce a revolution in bridge architecture'.

During his later exile in France, a bridge designed according to the principles of his model was built over the River Wear near Sunderland in County Durham, in the north of England. In 1803, as an epilogue to his 'pontifical works' – to use his own phrase – Paine wrote a memoir on the history of iron bridges in which he offered his knowledge and experience to the Congress of the USA.

Paine's practical involvement in bridge-building was brought to an end when Edmund Burke published an attack on the French Revolution in November 1790. Paine responded with his classic defence of representative government, *The Rights of Man*.

Whatever the form or constitution of government may be [he argued] it ought to have no other object than the general happiness. When, instead of this, it operates to create and increase wretchedness in any of the parts of society, it is on a wrong system, and reformation is necessary.[3]

Fifty thousand copies of the book were sold. The British Prime Minister William Pitt admitted in private that Paine was correct. 'What can I do?' he asked. 'As things are, if I were to encourage his opinions we should have a bloody revolution.'[4]

The government issued a proclamation against such inflammatory publications and Paine was indicted, but he none the less continued to promote his ideas at public meetings. One evening in Joseph Johnson's house here in St Paul's Churchyard he discussed his views with the poet and painter William Blake. As Paine rose to leave, Blake put a warning hand on his shoulder. 'You must not go home,' he said, 'or you are a dead man!'[5]

Paine left hurriedly for France, but on 8 December 1793 he was tried in his absence at the Court of King's Bench in London's Guildhall, found guilty of treason and declared an outlaw in England and all the British dominions. In France he was welcomed as a hero, and gained a seat in the National Assembly, but his opposition to the Jacobins led to his imprisonment under threat of the guillotine. It could not be decided whether he should be treated as a British, American or French citizen. 'The world is my country,' he said, 'to do good my religion.'

In prison he wrote *The Age of Reason*, arguing that religion was a private matter between man and his maker. He poured scorn on the Church establishment, organised religion and the theological doctrines. *The Age of Reason* aroused more hostility against him in Britain and America than any of his political works had done. Released from prison in 1794, he lived in France long enough to see Napoleon rise to power and his dreams of a more democratic society dashed. As it was still unsafe for him to return to England, in 1802 he travelled again to America, where he advised James Monroe in negotiations for the purchase of Louisiana.

Thomas Paine died in New York City on 8 June 1809 and was buried on his farm in New Rochelle. His remains were exhumed for reburial in Britain and were taken across the Atlantic in 1819 by William Cobbett, MP, who took care of them until his death in 1835. When his son inherited them he wrote the name Tom Paine on the skull and larger bones. He was then arrested for debt and the trunk containing the bones was seized. Cobbett had hoped for a funeral with twenty waggon-loads of flowers to be strewn in front of the hearse, but the bones were lost.

A year after Paine's *The Rights of Man* appeared, another radical and influential work was published by Joseph Johnson from St Paul's Churchyard: Mary Wollstonecraft's *Vindication of the Rights of Woman*.

At the end of St Paul's Churchyard lies the main entrance to the cathedral. St Paul's was founded as London's main church as long ago as AD 604, and the present magnificent building, built by Sir Christopher Wren, replaced the medieval cathedral, which was destroyed in the Great Fire of London after dominating London's skyline for more than five centuries.

Wren's St Paul's is unique among European cathedrals in having been completed in the lifetime of its architect, its chief stonemason (Edward Strong) and its chief woodcarver (Grinling Gibbons). The dome – the second largest cathedral dome in the world, beaten only by St Peter's in Rome – consists of outer and inner domes with a brick cone between, around which the public can climb to reach the Golden Gallery, which offers splendid views over London for those with strong legs and stomachs.

After a visit in 1856, Nathaniel Hawthorne wrote admiringly:

> St Paul's appeared to be unspeakably grand and noble, and the more so from the throng and bustle continually going on around its base, without in the least disturbing the sublime repose of its great dome, and indeed of all its massive height and breadth. Other edifices may crowd close to its foundation, and people may tramp as they like about it; but still the great Cathedral is as quiet and serene as if it stood in the middle of Salisbury Plain. There cannot be anything else in its way so good in the world as just this effect of St Paul's in the very heart and densest tumult of London.[6]

Benjamin Silliman described the cathedral as 'one of the finest and most sublime productions of modern architecture'. In particular he appreciated the Whispering Gallery:

> If you lay your mouth close to the wall and whisper in ever so low a voice, even so that the person who stands within a single yard cannot hear, such is the reverberation that anyone on the opposite side one hundred and forty feet off will, on laying his ear to the wall, hear every word distinctly, as if someone were speaking in a loud and audible whisper, and it is not easy to be persuaded that someone is not concealed behind the walls for the purpose of imposture. I could hardly banish this impression till [my companion] and I placed ourselves in opposite points of the gallery, and actually carried on a conversation of some minutes, although in very low whispers. When the door of this gallery is forcibly shut, it sounds to a person on the opposite side like thunder.[7]

Another American visitor was Oliver Wendell Holmes, the physician and author, who came in 1834. 'Admittance two pence,' he noted, 'but additional fees required by the banditti who show the different parts of the house – "but ye have made it a den of thieves." I suppose it is necessary; so I took twopence worth of magnificence.'[8]

John Quincy Adams visited St Paul's in 1817. The last time he had been there, he recorded, had been in 1797, when

> there was only one monument. . . . There are now more than twenty.
> . . . They are for the greatest part in honour of officers who have fallen
> in battle, and there is neither genius or variety in the designs. The
> inscriptions are all in English, and all marvelously insipid; generally a
> bare recital that they were erected at the public expense by a resolu-
> tion of Parliament.[9]

Today there are many more than twenty such monuments. Four con-
nected with American history are to be found in the south transept.

One is to General Cornwallis, Governor-General of India, who died on 5
October 1805 aged sixty-six, at Ghazipore in the province of Benares.
Cornwallis had previously commanded the British forces during the
American Revolution. He opposed the measures which provoked war
between Britain and the colonies but believed it his duty as a soldier and
loyal subject to accept a command in North America with the rank of major-
general.

Cornwallis aided the British victory in the Battle of Long Island, on 27–28
August 1776, and later that year pursued George Washington's army across
New Jersey, halting at New Brunswick on orders from General Howe.
Hurrying forward again after Washington's victory at Trenton on 26
December 1776, Cornwallis failed to entrap the American troops and retired
to winter quarters. He was largely responsible for the British victory at
Brandywine on 11 September 1777, and led the British forces into
Philadelphia.

After a brief return to England in 1778 Cornwallis was appointed lieu-
tenant-general, second-in-command to Sir Henry Clinton. He opposed the
evacuation of Philadelphia but accompanied the British Army on its retreat
to New York and repulsed the Americans under General Lee at the Battle of
Monmouth on 28 June 1778. He took part in the siege of Charleston in
April–May 1780 and, when Charleston fell and Sir Henry Clinton returned
to New York, Cornwallis took command of British forces in the South.

He marched his troops through the Carolinas, defeating but not crushing
the Americans. When he moved to Yorktown in August 1781, he was caught
between the French fleet and George Washington's land forces, which were
strengthened by a French army, and on 19 October 1781 he was forced to
surrender.

Around General Cornwallis stand statues of military leaders who fell in
the 1812–15 war between the USA and Britain, in alliance with Amerindian
forces. Neither Britain nor American merchants wanted war but there was
pressure from frontiersmen for the USA to take over Florida and Canada,
thus finally defeating the Amerindians and acquiring the Canadian fur
trade, farmlands and St Lawrence sea outlet.

High up on one of Sir Christopher Wren's huge pillars is a statue of
Tecumseh, leader of the Amerindian confederacy in the Great Lakes area. He

is accompanied by Major-General Brock, with whom he forced the Americans to surrender at Detroit without firing a shot. Brock 'gloriously fell', on 13 October 1812, 'resisting an attack on Queenstown in Upper Canada'.

At floor level, near the door, two officers stand together, one with his arm around the neck of the other. These are Major-General Edward Packenham and Major-General Samuel Gibbs, 'who fell gloriously on 8 January 1815 while leading troops to an attack of the enemy's works in front of New Orleans'. They were among the heavy British losses inflicted by Andrew Jackson when he arrived with his forces just in time to save the situation for the USA.

Above the entrance to the St Paul's crypt is a monument to General Ross, the British commander whose men set fire to the President's house while sacking Washington in 1814. President Madison and his wife had to escape in such a hurry that the British officers found their table still set for dinner, with wine in coolers of ice about to be served. The officers helped themselves to food and drink, then took one of the President's hats and a cushion from his wife's chair as souvenirs before leaving their troops to loot and burn in retaliation for the burning of York (Toronto). The scorch marks on the house were later covered with white paint and it became known as the White House. General Ross was killed attacking American forces outside Baltimore. It was during the British siege of Baltimore that 'The Star-Spangled Banner' was composed.

The crypt of St Paul's covers an area as large as the church itself. In a corner, reached by turning right at the bottom of the stairs, is the plain black tomb of Sir Christopher Wren. 'Reader if you require his monument', reads the Latin inscription, 'look around you.'

In 1924 the Architectural League of New York installed a plaque in the gallery above the cathedral's north aisle 'in recognition of the inspiration and enduring influence upon American architecture of the work of Sir Christopher Wren.'

Near to Wren an engraved slab on the floor marks the burial place of Benjamin West, alongside Sir Joshua Reynolds. Born at Springfield, Chester County, Pennsylvania, on 10 October 1788, West became President of the Royal Academy and died in London on 11 March 1820. At his funeral the hearse was drawn by six horses and there were between forty and fifty mourning coaches.

One of the eight pall-bearers at the funeral was Richard Rush, whose father was a signatory of the Declaration of Independence. Rush travelled to St Paul's with the Earl of Aberdeen, a future British Prime Minister. 'As the Cathedral came into full view,' Rush recorded, Lord Aberdeen

> remarked that he understood that the edifices in England which made the most impression upon the Americans were the gothic, as we had none in the United States; none at least that were ancient. I replied

that such was probably the case. He remarked that, although we had no antiquities among us, we had a long race to run which he hoped would prove fortunate. I said that we were proud of the stock we came from; on which Lord Aberdeen threw in a courteous quotation *matre pulchra filia pulchrior* [the daughter is more beautiful than the beautiful mother].[10]

On the wall close to Wren's tomb is an aluminium statue of a small girl wearing a peculiar hat and holding a replica of the Caldecott Medal awarded annually by the American Library Association for the most distinguished American picture book for children. The award was established in 1937 in honour of the English illustrator Randolph Caldecott, who died in Florida in 1886; he was buried there but is commemorated here in the crypt of St Paul's. The inscription on his monument describes him as 'an artist whose sweet and dainty grace has not been in its kind surpassed, whose humour was as quaint as it was inexhaustible'.

On the far side of the crypt is a memorial to Edwin Austin Abbey, Royal Academician, who was born in Philadelphia on 11 April 1852 and died in London on 11 August 1911. Best known for his illustrations in *Harper's Weekly* of scenes from Shakespeare's plays, in 1902 he also completed a fifteen-panel frieze, *The Quest of the Golden Grail*, for Boston Public Library; he also painted King Edward VII's Coronation portrait.

Near his monument is a bronze crucifix by the American artist John Singer Sargent, which was presented to St Paul's by his sisters. Their father was a prominent Philadelphia physician but the family lived abroad at the wish of their artistic mother. John Singer Sargent was born in Florence in 1856, and did not become an American citizen until he visited the USA for the first time at the age of twenty. One of the leading portraitists of his day, he painted more than seven hundred people, including Theodore Roosevelt, Henry James and the English actress Ellen Terry.

Further along in the crypt are the tombs of the Duke of Wellington and Admiral Lord Nelson (the latter's tomb was originally made for Cardinal Wolsey). Up three steps to the left of Nelson is a small glass case on the wall containing the gilded RAF wings worn by Pilot-Officer William Meade Lindsley Fiske III in the Battle of Britain on 18 August 1940: 'an American who died that England might live'.

Up three steps to the right of Nelson's tomb – close to the Treasury and Sir Christopher Wren's great wooden model of St Paul's – is a bust of George Washington, presented to the cathedral by President Harding in 1921. Similar busts were given to Liverpool Town Hall and Sulgrave Manor (the ancestral home of the Washington family near Banbury, Oxfordshire) President Harding hoped that

these gifts from the American people may be received as testifying anew their long-established friendship for the British nation, and may inspire a continual reciprocation of that sentiment by the British people. They may remind both peoples that Washington was an Englishman by birth and tradition before he became a leader in fighting for the new Anglo-Saxon nation of this continent.[11]

George Washington can also be seen upstairs in the American Memorial Chapel behind the cathedral's high altar. His face appears representing Washington among the state badges depicted in three stained-glass windows. Also colourfully displayed are the Utah beehive, the Kansas wild sunflower, California's Minerva, the Louisiana pelican, a Massachusetts Indian, the Rhode Island anchor and the flags of the five governments which have held sovereignty over Alabama. Below the windows are oak and limewood carvings of American birds, plants and animals.

The American Memorial Chapel was created as a British tribute to the twenty-eight thousand Americans based in Britain who lost their lives during the Second World War. The Roll of Honour in the chapel was presented to St Paul's by General Eisenhower in 1951, and the chapel was dedicated in the presence of the Queen and the Vice-President of the United States, Richard Nixon, in 1958. A Thanksgiving Day service is held at St Paul's each year for London's American community, usually attended by the US Ambassador. In the aisle leading from the American Memorial Chapel is a statue of John Donne (1573–1631), the poet and divine who was Dean of St Paul's from 1621 until his death. Donne is wearing his burial shroud – he posed for the statue wearing it while he was still alive. The statue was rescued from the flames that engulfed Old St Paul's during the Great Fire of London. Donne was a member of the Virginia Company and in 1623 preached the sermon at the last church service held under its auspices: 'You have made this island,' he told the Company congregation, 'which is but the suburbs of the old world, a bridge and gallery to the new; to join all to that world that should never grow old, the Kingdom of Heaven.'[12]

Martin Luther King, Jnr, preached his favourite sermon, 'The Three Dimensions of a Complete Life', in St Paul's on 6 December 1964. Four thousand people crowded in to hear him and many had to be accommodated in the crypt, where the sermon was relayed through loudspeakers. By chance Malcolm X was in London at the same time and King devoted one of his press conferences to minimising the political differences between black Americans. He also spoke on South African apartheid at the City Temple, where he was introduced by Canon John Collins of St Paul's. He spent three days in London before flying to Oslo to receive the Nobel Peace Prize.

Outside St Paul's the statue of Queen Anne is a replica of the one erected in 1712 to mark the completion of the cathedral. Around the Queen are female figures representing Britain, Ireland, France and America. The figure portraying America is an Amerindian woman popularly known as 'the American Princess'. In the year before the original statue was made, Queen Anne was visited by four Amerindian leaders who wished to assure her of their readiness to give service 'against all her enemies . . . and to secure her from the French in and about Canada and America.' The Queen ordered that the Amerindians be presented to the Lord Chamberlain and entertained at her expense. They were taken on the royal barge to Greenwich Hospital and the Woolwich Dockyard; in Hyde Park they watched a review of infantry and cavalry; New England and New York merchants in London invited them to a feast at which the Archbishop of Canterbury presented them with an English Bible; they attended a marionette show at Punch's Theatre in St Martin's Lane, for which their names were printed on the programme as Emperor Tee Ye Neen Ho Ga Row, King Sa Ga Yeau Qua Rah Toon, King Etow oh Koam and King Oh Nee Yeath Tow No Riow. After a three-week stay, the Amerindian diplomats went by way of Hampton Court and Windsor to Portsmouth, where they set sail in the *Dragon* for Boston.

Queen Anne was said to like a drink or two. When her statue appeared looking down from St Paul's towards Fleet Street it gave rise to the popular ditty:

> Brandy Nan, Brandy Nan,
> They've left you in the lurch,
> With your face towards the gin shops
> And your back towards the church.

FOUR

Fleet Street

'If slavery be thus fatally contagious, how is it that we hear the loudest yelps for liberty among the drivers of negroes?'

Dr Samuel Johnson, Taxation No Tyranny, *1775*

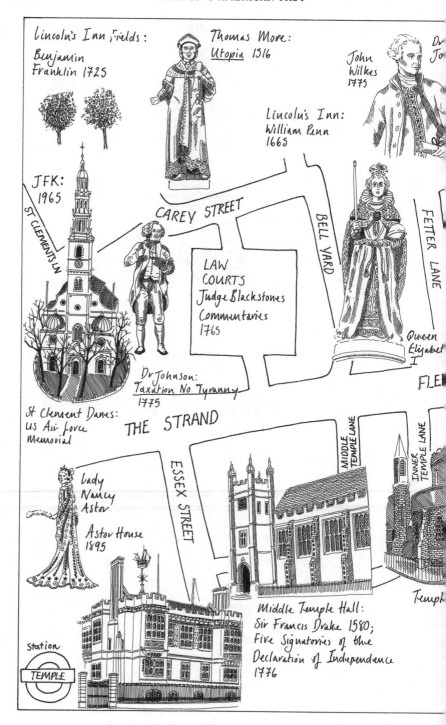

Lincoln's Inn Fields:
Benjamin
Franklin 1725

Thomas More:
Utopia 1516

John
Wilkes
1775

Lincoln's Inn:
William Penn
1665

JFK:
1965

ST CLEMENTS LN

CAREY STREET

BELL YARD

FETTER LANE

LAW
COURTS
Judge Blackstones
Commentaries
1765

Queen
Elizabeth
I

Dr Johnson:
Taxation No Tyranny
1775

FLE

St Clement Danes:
US Air Force
Memorial

THE STRAND

Lady
Nancy
Astor

Astor House
1895

ESSEX STREET

MIDDLE TEMPLE LANE

INNER TEMPLE LANE

Station

TEMPLE

Temple

Middle Temple Hall:
Sir Francis Drake 1580;
Five Signatories of the
Declaration of Independence
1776

Francis Barber 1765

Tom paine: Rights of Man 1792

station ST PAUL'S

St Paul's

Dr Johnson's English Dictionary

The American Princess

FARRINGDON STREET

WINE OFFICE COURT

Ye Olde Cheshire Cheese REBUILT 166

Edgar Wallace 1932

LUDGATE HILL

St Bride's

Poca Hontas 1613

Virginia Dare 1585

NEW BRIDGE STREET

John Donne 1600

American Memorial Chapel 1951

St Paul's
Fleet Street
and The Strand

The road down to Fleet Street from St Paul's Cathedral is Ludgate Hill, so called because it used to lead to Lud Gate, one of the gates in London's city wall from Roman times until 1760. It was here that the twenty-one-year-old Amerindian Princess Pocahontas – Lady Rebecca Rolfe – took lodgings with her royal party when they arrived in London after a hundred-day transatlantic crossing in June 1616. The tavern where they stayed had been known since the fifteenth century as the Savage Inn. After Pocahontas's visit it became the Belle Sauvage. In the eighteenth and early nineteenth centuries it was the American and Continental Hotel. 'I have known a princess, and a great one,' wrote the playwright Ben Jonson, 'come forth of a tavern . . . the blessed Pocahontas, as the historian calls her, and a great king's daughter of Virginia.'

When she was thirteen, Pocahontas had saved the life of Captain John Smith by laying her head beside his on a large stone as executioners were about to club out his brains. They hesitated and her father King Powhatan granted a reprieve. Smith called Pocahontas – whom he took to be only ten – his 'good little angel'. The incident led to a persistent belief that there was a romance between Pocahontas and Captain John Smith. It appeared in the popular song 'Fever'. In this they were said to have 'had a very mad affair, when her daddy tried to kill him she said – Daddy oh don't you dare.' The song was made a hit by Peggy Lee and later Elvis Presley.

Pocahontas certainly played an important political role as a peacemaker between her father and Captain John Smith and was a welcome figure in the settlement at Jamestown in its difficult early years. After Smith left for London with serious burn injuries Pocahontas assumed he had died and never expected to see him again.

Three years later, in 1612, with Virginia under the harsh military rule of Sir Thomas Dale, Pocahontas – aged seventeen – was taken prisoner in a bid to make her father return guns and swords he had captured and send back the colonists who had fled to him for sanctuary. Powhatan refused to comply and Pocahontas was kept a hostage to his good behaviour. She was sent to Henrico, an English satellite settlement near Jamestown, and lived there in the home of the Reverend Whittaker and his family. She soon learned English and began to attend church every Sunday.

Also living in Henrico was John Rolfe, a young widower whose wife and child had died on the voyage from England. Pocahontas helped him with his tobacco-breeding experiments. Rolfe was sent to Powhatan to bargain for her release, but, fearful of losing her, he begged Sir Thomas Dale and the Reverend Whittaker for permission to marry her. She was baptised and given the title Lady Rebecca.

The wedding was held in Jamestown on 15 April 1614 and Pocahontas's relatives came in all their finery. A peace treaty was agreed and lasted eight years, during which the English colony grew and prospered. Pocahontas had a son, Thomas, who travelled to London with her in 1616 when she was taken there by the Virginia Company, as a public-relations exercise, in the year when profits were due to be paid to those who had invested in the Company seven years earlier but for whom there were none.

Also with Pocahontas when she arrived in London were her husband John Rolfe, her son's godfather Sir Thomas Dale, her sister Matacanna, Matacanna's husband Uttamatamakin – a tribal leader and priest – and about a dozen other Amerindians. They did not find life in London very congenial. Used to daily bathing and exercise in fresh air, suddenly they were cooped up, surrounded by damp, smoke and open sewers. Three died within three months of their arrival.

Pocahontas, in European dress, attracted crowds and charmed Londoners. She was entertained by the Bishop of London and possibly visited the Queen of Denmark at Denmark House in the Strand. According to Samuel Purchas, she 'did not only accustom herself to civility but still carried herself as the daughter of a king.' At Christmas, when a great masque was presented at the Banqueting House in Whitehall, Pocahontas sat beside King James I on the royal dais while her husband – a commoner – had to be content with sitting in the balcony.

Early in 1617, Pocahontas and her party moved to Syon House, in the broad fields and woodlands of Brentford, at the invitation of its owners, the influential Percy family, who were financial backers of the Virgina Company. While she was here, Pocahontas received a surprise visit from Captain John Smith. Tradition has it that the shock broke her heart and caused her slowly to fade away. In fact she was probably suffering from consumption, and also possibly from smallpox. Her sister and child were also sick.

John Rolfe had incurred the King's displeasure by marrying royalty without his permission, and was keen to return to the freer atmosphere of Virginia. In March he and Pocahontas, with their party, boarded the *George* to go home to America. By the time the ship reached Gravesend, however, Pocahontas was dying and had to be taken ashore. "Tis enough that the child liveth,' she said on her deathbed, according to a letter from John Rolfe. 'All men must die.' The parish register at Gravesend records that on 21 March 1617 'Rebecca Wrolfe . . . a Virginia lady born, was buried in the chancel'. Her son, Thomas Rolfe, was left at Plymouth, England, in the charge of Sir Lewis Stukely. His English father perished in the 1622 massacre but he went to Virginia when he was twenty and was given land by his great-uncle Opechancanough. He married an Englishwoman in the colony and his descendants include John Randolph, Lady Mountbatten and Mrs Woodrow Wilson. One of his descendants was married at Cheam, near London, in 1930.

When the Belle Sauvage Inn was still flourishing, London's first daily newspaper, the *Daily Courant*, was published from a house at the bottom of Ludgate Hill in 1702. Printed on one side of the paper only, with two columns, the first edition, dated 11 March, contained five paragraphs translated from the *Haarlem Courant*, three paragraphs from the *Paris Gazette* and one from the *Amsterdam Courant*. It was printed by Edward Mallett but after forty days passed into the hands of Samuel Buckley, who produced it with two pages of news and advertisements. Buckley was briefly taken into custody by the sergeant-at-arms for publishing reports of Parliamentary proceedings but by 1724 the *Daily Courant* was described by officials as 'well-affected' and it became known as an organ of government propaganda. In 1735 it was absorbed into the *Daily Gazette*. It cost 1½ pennies. A sale of five to six hundred copies was probably adequate to finance production. Average sales were about three thousand, mainly within London.

The house in which the *Daily Courant* was first published stood beside the Fleet Bridge. Nowadays the River Fleet flows into the Thames at Blackfriars through a large pipe beneath Farringdon Street.

The Fleet Bridge, which led to Fleet Street, has been replaced by Ludgate Circus, on the far side of which – opposite the site of the house where the *Daily Courant* was first published – is a plaque commemorating Edgar Wallace, the adopted son of a Billingsgate fish-porter who became a respected Fleet Street journalist and prolific writer of popular thrillers. He also wrote the screenplay for the original *King Kong* and died in Hollywood in 1932. 'He knew wealth and poverty,' reads the inscription on his plaque, 'yet had walked with kings and kept his bearing. Of his talents he gave lavishly to authorship . . . but to Fleet Street he gave his heart.'

Fleet Street, which links the City of London to the Strand and the City of Westminster, became London's printing centre after Wynkyn de Worde, William Caxton's assistant, brought his press here in 1500. He set up shop at the sign of the Sun, opposite Shoe Lane, where the Reuters news agency building designed by Edward Lutyens was constructed 1938–40. Reuters began in the City of London in 1851 and its reporting of the American Civil War was a milestone in the history of journalism.

A few yards along Fleet Street on the left is the entrance to St Bride's church. The present building, much repaired after bomb damage in the Second World War, was designed by Sir Christopher Wren. The pre-Fire St Bride's that it replaced was the parish church of Ananias and Eleanor Dare, whose daughter Virginia was the first recorded European child to be born in North America. Eleanor Dare's father John White – also a St Bride's parishioner – sailed with the first settlement expedition sent by Sir Walter Ralegh to Roanoke in 1585, and produced many drawings of Amerindian life which were engraved and published in London when the disheartened settlers returned with Sir Francis Drake after a year. (White's drawings and paintings can now be seen at the Tower of London, in the Bloody Tower.)

In 1587, when John White led the second expedition to Roanoke, his daughter and son-in-law travelled with him. Soon after the settlers landed, Eleanor Dare gave birth to a baby girl and they named her Virginia. White left his new-born granddaughter and her parents in Roanoke and sailed back to London to organise the provision of supplies for the settlement. He was unable to return to Virginia until 1590, and when he arrived all fourteen families had disappeared. 'We let fall our grapnel near the shore,' he wrote to Richard Hakluyt, the theoretician of English colonisation, 'sounded with a trumpet a call, and afterwards many familiar English tunes of songs, and called to them friendly; but we had no answer.'[1] There is a small terracotta bust of Virginia Dare in St Bride's, sculpted by Marjorie Meggit.

The carved wooden reredos behind the altar at St Bride's was unveiled in 1957 by Queen Elizabeth II 'to the memory of Governor Edward Winslow and the Pilgrim Fathers'. Edward Winslow's parents were married in St Bride's in November 1594, and he was born at their home in Worcestershire the following year. At the age of fifteen he began work on his father's farm, but two years later, in 1613, he rode to London and became apprenticed to John Beale, a stationer. (The Worshipful Company of Stationers was then the governing body for the print trade in London.)

The young Edward Winslow attended church services at St Bride's and was greatly influenced by its preachers, Nathaniel Giffard and James Palmer, who were sympathetic to the ideas of Protestantism outside the Church of England. In 1617 he was allowed to break his apprenticeship and left London to join the English Separatists exiled in the Dutch town of Leyden. He became their printer and produced the books which were smuggled to England in wine-casks until King James I persuaded the Dutch authorities to seize the English Separatists' press.

Winslow sailed on the *Mayflower* in 1620. When a great storm broke the ship's mast, emergency repairs were successfully carried out using the iron screw of a printing press – presumably his. In the New World he was three times elected Governor of New Plymouth and he travelled to England many times representing the Pilgrim Fathers. On one visit he was thrown into the Fleet Prison for seventeen weeks, charged with dubious church teaching. After the Puritans came to power in England in 1649, Winslow was made Chief Commissioner in Oliver Cromwell's naval expedition to the Caribbean at a salary of £1000 a year. He died during the capture of Jamaica from Spain in 1655.

A reproduction of the entry in the St Bride's parish register recording the marriage of Edward Winslow's parents, Edward Winslow and Magdalene Ollyver, is on display in the small museum in the church crypt. Near it is an example of the so-called 'Breeches Bible', published in 1580, in which the word in Genesis 3:7 usually translated as 'aprons' appears as 'breeches', so that the verse reads: 'Then the eyes of them both were opened, and they knew that they were naked, and they sewed large fig tree leaves together, and made themselves breeches.' It was copies of the 'Breeches Bible' that the Pilgrim Fathers carried with them when they landed in the New World.

The St Bride's crypt museum also tells the story of the seven churches that have stood on this site since the seventh century, and traces the development of printing and newspaper publishing in Fleet Street over the past five centuries.

'If you wish to have a just notion of the magnitude of this great City,' wrote Dr Samuel Johnson, 'you must not be satisfied with seeing its great streets and squares but must survey the innumerable little lanes and courts.' One such alleyway is Wine Office Court, further along Fleet Street on the opposite side from St Bride's, where the Cheshire Cheese pub is to be found. It was built in 1667, but has pre-Fire cellars. Its visitors in the past included Theodore Roosevelt and Mark Twain. In 1907, during his last visit to London, Twain complained to a friend that literary giants were in the habit of dying. 'Shakespeare is dead,' he said, 'Milton also is dead, and I myself am not feeling very well.'[2]

The back alleys beyond Wine Office Court lead to Gough Square and the eighteenth-century merchant's house where Dr Johnson lived while compiling his famous dictionary. Commissioned by a syndicate of Fleet Street publishers in 1749, this huge work took Johnson ten years to complete. It was the first dictionary of the English language to define words scientifically, trace their history and give examples of their use by 'the best writers'. Johnson had no qualms about including his own interpretations.

LEXICOGRAPHER: a writer of dictionaries, a harmless drudge ... OATS: a grain which in England is generally given to horses, but in Scotland supports the people ... PATRON: commonly a wretch who supports with insolence and is paid with flattery . . . PIRATE: a sea robber, any robber; particularly a bookseller who seizes the copies of other men.

When he handed over the dictionary to be printed, Johnson did so 'with frigid tranquillity, having little to fear or hope from censure or from praise.'

Dr Johnson's dictionary was printed by one of the greatest of London's eighteenth-century printers, William Strahan. Strahan was also a close friend of Benjamin Franklin, with whom he discussed the possibility of a

marriage between his son and young
Sally Franklin. The plans came to
nothing and the two men became
estranged with the outbreak of the
War of Independence, particularly
when Strahan became an MP in the
House of Commons. They resumed
their friendship in 1784, after the war
had ended.

When the American Continental
Congress issued its Declaration of
Rights in October 1774 Dr Johnson
was commissioned by the British
government to write against the
arguments it put forward, which he
did in his essay 'Taxation No
Tyranny', 1775. The Continental
Congress had proclaimed in eleven
resolutions that Parliament had
deprived the colonists of the rights of Englishmen. It asserted their rights to
'life, liberty and property', to representation in Parliament and participation
in legislation, to trial by peers and the rights to assemble and petition the
King. In short, there should be no taxation without representation.

Dr Johnson argued that the right of governments to levy taxes had been
accepted 'by all mankind' until 'zealots of anarchy' denied the right of the
British Parliament to tax the American colonies. 'We are told that the
Americans, however wealthy, cannot be taxed . . . that the Continent of
North America contains three millions, not of men merely, but of Whigs, of
Whigs fierce for liberty and disdainful of dominion.' If these American
Whigs denied the British Parliament the right to tax them they implicitly
denied its rights to make laws for them. They claimed to have inherited
from their ancestors the privileges of Englishmen, but they were the
descendants of men who either had no vote or had left the country where
they had a vote for something

> in their opinion of more estimation . . . . They have not, by abandon-
> ing their part in one legislature, obtained the power of constituting
> another, exclusive and independent, any more than the multitudes,
> who are now debarred from voting, have a right to erect a separate
> Parliament for themselves.

Dr Johnson quite rightly saw that opposition to particular government
policies which had no way of influencing those policies became a challenge
to the legitimacy of the government itself. It was a democratic challenge, a
demand for greater political freedom. 'The Philadelphia Congress has taken
care to inform us that they are resisting the demands of Parliament as well

for our sakes as their own.' They had argued that 'when they are taxed, we shall be enslaved'. Slavery was a

> miserable state . . . and doubtless many a Briton will tremble to find it so near as in America; but how it will be brought hither, the Congress must inform us. . . . If slavery be thus fatally contagious, how is it that we hear the loudest yelps for liberty among the drivers of negroes?[3]

Johnson's antipathy to slavery was prac-tised in his personal life. When a man called Frank Barber was given to him as a slave brought from the Caribbean, Johnson freed him from legal bondage and employed him as a trusted servant. Barber was later seized on the streets of London by a Navy press-gang and Dr Johnson secured his release through the intervention of John Wilkes – a political thinker of very different views. A portrait of Frank Barber hangs in Johnson's house in the dining room, which is decorated with wood panelling imported from Virginia. When Johnson died Barber was the main beneficiary of his will, and he set up a school with his English wife outside London. The enter-prise was not a success, however, and Barber eventually went to the United States, where his descendants still live.

Turning sharp left from Dr Johnson's house and out of Gough Square, Pemberton Row leads to Fetter Lane, where Thomas Paine lived while he was writing *The Rights of Man*. In Fetter Lane stands a statue of John Wilkes – 'a Champion of English Freedom' – carrying a sheaf of papers inscribed 'for a just and equal representation of the people of England in Parliament.' The statue was erected 'by admirers' in 1988.

John Wilkes played a leading role in linking opposition in the American colonies towards George III's government with the opposition in Britain, particularly in London. Admirers in America contributed to the fund set up in 1770 to pay off Wilkes's debts. In 1774 the Society for the Defence of the Bill of Rights fought a British general election under his leadership on a

platform which included the defence of political rights in the American Colonies. Twelve of its candidates were elected as MPs. When the American Revolutionary War began Wilkes continued to defend the cause of American independence, even though many of his wealthier supporters benefited from government war contracts and his poorer supporters were swept up in war fever.

Wilkes is best known in British history for the battles he fought with the government of George III for freedom of the press. Asked by a French acquaintance how far freedom of the press extended in England, he replied 'I cannot tell, but I am trying to find out.' In 1763 he was expelled from the House of Commons, having been found guilty of seditious, obscene and impious libel, and was pronounced an outlaw for impeding royal justice. The charge of obscene and impious libel arose from his 'Essay on Woman', twelve copies of which were printed for his friends along with the 'The Maid's Prayer', a hymn of praise to 'Almighty Pego'. A spoof footnote explained that the 'the vegetation of Pego is most astonishing; even beyond what we know of American vegetation. It will shoot forth most amazingly, quite on a sudden, especially in a hot-bed, and as suddenly shrink back.'[4] Wilkes once declined to make up a table at cards saying, 'Do not ask me, for I am so ignorant that I cannot tell the difference between a king and a knave.'

From Wilkes's statue, Fetter Lane leads back to Fleet Street. In April 1783 Benedict Arnold – the most despised man in American history after he changed sides during the War of Independence – turned up uninvited at 135 Fleet Street, where his fellow American Silas Deane was lodging. Deane had been a delegate to the Continental Congress which was convened in Philadelphia on 10 May 1775 and for the next six turbulent years was the effective government of the American colonies as they struggled for independence. He had been chosen by the Congress to go to France in April 1776 to obtain arms to fight the British. Benjamin Franklin and Arthur Lee were later sent to join him, and within eighteen months seven shiploads of military supplies from France reached the American front line. Lee then accused Deane of profiteering and he was called before Congress. Although no formal charges were brought, Deane was dismissed, a ruined man.

Living penniless and depressed in France, in 1781 Deane wrote a letter to a friend in America saying that even if independence were won, it was questionable 'whether the revolution must ultimately be considered as a blessing or a curse.' He recommended accommodation with Britain and gave the sealed letter to his long-time American friend Dr Edward Bancroft, who was – unbeknownst to Deane – a British spy. Bancroft sent a copy of the letter to London and the British authorities published it in New York as part of their propaganda to persuade moderate Americans to abandon the war.

Deane's enemies viewed his recommendation of accommodation as tantamount to treason and it was under that cloud that he came to live in Fleet Street. One afternoon, as he sat in his lodgings discussing the possibility of land sales in upper New York State with some Americans, there was a knock at the door. Deane bade the visitor enter, and in walked Benedict Arnold, whom he had not met since 1775. Since then, Arnold had achieved important military successes for the American army but had become embittered by being passed over for promotion; had married the eighteen-year-old daughter of a Loyalist; had faced charges of misusing public funds and his authority; and finally, in 1780, had offered his services to the British for cash. After a five-minute chat, Deane escorted Arnold out into Fleet Street and asked him not to return.

But the damage was done. Two months later news of their meeting appeared in American gazettes and their names were linked as traitors. When Deane called on his old friend, the diplomat John Jay, he was not invited in. He wrote him two letters, and eventually Jay replied:

> You are either exceedingly injured, or you are no friend to America; and while doubt remains on that point, all connexion between us must be suspended. I was told by more than one that you received visits and were on terms of familiarity with General Arnold. Every American who gives his hand to that man, in my opinion, pollutes it.

Six years later, on a voyage to Canada, Deane died suddenly of a mysterious illness. The following day the *Gentleman's Magazine* wrote of him:

> The epicedium of Mr Deane may be this – he was second to very few politicians in knowledge, plans, designs and executions; deficient only in placing confidence in his compatriots, and doing them service before he got his compensation, of which no well-bred politician was before him ever guilty.[5]

In 1842, Congress voted Deane's heirs $37,000 as a partial restitution of his expenses and reputation.

On Fleet Street, between Fetter Lane and Chancery Lane, stands the church of St Dunstan-in-the-West. The statue on its outside wall of Queen Elizabeth I was carved during her lifetime. It originally decorated Lud Gate but was moved to St Dunstan-in-the-West when the gate and city wall were demolished in 1760. The present St Dunstan-in-the-West is an octagonal Victorian building. Below Queen Elizabeth, hidden in an alcove, are three less well-preserved statues: James I and his sons Prince Henry and Prince Charles. It was in honour of these two young princes that the two capes off the coast of Virginia were named, after the ships *Susan Constant*, *Discovery* and *Godspeed* were driven between them by a violent storm when they reached America in 1607.

Beyond St Dunstan's are an alley and gateway, the only remains of Clifford's Inn. When Clifford's Inn was still functioning as an Inn of Chancery, one of those who studied and practised law here was Thomas Morton, founder of the ill-fated Merry Mount settlement. A further link with America comes through a lawyer called Master Hore, who in 1536 persuaded 'divers young gentlemen of the Inns of Court and Chancery' to join him on one of the first expeditions to set sail for America. At Gravesend 120 of them procured two vessels and took the sacrament together, but made no other preparations. When they reached Newfoundland their supplies ran out and their ships were grounded. In the land of fish they could not use a line and bait. They ate roots and bilberries, picked fishbones from ospreys' nests and eventually began to eat each other, ignoring Master Hore's warnings that for cannibalism they would go to unquenchable hellfire. When a French vessel appeared they seized it and the food on board, then sailed away, leaving behind the French crew, who were lucky enough to be rescued. The French complained to King Henry VIII about their treatment. He ordered an inquiry but was moved by the plight of Master Hore's party and did not punish them. Instead he made recompense to the French out of his own purse.

The Inns of Chancery, which began in the fourteenth and fifteenth centuries, were centres for housing law students and training them for entry to the Inns of Court. By the eighteenth century they had become social clubs for lawyers, but those that continued were dissolved in the legal reforms of the late nineteenth century. The names of some of the Inns of Chancery are still used for the sites they used to occupy: Thavies Inn, Furnival's Inn, Clement's Inn, Staple Inn, Barnard's Inn and Clifford's Inn.

The four ancient Inns of Court, similar but senior to the Inns of Chancery, have survived. They are Lincoln's Inn, Inner Temple, Middle Temple and Gray's Inn. They call lawyers to the Bar, provide chambers for barristers practising in the Courts of Law and are the august organisations of the legal profession.

The entrance to Inner Temple and Middle Temple is in Fleet Street, opposite Chancery Lane, through Inner Temple Lane. Built over the gateway of the lane is a dark, wooden-fronted house – 17 Fleet Street – dating from 1611. Decorated with carvings of the Prince of Wales feathers and known as Prince Henry's Room, it was originally used as an office for King James I's son Prince Henry, the boy whose death in 1613 at the age of eighteen caused his imprisoned tutor, Sir Walter Ralegh, to abandon his *History of the World*.

FIVE

Inns of Court and Law Courts

'In the two hundred years between Sir Walter Ralegh's expedition to Virginia and the adoption of the Constitution of the United States, it was in this very hall that many of those who later became prominent in law and government in the Colonies and in the newly independent United States, learnt those principles of liberty under the law which were the inspiration of the American Constitution.'

Lord Diplock,
Links between the Middle Temple and
the United States of America, *1971*

At the bottom of Inner Temple Lane is the round church built in 1185 for the Knights Templar, whose full title was the Poor Knights of Christ and of the Temple of Solomon of Jerusalem. The Knights Templar were an armed religious order founded in Jerusalem in 1099, on the site of Solomon's Temple. They fought in Palestine in the Crusades against the Islamic world, and throughout Europe branches of their organisation were set up with churches modelled on the round church of the Holy Sepulchre in Jerusalem. The wealth and power of the Knights Templar were coveted and feared by medieval monarchs. In 1307 King Philip V of France, in collusion with the Pope, crushed the French 'tongue' of the Knights Templar organisation. Edward II followed suit in England.

The land occupied by the English 'tongue' of the order, alongside the Thames at the western edge of the City of London, was given by Edward II to the Knights of St John of Jerusalem, a rival religious order which leased the land to men who practised law in the Kings's courts but were not clergy. These early professional lawyers soon formed themselves into 'honourable societies' living in the Inns of Court.

When Henry VIII dissolved the Knights of St John of Jerusalem in 1559, the Honourable Society of the Middle Temple and the Honourable Society of the Inner Temple became tenants of the Crown. In 1608 they secured the freehold of the land by a charter from King James I, on condition that they maintained the Temple Church and its services for ever. In 1610 a special farewell service was held in the Temple Church for the adventurers about to sail to Virginia with their governor, Lord de la Warre. They heard a stirring sermon applauding Lord de la Warre's patriotism and comparing him to Abraham because he was forsaking his father's house and kindred for 'a land which God will show thee'. When he arrived at the Jamestown settlement in Virginia he found the colonists in a desperate state. His intervention restored their confidence and ensured that the colonising project was not abandoned.

From the Temple Church, Pump Court Cloisters leads to Middle Temple Lane and Middle Temple Hall in Fountain Court. Middle Temple Hall, with its fine Tudor hammerbeam roof, was built in 1571. At that time the Inns of Court not only prepared students for the practice of law but they 'rivalled the universities as centres of intellectual life,' as Lord Diplock, Master of the Middle Temple Bench, explained to visiting members of the American Bar Association in 1971.[1] The training that they offered was regarded as the fittest preparation for a leading role in government and affairs of state. Many famous statesmen and men of action in the first Elizabethan age were members of one or other of the four Inns, including Sir Francis Drake. A great banquet in his honour was held in Middle Temple Hall in 1581 to celebrate his return from circumnavigating the globe and staking England's claim to the west coast of North America. Drake had given up supplying slaves to the Spanish empire in Central and Southern America in favour of the more

Middle Temple Hall

lucrative business of pirating Spanish treasure ships. His victories in the Spanish Maine opened up the eastern shores of America for English settlement.

Francis Drake set out from Plymouth, England in the *Pelican* to sail around the world in November 1577, telling his crew that they were going to the Middle East. Around the cape of South America they ran into 'a tempest the like of which no traveller hath felt since Noah's flood.' They weathered it and went on to sack the cities on the west coast of South America, then, loaded with Spanish treasure, landed on the west coast of North America in what is now California, which Drake called Nova Albion. Before returning to England, he renamed his ship the *Golden Hind*.

When the *Golden Hind* sailed home to Plymouth the Spanish King demanded Drake's head for piracy, but Queen Elizabeth I invited the great sea-dog to bring the *Golden Hind* up the Thames and moor it in Deptford, near her palace at Greenwich. There she provided on board 'a finer banquet', as the Spanish Ambassador noted, 'than has ever been seen in England since the time of King Henry.' She laid a gilded sword on Drake's shoulder and dubbed him Sir Francis.

In his four-year voyage Drake had made world history, and a fortune for himself. Those who invested in the enterprise – including the Queen and the City of London merchants – realised profits of three thousand per cent.

The merchants were so delighted that some of their number suggested mounting the *Golden Hind* on top of the spire of the Old St Paul's. The idea was abandoned as impractical, but the hatch-cover of the ship was made into a table which still stands in Middle Temple Hall. On it students 'called to the Bar' still sign the roll, beneath the gaze of a portrait of Elizabeth I painted in her lifetime.

Philip Amadas, who captained the first expedition sent in 1584 by Walter Ralegh to explore the land later named Virginia, was also a member of the Middle Temple. When he returned with the news that gained Ralegh his knighthood, he was fined by the Middle Temple Benchers for being absent from his legal studies without permission. Ralegh was himself a Middle Templar, as was Sir Edwin Sandys of the Virginia Company.

In the eighteenth century increasing numbers of American-born students came to London to learn the principles of the common law in its birthplace – the Inns of Court. Middle Temple was particularly favoured. It was a centre of Whiggery and sympathetic to the cause of the American colonists. Peyton Reynolds, who presided over the first meeting of the Continental Congress in 1774, was a Middle Templar. So was John Dickinson, the 'penman of the Revolution', who drafted the Articles of Confederation. Thomas McKean, a delegate from Delaware who signed the Declaration of Independence, was also a member of Middle Temple. (He later served as President of Delaware and Governor of Pennsylvania.) All four delegates from South Carolina who signed the Declaration were Middle Templars, including Edward Rutledge, who became Governor of the state. Rutledge was also one of three Middle Templars who drafted the Constitution; the others were Jared Ingersoll of Pennsylvania and William Livingston, Governor of New Jersey. Rutledge went on to become second Chief Justice of the United States.

In the twentieth Century the Middle Temple began to elect distinguished American citizens as Honorary Masters of the Bench – the ancient governing body of the Inn. The first, in 1905, was Joseph Choate, American Ambassador in London and former President of the American Bar Association. Subsequent American Ambassadors in London who were lawyers were intermittently elected as Honorary Benchers. Since 1947 it has been customary for the current American Ambassador in London to be numbered among Benchers of the Inn. William Howard Taft, who was the twenty-seventh President (1909–13), and General Charles Dawes (Vice-President 1925–9) were both Honorary Benchers of Middle Temple.

Next to Middle Temple Hall is Temple Garden. This is where William Shakespeare set the plucking of red and white roses by the supporters of the Houses of Lancaster and York, whose enmity led to the fifteenth-century Wars of the Roses which wiped out England's medieval nobility. 'Within the Temple Hall we were too loud,' says the Earl of Suffolk in Act II, scene iv of *Henry VI, Part One*. 'The garden here is more convenient.' At the end of the scene the Earl of Warwick concludes:

> . . . this brawl today,
> Grown to this faction in the Temple Garden,
> Shall send between the red rose and the white
> A thousand souls to death and deadly night.

From the Temple Garden, steps lead down and out of the Middle Temple to Milford Lane, which was on mudbanks of the Thames before the building of the Embankment. On the corner stands Astor House – 2 Temple Place – which John Betjeman, the English poet and architectural historian, described as 'one of the most attractive late-Victorian private houses in London . . . an oasis in a sad district beset by railways'.[2] Astor House was built in 1895 as a residence and estate office for William Waldorf Astor, afterwards first Viscount Astor. He was the great-grandson of John Jacob Astor, the German butcher's boy who emigrated from the village of Waldorf to America in 1783 and founded the great fur-trading and shipping empire of the Astor family. After a distinguished career in America as businessman, politician, diplomat, novelist, newspaper proprietor and a gentleman-farmer, he emigrated to Britain in 1890, became a naturalised British

Astor House, 2 Temple Place

subject nine years later, and soon after bought the thirteenth-century Hever Castle in Kent. He was created Baron Astor in 1916 and Viscount Astor of Hever in 1917, two years before his death.

When William Waldorf Astor entered the House of Lords in 1916, his American-born wife Nancy was elected to his seat in the House of Commons as Conservative MP for Plymouth. She was the first woman to sit in Parliament and kept her seat until 1945. Nancy Astor distinguished herself as a crusading advocate of temperance, a champion of women's and children's welfare, and a spirited opponent of socialism, though in the late 1930s her political reputation suffered from her involvement with the 'Cliveden set', who were suspected of sympathy with Hitler. She died in England in 1964. Astor House is now a commercial headquarters, but it has – as a reminder of its American past – a beautiful and detailed beaten-copper weathervane in the shape of Christopher Columbus's caravel, the *Santa Maria*.

From Milford Lane, steps lead up to the Essex watergate, which in the sixteenth century gave access from boats on the Thames to Essex House. This was the home of Robert Devereux, Earl of Essex, stepson of Elizabeth I's beloved Robert Dudley, Earl of Leicester. Essex was a handsome young man who tried to charm the ageing Queen to rescue him from military and financial disaster. When she refused to underwrite his debts, he resorted to conspiracy but his plot to put himself on the throne was uncovered. He was surrounded and seized in Essex House, taken to the Tower of London and executed in 1601 for treason.

Essex Street leads past the Edgar Wallace pub to the Strand, which is in the City of Westminster. The Strand is a continuation of Fleet Street but the name changes at the City of London boundary marked by a dragon on the site of the old Temple Bar. In the Strand is the late nineteenth-century building which houses the Royal Courts of Justice – the highest civil courts in England and Wales – usually known as the Law Courts.

The imposing public lobby of the Law Courts contains a statue of Judge William Blackstone (1723–80), presented by the American Bar Association in 1924. Judge Blackstone's *Commentaries on the Laws of England* (1765) were an important source of American knowledge of English law and were used in drafting the Constitution and establishing the legal system of the

USA. After publication of the four volumes of *Commentaries* in England there were more than a thousand copies in circulation in the American colonies. Fourteen hundred copies of the American edition were ordered in advance of publication in 1771. In his *History of the American Bar*, Charles Warren wrote that the advent of Blackstone

> opened the eyes of American scholars to the broader field of learning in the law. He taught them for the first time, the continuity, the unity, and the reason of the Common Law – and just at a time when the need of a unified system in both law and politics was beginning to be felt in the Colonies.

Most of the specific powers given to the President by Article III of the Constitution are listed by Judge Blackstone as the prerogatives of the Crown, though the powers of the President are usually limited or qualified. Article III of the Constitution – which deals with treason – in effect states much of Blackstone's summary of procedures developed over several centuries in England. The first ten Amendments to the Constitution – often referred to as the Federal Bill of Rights – contain rights discussed by Blackstone, such as liberty of the press and the right of petition. The use of torture, which Blackstone said was unknown to English law, though 'occasionally used as an engine of State', is forbidden by the provision against compulsory self-incrimination in the Fifth Amendment.

Judge Blackstone's principal influence on American law lay not in the writing of the Constitution but in the development of law in general after the Constitution had been adopted. The American revolutionists differed with his views, but 'the final irony', writes Stanley Katz in the Chicago Press facsimile edition of the *Commentaries*, 'runs in Blackstone's favor, for with the establishment of the new American nation in 1789, Americans increasingly turned to the *Commentaries* as a model for the legal system of a democratic republic.' After the Revolution, Americans chose the Common Law rather than any other legal system because it was accessible in the *Commentaries*.[3]

Next to Judge Blackstone's statue is a painting of John Singleton Copley, Lord Lyndhurst (1772–1863), the Boston-born son of the American artist John Singleton Copley. Lord Lyndhurst was a barrister at Lincoln's Inn and is shown here as Solicitor-General, conducting the prosecution of Queen Caroline in 1820. The future King George IV married his cousin Caroline of Brunswick in 1795 when he was still Prince of Wales, in order to persuade Parliament to write off his debts. After the birth of their daughter Princess Caroline in 1796 the couple separated and Caroline went to live in Italy. When George III – the last King of America – was incapacitated by illness, the Prince of Wales became Prince Regent, and on his father's death in 1820 he succeeded to the throne. Caroline returned to England to claim her rights as Queen, quickly becoming a focus of popular discontent against

George IV and his government. A Bill was introduced in Parliament depriving Caroline of the title of Queen and declaring the royal marriage 'for ever wholly dissolved, annulled and made void'. When Caroline tried to attend George IV's Coronation she was turned away from the doors of Westminster Abbey. She died suddenly in 1821.

The exit from the Law Courts is on the first floor and leads to Carey Street, opposite Lincoln's Inn. On the corner of Lincoln's Inn is a statue of one of its most illustrious past members, Sir Thomas More, 'some time Lord Chancellor of England, martyred 6 July 1535'. More's famous book *Utopia* was published abroad, in Louvain, in 1516, and at St Paul's Churchyard in 1551 by Abraham Uete. *Utopia* had an immediate and far-reaching impact. In it More turned his back on the wars and dissension of Europe to imagine life in the new-found lands where there was room for expansion and experiment. Humanity had a chance, he argued, which might never return, to build a new and better society. He was inspired to write *Utopia* by discussions with Amerigo Vespucci and his seamen, as well as by his studies of Plato and the New Testament. He had read Vespucci's

Quattuor Americi Vesputi Navigationes, which portrayed a people 'who hold all their goods in common, and . . . gold, pearls, jewels were things of no account.' In the land of Utopia, More wrote,

> it should be lawful for every man to favour and follow what religion he would, and that he might do the best he could to bring others to his opinions, so that he did it peaceably, gently, quietly and soberly, without harty and contentious rebuking and inveighing against others.

He envisaged a world in which there would be no unemployment, no excessive labour, no monopolies, and no wars, 'except to right grievous wrongs'. His Utopians regarded war 'as a thing very beastly'. They worked only six hours a day, leaving ample leisure time for the 'free liberty of the mind and garnishing of the same'.[4]

Sir Thomas More was executed by Henry VIII in 1535 for his religious views. His parboiled head was impaled on a spike and publicly displayed on London Bridge until it was retrieved by his daughter Mary Roper, a scholar of international repute.

Soon after the first publication of *Utopia*, More's brother-in-law, John Rastell, gained royal approval for a transatlantic voyage of exploration. In

1517, he set sail for America from the Thames, with a small fleet of vessels and a letter from Henry VIII 'to all Christian princes'. Rastell was a printer and lawyer, not a sailor, and could not keep order on board ship; his rebellious crew bundled him ashore at Cork, in Ireland, and returned home. Rastell drew on this fiasco for his play *An Interlude of the Four Elements*, published in 1519. The play was a mixture of scientific dissertation and comedy, but in it Rastell was arguably the first to put the case for English colonisation of the new-found lands. A character called Experience explains to another called Studious Desire:

> Westward be found new lands
> That we never heard tell of before this
> By writing nor other means
> Yet many now have been there
> And that country is so large of room
> Much longer than all Christendom
> Without fable or guile
> For divers mariners have tried
> And sailed straight by the coast side
> About five thousand mile
> But what commodities be within
> No man can tell nor well imagine. . . .
> And what a thing had be then
> If that they be Englishmen
> Might have been the first of all
> That there would have taken possession
> And made first building and habitation
> A memory perpetual
> And also what an honorable thing
> Both to the realm and to the king
> To have had this dominion extended
> There into so far ground
> Which the noble king of late memory
> The most wise prince the vii Henry
> Caused first to be found
> And what a great and meritous deed
> It were to have the people instructed
> To live more virtuously . . .
> Which as yet live all beastly
> For they neither know god nor the devil
> Nor never heard tell of heaven or hell
> Writing nor other scripture
> But yet in the stead of god almighty
> They honour the sun for his great light. . . .
> For that doth them great pleasure
> Building nor house they have none at all
> But wood cots and caves small

No marvel though it be so
For they use no manner of iron
Neither in tool nor other weapon
That would help them thereto.
How the people first began
In that country or whence they came
For clerks it is a question.
Other things I have in store
That I could tell thereof but now no more
Til another season.
But this new land found lately
Been called America by cause only
Americans did first find them.[5]

Lincoln's Inn is entered from Carey Street through an archway built in 1697. The path leads to New Square, which dates from around 1690. At the end of the square is the Old Hall built in 1490 and much used by Sir Thomas More. Next to it stands the Lincoln's Inn Chapel, which was probably designed by Inigo Jones and is an example of early seventeenth-century Gothic style. The chapel stands on pillars over an 'undercroft' at ground level. This 'undercroft', with its beautiful carved stone ceiling, provided gentlemen of Lincoln's Inn with shelter against stormy weather; it was also a place where distressed and unsupported mothers could leave their babies, secure in the knowledge that the Inn would see that they were looked after and well brought up. Babies found in the chapel undercroft were usually given the surname Lincoln and, when they became teenagers, the boys were apprenticed and the girls provided with a marriage dowry. The girls were not allowed to work in the Inn once they reached puberty. In 1565 the Benchers of Lincoln's Inn issued a decree banning from the premises all laundresses and other female servants 'except under the age of twelve years or above the age of forty years'.

The foundation stone of Lincoln's Inn Chapel was laid by John Donne, a member of the Inn, who also preached the consecration sermon on Ascension Day in 1623. The finely carved chapel pews – which are still in use – were that day filled with a 'great concourse of noblemen and gentlemen; whereof two or three were endangered, and taken up dead for the time, with the extreme press and thronging.'[6] The bell which was rung to celebrate the consecration of the new chapel had been captured as part of the spoils of the English sacking of the Spanish town of Cadiz in 1596. When John Donne was a student at Lincoln's Inn, he would have heard it being rung to announce important events. It is still tolled today at 9 p.m. to announce the nightly curfew, and between 12.30 and 1 p.m. when news of the death of a Bencher is received. 'No man is an Island, entire of it self,' wrote Donne in his *Devotions Upon Emergent Occasions*, first published in 1624. 'Every man is a piece of the continent, a part of the main. . . . Any man's death diminishes me, because I am involved in Mankind; And therefore never send to know for whom the bell tolls; It tolls for thee.' These lines have inspired, among others, Ernest Hemingway, and were quoted by Mikhail Gorbachev to the United Nations in 1988.

The main exit from Lincoln's Inn, alongside the nineteenth-century mock-Tudor dining hall, leads to Lincoln's Inn Fields, a public garden which in the fourteenth century was the playing fields for students of Lincoln's Inn. As a child Giulielma Springett played here with young Thomas Ellwood, who later described how he used to 'ride with her in a little coach drawn by her footmen about Lincoln's Inn Fields.'[7] Ellwood had to give up hopes of marrying Giulielma once she decided to become the wife of William Penn. Penn, a member of Lincoln's Inn, married her in 1672. She was, he wrote, 'the love of my youth and much the joy of my life.'

When the young Benjamin Franklin left employment at Palmer's printing house in Bartholomew Close in Smithfields, he went to work

at Watt's, near Lincoln's Inn Fields, a still greater printing-house. Here I continued all the rest of my stay in London. At my first admission into this printing-house I took to working at press, imagining I felt a want of the bodily exercise I had been used to in America, where presswork is mixed with composing. I drank only water; the other workmen, near fifty in number, were great guzzlers of beer. On occasion, I carried up and down stairs a large form of types in each hand, when others carried but one in both hands. They wondered to see, from this and several instances that the *Water-American*, as they called me, was *stronger* than themselves, who drank *strong* beer! We had an alehouse boy who attended always in the house to supply the workmen. My companion at the press drank every day a pint before breakfast, a pint at breakfast with his bread and cheese, a pint between breakfast and dinner, a pint at dinner, a pint in the afternoon about six o'clock, and another when he had done his day's work. I thought it a detestable custom; but it was necessary, he supposed, to drink *strong* beer, that he might be *strong* to labour. I endeavoured to convince him that the bodily strength afforded by beer could only be in proportion to the grain or flour of the barley dissolved in the water of which it was made; that there was more flour in a penny-worth of bread; and therefore, if he would eat that with a pint of water, it would give him more strength than a quart of beer. He drank on, however, and had four or five shillings to pay out of his wages every Saturday night for that muddling liquor; an expense I was free from. And thus these poor devils keep themselves always under.[8]

A house at 58 Lincoln's Inn Fields – on the far side from Lincoln's Inn – was the scene of an all-male dinner party on 15 April 1848, where the guests included Ralph Waldo Emerson, Charles Dickens and Thomas Carlyle. After dinner, Emerson recorded, the conversation 'turned on the shameful lewdness of the London streets at night.' One of the company said that he heard 'whoredom in the House of Commons. Disraeli betrays whoredom, and the whole House of Commons universal incontinence in every word they say.' Carlyle and Dickens thought 'chastity in the male sex was as good as gone in our times, and in England was so rare that they could name all the exceptions.' Emerson was shocked and disputed Carlyle's assertion that the same was true in America: 'I assured them it was not so with us; that, for the most part, young men of good standing and good education, with us go virgins to their nuptial beds as truly as their brides.' Charles Dickens then remarked that 'incontinence is so much the rule in England that if his own son were particularly chaste, he should be alarmed on his account, as if he could not be in good health.'[9]

Nearby is the so-called Olde Curiosity Shop, dating from 1562. From here, Clement's Lane leads past the London School of Economics, where John F. Kennedy was a student in the summer of 1935 at the age of eighteen, before he went to Princeton. At the end of Clement's Lane is Clement's Inn, which becomes Mobil Court opposite the church of St Clement Danes in the Strand.

The present St Clement Danes was built by Sir Christopher Wren in 1679, with a steeple added by James Gibbs in 1719. The church was badly damaged by enemy action in 1941 but restored and re-dedicated in 1958 as the central church of the Royal Air Force. Among the World War II rolls of honour on display inside is one to US airmen which is inscribed with Abraham Lincoln's famous words: 'we here highly resolve that these dead shall not have died in vain: that this nation under God, shall have a new birth of freedom and that government of the people, by the people, for the people shall not perish from the earth.' The organ in St Clement Danes was a gift in 1956 from 'members of the United States Air Force, their families and friends.'

Alongside the organ flies the flag of modern Denmark. By the Treaty of Wedmore, made in AD 878 between the Anglo-Saxon King Alfred and the Danish King Guttram, the Danish community in London was allowed to settle here in Aldwych around the church of St Clement Danes. A wooden church on this site is known to have been replaced by a stone church by the start of the eleventh century. When the Danish community came under attack from King Ethelred the Unready, many people fled to the church for safety, only to be butchered on the steps of the altar. Ethelred the Unready died in 1016; his son Edmund Ironside continued the war with King Canute of Denmark, who eventually added England to his domains. The Danes were part of the seafaring Norse civilisation which expanded from Scandinavia between AD 750 and 1000. Many ventured much further afield than London. In AD 986 Bjarni Herjulfsson became the first recorded European to sight North America; Lief Eriksson landed at three places on the east coast; and Thorvald Eriksson and Thorfinn Karlsefni established a settlement of sixty-five men and women which lasted for a few years before they returned to their homeland.

From St Clement Danes, Aldwych curves round to Kingsway, built in 1905 at a cost of £5 million and the last great road in London designed for horse-drawn traffic. At the end of Kingsway is Bush House – now the home of the BBC World Service – which owes its name to Irving T. Bush, the American who planned the building in 1919 as a vast and luxurious trade centre where manufacturers could show and sell their goods. Bush House was designed by the American architect Harvey W. Corbett and completed in 1935.

Across Kingsway stands the Aldwych Theatre at the foot of Drury Lane, birthplace of London's modern theatreland.

Bush House

SIX

Theatreland

'Walking to Westminster . . . I did see many milkmaids with their garlands upon their pails, dancing with a fiddler before them; and saw pretty Nell Gwynn standing at her lodgings' door in Drury Court in her smock sleeves and bodice looking upon me; she seemed a mighty pretty creature.'

Samuel Pepys, Diary, *1667*

Fred and Adéle Astaire 1923

Shaftesbury Theatre

DRURY LANE

SHAFTESBURY AVENUE

Alexander's Ragtime Band 1913

MONMOUTH ST

Royal Opera House

LONG ACRE

COVENT GARDEN

GARRICK STREET

Lucretia M. and Elizabe. Cady Stanto.

Hippodrome

CRANBOURN STREET

CHARING CROSS ROAD

George Washington

ST MARTIN'S LANE

Harry Houdini 1900

LEICESTER SQUARE

John Singleton Copley 1782

Nelson's Column

St Martin-in-the-Fields

Qu. H. 18.

Tennessee Williams 1948

PANTON St

TRAFALGAR SQUARE

HAYMARKET

THEATRE ROYAL HAYMARKET

PALL MALL

King George III

COCKSPUR ST

Patience Lovell Wright

Covent Garden
Theatreland

Peabody Buildings

DRURY LANE

RUSSELL STREET

KINGSWAY

Bush House
Irving T. Bush
1919

Theatre
Royal
Drury Lane

ALDWYCH

WELLINGTON STREET

Edwin
Forrest
1836

ALDWYCH

THE STRAND

Station

TEMPLE

Ethel
Barrymore
1897

SAVOY

Robert Fulton's
Submarine 1897

Paul
Robeson
1929

LANCASTER PLACE

WATERLOO BRIDGE

VICTORIA EMBANKMENT

RIVER
THAMES

Benjamin Franklin's
House 1757-1775

CRAVEN STREET

TO WESTMINSTER

The road from Aldwych north to High Holborn was known until the beginning of the seventeenth century as Via de Aldwych, but after Sir Thomas Drury built a house there in the reign of Queen Elizabeth I its name was changed to Drury Lane. It became the birthplace of London's modern theatreland when the first Theatre Royal Drury Lane was opened in 1663. Drury Lane was also one of the places where the Great Plague began, as Samuel Pepys noted in his diary in June 1665:

> This day, much against my will, I did in Drury lane see two or three houses marked with a red cross upon the doors, and 'Lord have mercy upon us' writ there – which was a sad sight to me, being the first of that kind that to my remembrance I ever saw.[1]

By the eighteenth century Drury Lane was notorious for gin shops, prostitution and poverty. John Gay, in *The Art of Walking the Streets of London by Night*, published in 1716, wrote:

> O! may thy virtue guard thee through the roads
> Of Drury's mazy courts and dark abodes!

The street became one of London's densely overcrowded 'rookeries', a byword for bad living conditions and social deprivation. In 1816 a surgeon reported that 'Some of the lower habitations have neither windows nor chimneys nor floors, and some are so dark that I can scarcely see at mid-day without a candle.'

Drury Lane slums were eventually replaced by Peabody Trust apartment blocks, still in use today. The philanthropic housing organisation founded by the American merchant-banker George Peabody tried hard to discipline its tenants into cleanliness, orderliness and thrift. A London woman who grew up in Peabody Buildings before the First World War recalled that

> The stairs and the landing had to be polished until they were shining every week. All us children had to be vaccinated and you weren't allowed to play in the square outside after seven in the winter or after eight in the summer. And if you broke the rules or you didn't pay the rent each week, you were given a couple of hours to do it, to put your house in order, or you were out. Our superintendent was a real sergeant-major type, a stickler for the rules, and we were a bit frightened of him, so most people did as they were told.[2]

Opposite the Peabody Buildings, at the corner of Drury Lane and Russell Street, is the back of the Theatre Royal Drury Lane; the front of the theatre is further along Russell Street, at the corner with Catherine Street. James Boswell, the biographer of Dr Johnson, once took two vivacious young women to the Shakespeare's Head Tavern in Catherine Street and there enjoyed 'high debauchery'.[3]

Peabody Buildings

The first Theatre Royal Drury Lane was where King Charles II met Nell Gwynne, the orange-seller who became a popular London actress. Her first known appearance on the stage was in 1665 as Cydaria in Dryden's *Indian Emperor*. She usually played piquant, bustling parts and her dancing was much admired. She had various adventures with lovers other than the King, whose mistress she became in 1669. She once threatened to drop her royal baby out of a window unless the King gave him a title, which he did: the Duke of St Albans. Nell left the stage in 1682.

The present Theatre Royal, dating from 1812, is the fourth on the site. It was to the second Theatre Royal that Abigail Adams came in 1785 when Sarah Siddons was playing Desdemona in *Othello*. Mrs Adams wrote to her sister in America that Mrs Siddons was

> interesting beyond any actress I have ever seen; but I lost much of the pleasure of the play, from the sooty appearance of the Moor. Perhaps it may be early prejudice, but I could not separate the African color from the man, nor prevent that disgust and horror which filled my mind every time I saw him touch the gentle Desdemona.[4]

In March 1813 the Theatre Royal manager received a letter from the twenty-one-year-old New York actor John Howard Payne, who was then living at the Tavistock Coffee House in Covent Garden:

I am an American recently arrived in this country. My pursuit is theatrical. It is my wish to appear at Drury Lane Theatre as soon as it may be convenient. Lest my playing might prove unworthy of a refined British audience, I should wish to make my earliest efforts without being publicly known.[5]

When Payne made his Drury Lane début two months later, the *Weekly Despatch* expressed the opinion that it was 'remarkable that a youth from a remote country – a country nearly 200 years behind us in the improvement of every art – should have the courage to come before a London audience under every possible disadvantage.'

In 1820 Payne leased the Sadler's Wells Theatre in Rosebery Avenue, but got into debt and was sent to the Fleet Prison. He noted in his diary how crucial it was 'never to owe money to one's landlord. Little debts are always worse than big ones.' His imprisonment, however, was relieved by visits from the attractive English actress Mrs Glover. Working frenziedly for a few days, Payne produced a translation of the French play *Thérèse*, by Victor Ducange, which had been sent to him in prison anonymously. Mrs Glover took his translation to the manager at the Theatre Royal Drury Lane – where she was appearing in *The School for Scandal* – and *Thérèse* opened soon after to rave reviews. The published play was also an enormous success, selling out immediately, and with the £140 he received Payne was able to pay off enough creditors to secure his release from prison. Other creditors were hot on his heels, so he reclaimed his possessions from his landlady at 4 Southampton Street and left for Paris, where he wrote the words of 'Home Sweet Home'. When he returned to the USA in 1832, he was warmly welcomed but still had financial problems. With the help of influential friends, including Daniel Webster, he was appointed American consul at Tunis, and died there in 1852. He was buried in Washington, DC.

In October 1836, the Philadelphia-born tragic actor Edwin Forrest opened at the Theatre Royal, Drury Lane in *The Gladiator*, a play by the American playwright Robert M. Bird. Forrest was bombarded with bravos and a chorus of 'Welcome to England!' from the audience. William Macready – London's foremost actor of the day, who played at the rival Theatre Royal Covent Garden – came backstage to greet Forrest and initially liked him. But after Forrest had played to full houses at Drury Lane for two months in *Othello*, *Macbeth* and *King Lear*, Macready viewed him as a dangerous competitor, even while he presented him with a gold snuffbox on his last night. When Forrest returned from a provincial tour to open at the Theatre Royal Drury Lane in *Richard III*, Macready began performing *Richard III* himself at the Theatre Royal Covent Garden. This drew audiences away from Drury Lane and the manager there had to cut back Forrest's performances to one a week.

The thirty-one-year-old Edwin Forrest had fallen in love with nineteen-year-old Catherine Sinclair. When her father asked Forrest what financial settlement he intended to make he was told that if she could not trust him for her money she had better not trust him for her happiness. The couple were married without Mr Sinclair's blessing on 23 June 1837 at St Paul's Church in Covent Garden. 'Forrest led his young and lovely bride', one newspaper reported, 'to a new and splendid carriage expressly manufactured for the occasion, and with the aid of four beautiful gray horses, richly caparisoned, the young couple started for Windsor where they were to pass the first portion of their honeymoon.'[6] From Windsor the Forrests went to Paris, returned to London and then sailed to New York, where the beautiful and vivacious Catherine became the talk of the town. Ten years later Edwin and Catherine Forrest vigorously accused each other of multiple adultery in a sensational court case and were divorced.

In 1849, when William Macready arrived in New York from London to play *Macbeth* at the Astor Place Opera House, Edwin Forrest supporters howled him down. On the second night a mob gathered outside the theatre, threw stones and threatened to seize Macready. The militia were called in. They opened fire and many New Yorkers were killed. Forrest was blamed for the tragedy and socially ostracised, but he continued to play to large audiences and amassed a fortune. He became lame in 1865 and died in Philadelphia in 1872.

At the end of Russell Street, to the left, is Wellington Street, at the bottom of which stands the Lyceum Theatre. Gouverneur Morris – the American statesman and diplomat who played an important role in the War of Independence and the drafting of the Constitution – came here in 1790 to see a large Lincolnshire ox on show. 'It is,' he wrote,

> truly a wonderful creature, now seventeen years old, nineteen hands high and three feet four inches across the hips. . . . According to my little judgement on subjects of this sort I think that his beef, hide and tallow will weigh above 3000 lbs. He is to be sold in a day or two, the owner having too much to attend to as he says to continue here for the purpose of exhibiting him. I tell him that he had better have him killed as much for the show and spare the expense of feeding and attendance upon the beast.[7]

In July 1881 a party was held at the Lyceum for Edwin Booth, the greatest American actor of the nineteenth century. Booth had been playing in *Othello* with the English stars Henry Irving and Ellen Terry, and his performance was hailed by the London critics as a triumph, although it was given at a time when his young wife was dying. His American friends at the party included Thomas B. Aldrich, editor of *Atlantic Monthly*, and William

Winter, drama critic for the New York *Tribune*. Winter conveyed Booth to his hotel room after the men-only party broke up at dawn and the actor later recorded that when he awoke at 2.30 p.m. he was 'feeling quite decent'; he remembered nothing of the previous evening 'beyond the fact that the table was luxurious, the lager cold and the spirits warm'.[8]

Wellington Street leads down to the Strand, which for centuries was lined with great aristocratic houses overlooking the Thames. One of them was the Savoy Palace, the site of which is now occupied by the Savoy Hotel, built in 1889. The hotel's forecourt is the only place in Britain where traffic must drive on the right.

In 1914 the Savoy became the rallying point for Americans caught in Europe at the outbreak of the First World War. Tens of thousands of Americans fled from the Continent to London but could find no banks to cash money, no hotel accommodation and no places on ships to take them home. Herbert Hoover – then a mining consultant representing San Francisco's Panama–Pacific Exposition in London – was persuaded by the American Ambassador Wallace Hines Page to organise a Relief Committee for his stranded countrymen, and the Savoy Hotel provided him with reception rooms free of charge so that he could do so. Volunteers working for the Relief Committee telephoned American firms with London branches to borrow cash from their safes and by these means a limited number of pounds were exchanged for each tourist at the normal rate of $4.85. Those who had run out of money were loaned ten shillings a day. In addition, twelve American businessmen guaranteed an account of $1 million with the British Treasury, which then supplied cash against paper dollars, including personal cheques. In six weeks

Hoover's committee helped 120,000 Americans get home and paid out over $1.5 million. Its loss in bad cheques and non-repayments amounted to less than $300. Hoover's work in setting up and administering the committee launched him on the career in public service which led eventually to the White House.

Among the stranded Americans who thronged to the Savoy in 1914 were a dozen Amerindians who had been performing in a Wild West Show in Poland. Penniless, but wearing full costume, they camped in the hotel lounge until the management had made sure that places were found for them on a transatlantic steamer. Another memorable incident occurred when high-class clothes delivered to the hotel by London shops for a wealthy young Michigan lady whose trunks had gone astray were inadvertently commandeered by Mrs Hoover and distributed free of charge to women and children arriving from the Continent in distress.

In 1929 the great American singer and actor Paul Robeson was, on account of his colour, refused admission to the Grill Room of the Savoy during a party given for him by Lady Sybil Colefax. In the protests which followed, the hotel management expressed astonishment that such a mistake could have been made. Prime Minister Ramsay MacDonald told Parliament that the government was powerless to prevent such behaviour.

Robeson had become a celebrity in London overnight after his singing of 'Ol' Man River' in the production of *Showboat* at the Theatre Royal Drury Lane. He gave a concert in the Royal Albert Hall, sang for private receptions, lunched at the House of Commons and met English writers such as Rebecca West and H. G. Wells. In May 1930 he opened in *Othello* at the Savoy Theatre with an all-star cast, including Sybil Thorndike and Peggy Ashcroft. Despite his concern over his lack of acting experience, on the first night there were thirty curtain calls. *The Times'* critic wrote that Robeson's portrayal of Othello contained 'a sadness that never lifts from the stage, growing as the tempest of fury, scorn and hatred draws to its full, possessing our minds and giving a kind of noble plainness to the tragedy.' After touring Britain with *Othello*, Robeson returned to London to perform in Eugene O'Neill's *The Hairy Ape* at the Ambassador Theatre and in *All God's Chillun Got Wings* at the Piccadilly Theatre. His artistic achievement and popularity were recognised by an entry in the British *Who's Who*, which was rare both for a performer and for an American.

Room 360 of the Savoy, overlooking a narrow alley off the Strand, was where William Saroyan wrote *The Adventures of Wesley Jackson*, working non-stop for thirty-eight days in 1944. Saroyan – who had won the Pulitzer Prize in 1939 for *The Time of Your Life* – was in England as a private in the US army. He had suggested to the Office of War Information that he should write a novel which would enhance Anglo-American relations and was allowed time to do so, living in the Savoy Hotel at his own expense. In the novel he presents a vivid view of wartime London through the eyes of his

American hero, Wesley Jackson, a nineteen-year-old born in San Francisco, with an Irish mother and a father from London. When he crossed the Atlantic as an Army conscript in a convoy of thirty-seven ships, the first land they sighted after a terrible voyage was Ireland, which Jackson thought was beautiful. They docked at Swansea in Wales and went by train to London,

> where we were taken in a truck to a building that was to be our barracks. . . . London was cold and sad. None of us had had a bath for two weeks, so we were cold and sad too, and homesick and angry, because the barracks were cold and sad. We made mattresses for our bunks out of straw that was piled on the floor. . . .
>
> We went out and started to prowl. We prowled from Soho to Piccadilly Circus where all the streetwalkers work. The place was like a sore. Everybody had a flashlight, so you got flashes of everything but not enough light at one time to give you anything like a real picture of what was going on. The sidewalks were jammed with soldiers and English girls, swarming together as if they were red and white corpuscles in sick blood. . . .
>
> In the midst of all this the Air Raid siren started to wail and a lot of people in the streets started hurrying to the shelters, but a lot of them *didn't* too. A couple of MPs told us it would be a good idea to duck down into the subway station right there – Piccadilly Circus. It was a *real* sight down there. Along the walls of the station bombed-out families had their little homes – double-decker bunks with sometimes a little bit of carpet in front of them. You'd see a whole family: father, mother and two or three children, the kids asleep and the father and mother talking quietly in spite of all the people around, as if they were in their own parlour. The place didn't smell very good, but the people were used to it. Every once in a while a train would roar up and stop. A lot of people would get off, a lot would get on, and a woman in overalls who worked on the train would holler at everybody to step lively, move along, hurry up there now, and all that. . . . The trains came and went and came and went, and then one train came that was headed for Cockfosters, so Joe suggested that we go out there, and hell, we'd got across the water [the Atlantic] safe and sound, and the city was being bombed, and a lot of people were hanging onto themselves under the ground that way, so a train headed for Cockfosters seemed very funny to us. We started to laugh about that and make jokes about it and the English people smiled and said to one another, 'More Americans – always laughing.' There's nothing funny to the English about a place being called Cockfosters. Cockfosters is somewhere where people live, and nobody in England thinks it's a joke at all – you've got to come from America to think it's funny, and of course it really isn't, but we thought it was the funniest thing in the world.

Wesley Jackson meets and marries a young Englishwoman called Jill, from Gloucester, and together they explore the streets of London:

London is the loveliest city in the whole world for those who love one another. Jill and I loved every bit of the city and found beauty and tenderness in everything that was part of it. Coming to Trafalgar Square one Sunday morning we looked up and saw a word we had seen many times before, but now it was so beautiful to us that I took Jill in my arms and kissed her and said the word to her as if it meant all the secret loving things of the heart that no other word could ever say.

'Bovril.'

. . . Then we crossed London Bridge and went down the steps to the Fishmongers Shops along Lower Thames. Then up Upper Thames to Fye Foot Lane where we stopped to chat with a bobby who told us that according to Stowe's *Survey of London* published in 1665 or somewhere along in there the name of the Lane had been Five Foot Lane, but it had come to be called Fye Foot Lane, which was just as good, if not better.[9]

In 1945 Edna Ferber – the American journalist and novelist who won the 1925 Pulitzer Prize for her book *So Big* – stayed at the Savoy Hotel while on a writing assignment. Other well-known Americans who have stayed here include Laurel and Hardy, Jimmy Durante, Errol Flynn, Clark Gable, Gene Autry, James Stewart, Edward G. Robinson, Gloria Swanson, Bob Hope, Bing Crosby, Paulette Goddard, John Wayne, Danny Kaye and Ava Gardner.

Beyond the Savoy Hotel – to the right off the Strand – is Southampton Street, where the future President Woodrow Wilson lodged in the Covent Garden Hotel during his first visit to London in 1896. He was on holiday to recover from a 'derangement of the bowels' caused by nervous indigestion.

In the Strand beyond Southampton Street stands the Adelphi Theatre. Here the American actor Joseph Jefferson starred in *Rip Van Winkle* for 170 nights, beginning on 5 September 1865. During the Civil War Jefferson, then aged thirty-six, had been acting in Australia and stopped off in London on his way back to New York. After his return to the USA he played Rip Van Winkle for a further fifteen years.

Off the Strand to the right, beyond the Adelphi, is Bedford Street. Benjamin West lived here at No.19 in 1763, while establishing himself as a leading portrait painter. One of the young American artists who later studied under West in London was Robert Fulton, who arrived from Philadelphia in 1786. He exhibited two portraits at the Royal Academy but then devoted himself to engineering and in 1796 published his *Treatise on the Improvement of Canal Navigation*, a copy of which he sent to President Washington. Fulton then went to Paris for four years, and received 10,000 francs from the Emperor Napoleon to develop a submarine and 'submarine bombs' – i.e. torpedoes. His submarine, *Nautilus*, was launched at Rouen in 1800. Once, in an experiment, *Nautilus* successfully blew up a sloop and on two occasions approached British warships but they escaped and French interest in the project waned. The British government, however, had sent a secret agent to France to find Fulton, who demanded £100,000 for a demonstration of his submarine and torpedo. The Foreign Secretary, in a personal letter, told him that his inventions had to be tested in England before such a fee could be considered, but promised that he would be treated 'with the utmost liberality and generosity'.

Fulton therefore returned to London in April 1804 and took rooms in Bedford Street. He made drawings of a nine-foot, one-man submarine and of a thirty-five-foot, six-man submarine which could remain anchored under water for twenty days. A top-level scientific and military committee, headed by the President of the Royal Society, studied the drawings and decided that, although his submarines were technically accurate, they would prove impractical in combat.

Undeterred, Fulton managed to secure an invitation to visit the Prime Minister, William Pitt, at his country estate near Dover in July, to put forward his torpedo idea. Pitt and his naval advisor were impressed and a contract was signed under which Fulton would be paid £200 a month and up to £7000 for his 'mechanical preparations'. The royal docks, yards and arsenals were to supply all the materials, and Fulton would receive £40,000 for every French vessel destroyed by his 'submarine bombs'.

Napoleon was amassing warships and troops at Boulogne to invade England, and when the British attacked them that October, Robert Fulton was on board HMS *Monarch* to oversee the use of his 'submarine bombs'. The bombs were fixed to either end of a line pulled by cutters to within five hundred yards of the enemy. Their clockwork timers were set and it was hoped they would be washed by the tide to the anchor cables of the French ships. One French ship was caught this way and went down, but most of Fulton's bombs failed to explode, sank or drifted ashore.

A year later, in a final attempt to convince sceptical British naval officers, Fulton staged a demonstration attack on the 250-ton *Dorothea*. This time his bombs were kept buoyant by cork-filled boxes and the small warship was successfully blown into two pieces: 'in one minute nothing of her was to be seen but floating fragments'. All doubts about the 'submarine bomb' were dispelled, but Admiral Lord Nelson's victory over the French at the Battle of Trafalgar six days later meant that Robert Fulton's contribution to modern naval warfare ceased to be needed for the time being. He was given £14,000 and back-pay of £1640, then returned to the USA, where he tried without success to win President Jefferson's support for development of the submarine and torpedo. Fulton's main achievement was establishing the commercial use of steamboats on the Hudson, Raritan, Potomac and Mississippi rivers.

Two other American residents of Bedford Street were the Barrymore siblings Ethel and John, who lived in rooms above the publisher William Heinemann in 1897, when they were aged twenty and fifteen. Young John Barrymore had been sent by his father to attend King's College School in Wimbledon, but he spent most of his time with his sister at 21 Bedford Street while awaiting acceptance into the Slade School of Art. Ethel Barrymore was earning £10 a week at the Lyceum Theatre in *The Bells* with Ellen Terry and Henry Irving. When she got engaged to Irving's son Laurence, her father sent a cable saying 'Congratulations, love Father'. He sent her an identical cable a few weeks later when she broke off the engagement. Described by Henry James as rather 'Gothic', Ethel Barrymore was to play many West End seasons under the American theatrical manager and producer Charles Frohman, whose first modest offices were off Bedford Street, in Henrietta Street.

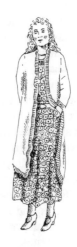

Charles Frohman, born in Sandusky, Ohio, in 1860, was raised in New York and began working in the theatre at the age of eight as a programme-seller. By the age of fourteen he was a ticket-seller. He later became an advance agent for his brother's touring company, which meant he had to ensure that posters for the show were up in the most conspicuous sites in town before the company arrived, and that they stayed up. By the time he was twenty-three he was an independent manager. His first important success came in 1889 when he presented Bronson Howard's *Shenandoah* in New York. In 1893 he opened the New York Empire Theatre and for many years he maintained there one of the finest companies in the USA. Frohman's promotion of the careers of performers such as William Faversham, Maude Adams and Ethel Barrymore earned him the nickname 'star-maker'.

In 1894 he came to England, because he believed that to produce the best English-speaking plays in the USA and to produce American plays in London he had to know English playwrights, actors and actresses on their own ground. He spent two seasons watching the London stage and meeting theatre people. His first London production was *The Lost Paradise* at the Adelphi Theatre. The New York production had been a success, but the London one failed. Then, in 1897, Frohman backed the American actor–playwright William Gillette in his own play *Secret Service*, also at the Adelphi, and scored his first major London success. He introduced his first female American star – Annie Russell – in *Sue*, and took a nineteen-year lease on the prestigious Duke of York Theatre in St Martin's Lane. He replaced the foyer statues of William Shakespeare and David Garrick with huge photographs of live American stars, engaged the best-known and highest-paid producer in London, Dion Boucicault, and embarked on a series of impeccable productions.

Frohman enjoyed working in England, where he felt the theatre had a distinction and dignity lacking in America. He said he would rather make

£15 in London than $15,000 in New York. When in London, as he was for part of every season, he always stayed in the same suite, overlooking the Thames, at the Savoy Hotel, where one of his favourite dinner guests was Mark Twain.

Between 1900 and 1910, Frohman and five other men of the American Theatrical Syndicate held a virtual monopoly over theatrical touring in the USA. At the height of his career Frohman employed more than ten thousand people and owned theatres valued at over $5 million dollars. At one time he had several theatres in London and rented others. Among the 125 plays and musicals he produced in London were J. M. Barrie's *Peter Pan* – which was revived each year at Christmas – and typical American dramas such as *The Great Divide*, *Brewster's Millions*, *Alias Jimmy Valentine*, *A Woman's Way*, *On the Quiet* and *The Dictator*. From 1913 onwards he ruled his West End entertainment empire from one of London's finest suites of theatrical offices at Trafalgar House in Waterloo Place. So great was Charles Frohman's influence on both sides of the Atlantic that he was known as 'the Napoleon of drama'. He died at sea in the sinking of the *Lusitania* on 7 May 1915. 'One can conceive him so often,' wrote J. M. Barrie in tribute, 'sitting at ease, far back, in his chair, the humorous, gentle, roughly educated, very fine American gentleman in the chair.'[10]

Henrietta Street, Covent Garden, was also the scene for the marriage of Sinclair Lewis and Dorothy Thompson, in St Martin's Registry Office on 14 May 1928, before they went on to have a church ceremony at the Savoy Chapel. Lewis, then aged forty-three, had been born in a raw little village on the Minnesota prairies called Sauk Center, where his father was one of the two doctors, and he spent a wretched youth there. In the 1920s he published five extraordinarily successful novels: *Main Street*, *Babbit*, *Arrowsmith*, *Elmer Gantry* and *Dodsworth*. These novels attacked the manners of the American middle class in the Midwest by satirically exposing conformism, hypocrisy, commercialism and cant. Their main theme was the stupidity of refusing to be free in a free country. Like Thoreau and Whitman, Sinclair Lewis idealised mid-nineteenth-century America as somewhere vast and formless but holding the promise of a wide, casually human freedom in which personal life could be lived in honest – even eccentric – effort, and where social life above all tolerated variety and individuality. Lewis's underlying concern was the contradiction between this idealisation and the reality of the twentieth-century America he knew. His bride, thirty-four-year-old Dorothy Thompson, was an American newspaper correspondent who had won a wide readership for her reports from Vienna and Berlin. At their wedding Lewis looked the typical English gent, in a Savile Row pin-striped suit, wing-collared shirt and pearl-grey top hat, carrying a cane and sporting a yellow flower in his lapel.

In 1930 Lewis became the first American to win the Nobel Prize for Literature. Dorothy Thompson – an early critic of Adolf Hitler – became one of the best-known journalists of her time. Her books included *The New*

Russia, A Political Guide and *Let the Record Speak*. Their marriage – the subject of *Dorothy and Red* by Vincent Sheean, published in 1963 – ended in divorce in 1942.

Henrietta Street – named after Queen Henrietta Maria, wife of Charles I, who also gave her name to Maryland – leads into the Covent Garden Piazza. When King Charles I granted a license to the fourth Earl of Bedford to build on the open land of Covent Garden houses 'fit for the habitations of gentlemen and men of ability', the result was London's first residential square, designed by Inigo Jones in the 1630s. In 1671 the fifth Earl of Bedford acquired the right to hold a fruit, vegetable and flower market in Covent Garden, which the Bedford family retained until the early twentieth century. With the coming of the market the fashionable residents moved out westwards and Covent Garden became the main red-light district of eighteenth- and nineteenth-century London. As the English poet John Dryden put it:

> This town two bargains has not worth one farthing.
> A Smithfield horse and a wife of Covent Garden.

The mixture of market produce and prostitution was also captured by John Gay in *The Beggar's Opera*, written in 1728. In this outstandingly successful early musical Polly Peachum sings:

> Virgins are like the fair flower in its lustre,
> Which in the garden enamels the ground:
> Near it the bees in play flutter and cluster,
> And gaudy butterflies frolic around.
> But when once plucked 'tis no longer alluring,
> To Covent Garden 'tis sent (as yet sweet),
> There fades and shrinks, and grows past all enduring,
> Rots, stinks and dies, and is trod under feet.[11]

In 1830 the present glass-roofed Covent Garden market building went up. Charles Dickens's son described how

On each side of the main avenue within the Central Market . . . are enclosed squares and here the wholesale fruit market is carried on. In

Covent Garden

winter there are thousands of boxes of oranges, hundreds of sacks of nuts, boxes of Hamburg grapes and French winter pears, barrels of bright American apples. At ten o'clock the sale begins; auctioneers stand on boxes, and while the more expensive fruits are purchased by the West End fruiterers, the cheaper are briskly bid for by the coster-mongers.[12]

Most of the portering in the fruit-and-vegetable market was done by women, who often tramped thirty miles a day with loaded baskets and were paid five shillings a week. There were also girls who lived by making and selling posies of flowers. They inspired the English dramatist George Bernard Shaw to create the character of Eliza Doolittle in his play *Pygmalion* (1913), later made into the hit musical and film *My Fair Lady*. Eliza Doolittle meets Professor Higgins as she sells flowers in the portico of St Paul's church, overlooking the Covent Garden Piazza.

The Earl of Bedford is said to have told Inigo Jones that he did not want to spend much money on St Paul's, Covent Garden, so the church should be built like a barn – to which Jones replied, 'Sire, you shall have the handsomest barn in Europe.' St Paul's is traditionally London's 'Theatre Church' and contains the ashes of Ellen Terry as well as memorial plaques to theatrical figures such as Vivien Leigh, Boris Karloff and Charlie Chaplin.

When London's wholesale fruit-and-vegetable market moved to a new site at Nine Elms, near Battersea, in 1974, Covent Garden was threatened by the bulldozer and by a bypass plan, but fortunately it was spared and preserved as a tourist attraction, modelled on San Francisco's Fisherman's Wharf, formerly the Cannery Row written about by John Steinbeck.

On the far side of the Covent Garden Piazza is the Theatre Royal Covent Garden, now the Royal Opera House. It was first called the Royal Italian Opera House in 1847. That building was destroyed by fire and the present one dates from 1856. Pittsburg-born Louise Homer – one of the foremost concert contraltos of her day – first sang here in 1899, when she was twenty-eight. Her début performance in *Aida* won an ovation – as she wrote to her mother – 'in the *middle* of the act'. Louise Homer was invited to sing for Queen Victoria at Windsor Castle and the following year joined the Metropolitan Opera Company in San Francisco.

In 1919 *Lawrence of Arabia*, a silent movie about T. E. Lawrence, was shown in the Royal Opera House, accompanied by a spoken commentary from its American director Lowell Thomas. The audience was so impressed that it stood and clapped for ten minutes and the *Daily Telegraph* critic said he could 'conceive of no more invigorating tonic than two hours spent in the company of Lowell Thomas. This illustrated event is a triumphant vindication of the power of moving pictures.'

The front of the Royal Opera House is in Bow Street, the birthplace in 1749 of London's first police force, the Bow Street Runners (although they were not known by that name for another fifty years). Financed by secret-service funds, the Bow Street Runners were the brainchild of two reforming Covent Garden magistrates, Henry Fielding (author of the novel *Tom Jones*) and his brother Sir John Fielding, known as 'the blind beak of Bow Street'. Although Sir John Fielding had lost his sight, he was able to identify by their voices the hundreds of people who came regularly to his Covent Garden court-room. 'One would imagine', he said of Covent Garden, 'that all the prostitutes in the kingdom had picked upon that blessed neighbourhood, for here are lewd women enough to fill a mighty colony.'

At the top of Bow Street is Long Acre, once a narrow strip of vegetable gardens owned by the monks of Westminster Abbey. In the mid-seventeenth century, Long Acre became a centre for coachbuilding, cabinetmaking and furniture-design. Turning to the right, the street leads back to Drury Lane and the imposing Freemasons' Hall in Great Queen Street. Delegates from Massachusetts and Pennsylvania were among the five hundred people who participated in the first World Anti-Slavery Convention which was held in an earlier Freemasons' Hall here in 1840. Two of the American delegation-leaders were women – Elizabeth Cady Stanton and Lucretia Mott – and many other women from various parts of the world attended. The British Executive Committee of the World Anti-Slavery Convention, however, ruled that 'ladies were inadmissable as delegates', a ruling which was backed by British clergymen on the grounds that the Bible made clear the fact that woman's subordination was divinely decreed. One of the American delegates, George Bradburn, declared that if the Bible taught 'the entire subjection of one-half of the human race to the other', all Bibles should be made into a bonfire and burned.[13] A men-only ballot eventually decided that the women could remain at the convention, but only as observers seated in the gallery and unable to speak or vote. In protest, William Garrison, an American delegation-leader, together with some (but not all) of the American male delegates, spent the entire twelve days of the convention in silence in the gallery, keeping the women company. Elizabeth Cady Stanton and Lucretia Mott became close friends and on their return to the United States they organised the first American women's rights convention, held in Seneca Falls, New York, in 1848.

Drury Lane continues north from Great Queen Street towards High Holborn. Beyond the New London Theatre, on the right, is Macklin Street, formerly called Lewknors Lane and described in 1715 as 'a rendezvous and nursery for lewd women first resorted to by the Roundheads.' Such was the reputation of Lewknors Lane that its fame crossed the Atlantic and cropped up in an early Maryland court report. Women who came to Maryland from England, it was said,

> have the best luck here as in any place of the world besides; for they are no sooner on shore, but they are courted into a copulative matrimony, which some of them (for aught I know) had they not come to such a market with their virginity, they might have kept it by them until it had been mouldy, unless they had let it out by a yearly rent to some of the inhabitants of Lewknors Lane.[14]

Opposite Macklin Street is Shorts Gardens, so called because William Short of Gray's Inn cultivated a garden here in the late sixteenth century. Bisecting Shorts Gardens is Endell Street, built in 1845 and named after the reforming Rector of St Giles, James Endell Taylor. Endell Street, turning right, leads to the Shaftesbury Theatre, where Fred and Adèle Astaire made their London début in *Stop Flirting* in 1923. The London theatre critics called the Astaires 'dancers of genius' and said that Adèle 'could dance the depression out of an undertaker'. The following year the twenty-one-year-old Tallulah Bankhead played at the Shaftesbury Theatre. When she saw her name in lights there for the first time she was so surprised she went round and round the block to have a good look at it.

From the Shaftesbury Theatre, Shaftesbury Avenue leads to Cambridge Circus. Off to the right, in Charing Cross Road, is the Phoenix Theatre, where Arthur Miller's *Death of a Salesman* was first performed in London on 28 July 1949, with a mainly American cast headed by Paul Muni. During rehearsals for the play, Muni received an invitation to the Ambassador's Fourth of July party at the American Embassy, but he turned it down, saying he was by then not himself but the salesman Willy Loman, who would not have been invited. Feeling ill-prepared for the first night, Muni was convinced by the final curtain that he had destroyed the play, but the audience applauded him back for fifteen curtain-calls. He had rendered Willy Loman, said the London critics, 'helplessly and hopelessly amiable and pitifully, if exasperatingly, immature.'

Opposite the Phoenix is Old Compton Street, in Soho, where the American literary critic and cultural historian Van Wyck Brooks lived as a young man, in 1907, in a chilly room above a restaurant at No. 16. Brooks was working at Ludgate Circus for the Curtis Brown news agency, rewriting English human-interest stories in the 'breezy style' demanded for American readers. From Soho he moved to a Sussex village and wrote *The Wine of the Puritans*, arguing that the strong influence of Puritanism on American culture meant neglect of the artistic side of life. This theme was to be developed in his later works, including *The Flowering of New England*, published in 1936, for which he won the Pulitzer Prize.

Across Cambridge Circus, beyond the Palace Theatre, Charing Cross Road leads to the London Hippodrome , which opened as a music hall in 1900. It was from the Hippodrome that ragtime music burst upon London in June 1913, when twenty-five-year-old Irving Berlin performed a song he had sketched out during his transatlantic crossing: 'Alexander's Ragtime Band'. 'Go where you will,' the London *Daily Express* reported, 'you cannot escape from the mazes of music he has spun. Ragtime has swept like a whirlwind over the earth and set civilization humming.'

From the Hippodrome, Cranbourn Street leads into Leicester Square. The public garden in this square was once Lammas Land – that is, land where local people had the right to dry their clothes and pasture cattle after Lammas Day on 12 August. When the Earl of Leicester had a grand house built here for himself in 1633, he was told by a Privy Council committee that he had to turn the former Lammas Land 'into walks . . . planted with trees . . . and fit spaces for the inhabitants to dry their clothes there as they were wont, and to have free use of the place.' In the 1670s the so-called Leicester Fields became Leicester Square when fine houses were built 'for the benefit of the family, the advancement of their revenue and the decency of the place before Leicester House.'[15]

In the eighteenth century the Leicester Square houses were occupied by

aristocrats – the Earls of Aylesbury, Sunderland, Rockingham, Scarsdale, Westmorland and Deloraine – and by well-established artists and writers. William Hogarth lived at 30 Leicester Square, producing some of his best-known satirical paintings, such as *Marriage à La Mode*, *The Rake's Progress*, *Gin Lane*, *Beer Street* and *Industry and Idleness*. Sir Joshua Reynolds lived at No. 47, installing 'a splendid gallery for the exhibition of his works, and a commodious and elegant room for his sitters.' The American artist John Singleton Copley moved into No. 28 in 1776, when he

was on the threshold of his successful career as a
painter of fashionable portraits and dramatic historical
events, such as *The Offer of the Crown to Lady Jane
Grey*, *Charles I's Attempt to Arrest the Five Members*
and *The Death of the Earl of Chatham*.

On 5 December 1782 Copley broke off working on a
portrait of Elkanah Watson – a fellow American – so
that they could hurry over to the House of Lords to
hear King George III formally acknowledge American
victory in the War of Independence. As Elkanah Watson
later recorded:

> The painting was finished in most admirable style, except the back-
> ground, which Copley and I designed to represent a ship bearing to
> America the acknowledgement of our independence, with the sun just
> rising upon the Stripes of the Union streaming from her gaff. All was
> complete save the flag, which Copley did not deem it proper to hoist
> under the present circumstances, as his gallery is a constant resort for
> the Royal family and the nobility.

When the two men returned from the House of Lords that day, however,
Copley, 'with a bold hand, a master's touch, and, I believe, an American
heart . . . attached to the ship the Stars and Stripes; this was I imagine the
first American flag hoisted in old England.'[16]

The house next door to Copley's – No. 27 – had been converted in 1725
into a *bagnio* – a not altogether respectable public baths. It was here that an
illiterate woman from Surrey called Mary Tofts for a while attracted serious
attention with her claim that she had given birth to a litter of fifteen rabbits
after being frightened by a rabbit while she was working in the fields. The
anatomist Nathanael St André, then a surgeon at Westminster Hospital,
believed her claim, particularly after he himself – so he claimed – had delivered her of a further two rabbits.

Leicester Square was, in the words of the modern *Survey of London*
(Volume 34),

> essentially masculine – its popularity with the *demi-monde* meant
> that it was no place for unescorted ladies – and when the war engulfed
> its clientele nostalgic memories of it were universally evoked by the
> phrase 'Farewell, Leicester Square' in the song 'It's a Long Way to
> Tipperary'.[17]

Harry Houdini, the American escape-artist and magician, was a tremen-
dous hit when he played in Leicester Square at the Alhambra Theatre for six
months in 1900, earning £60 a week. Arriving in London unknown, Houdini
caught the interest of the Alhambra's manager with his offer of a 'challenge'
act in which he would escape from handcuffs, chains, straitjackets, etc.,

brought by members of the audience. To test him, the manager took Houdini to Superintendent Melville at Scotland Yard, who handcuffed Houdini's wrists together behind his back around a pillar. He gave him an hour to escape but Houdini was standing beside his two captors before they were out of the room: 'Here, I'll come with you,' he quipped. Houdini's later acts included escaping from a water-torture cell in which he was submerged upside down, and walking through a wall. He went on to star in silent movies and – as part of his crusade against fraudulent mediums – wrote *Miracle-Mongers and Their Methods* (1920) and *A Magician Among the Spirits* (1924). When he died from acute appendicitis in Detroit in 1926, at the age of fifty-two, he left his magic books to the Library of Congress and his show to his brother, Hardeen Houdini.

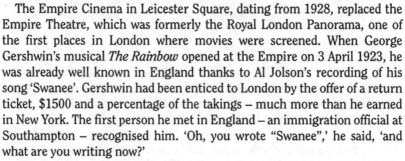

The Empire Cinema in Leicester Square, dating from 1928, replaced the Empire Theatre, which was formerly the Royal London Panorama, one of the first places in London where movies were screened. When George Gershwin's musical *The Rainbow* opened at the Empire on 3 April 1923, he was already well known in England thanks to Al Jolson's recording of his song 'Swanee'. Gershwin had been enticed to London by the offer of a return ticket, $1500 and a percentage of the takings – much more than he earned in New York. The first person he met in England – an immigration official at Southampton – recognised him. 'Oh, you wrote "Swanee",' he said, 'and what are you writing now?'

The Rainbow had an Anglo-American cast. During rehearsals Gershwin took some of the jokes from one of the English actors and gave them to one of the American actors. This made the Englishman so angry that he stopped the show's finale on the first night and made a public protest which attracted more attention than the show itself. *The Rainbow* closed after a few days. Three years later, however, Gershwin was back at the Empire Theatre with his musical *Lady Be Good*, which was a rip-roaring success.

On the far corner of Leicester Square is Panton Street, named after King Charles II's friend Colonel Thomas Panton, of whom it was said that at the card table he was 'an absolute artist, either upon the square or at foul play'. The Comedy Theatre in Panton Street was where John Barrymore made his London début in *The Dictator* in May 1905.

Panton Street leads to the Haymarket, famous in Queen Victoria's day, according to London journalist Henry Mayhew, for

> the architectural splendour of the aristocratic streets, the brilliant illumination of the shops, cafés, Turkish divans, assembly halls and concert rooms, and the troops of elegantly dressed courtesans, rustling in silks and satins, and waving in laces, promenading . . .

among throngs of fashionable people, and persons apparently of every order and pursuit, from the ragged crossing-sweeper and tattered shoe-black to the high-bred gentleman of fashion and scion of nobility.

In a social survey of prostitution in London, Mayhew noted that apart from women kept by

men of opulence and rank in the privacy of their own dwellings, the whole of the other classes are to be found in the Haymarket, from the beautiful girl with fresh blooming cheek, newly arrived from the provinces, and the pale, elegant, young lady from a milliner's shop in the aristocratic West End, to the old, bloated women who have grown grey in prostitution, or become invalid through venereal disease.[18]

The present Theatre Royal Haymarket, designed by John Nash, dates from 1821. In the previous building fifteen people were crushed to death in 1794 during the theatre's first performance, and in 1805 the satirical play *The Tailors* led to a riot of outraged tailors, quelled only by the arrival of the Life Guards. On 30 December 1845 Charlotte Cushman, America's first great tragedienne, opened here as Romeo to her sister Susan's Juliet. 'Miss Cushman's Romeo', said *The Times*, 'is a creation; a living, breathing, animated, ardent human being.' Having taken London by storm, the production had an exceptionally long run of eighty nights.

Born in Boston in 1816, Charlotte Cushman began her career as an opera-singer in 1835. She switched to the dramatic stage with a performance of Lady Macbeth and scored her first New York success in 1837 as Nancy in *Oliver Twist*. In 1844 she accompanied William Macready on an American tour, and from 1845 to 1849 she acted in England. After touring America for a further three years Cushman retired, although she frequently played return engagements and her last stage appearance was in 1874. She died in Boston in 1876.

The Theatre Royal Haymarket was also where Tennessee Williams's play *The Glass Menagerie* first opened in London, on 28 July 1948, when Williams had just won both the New York Drama Critics' Circle Award and the Pulitzer Prize. He did not get along with the play's English director, John Gielgud, and stayed in Paris on the opening night, missing the gala

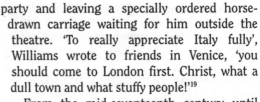

party and leaving a specially ordered horse-drawn carriage waiting for him outside the theatre. 'To really appreciate Italy fully', Williams wrote to friends in Venice, 'you should come to London first. Christ, what a dull town and what stuffy people!'[19]

From the mid-seventeenth century until 1830 Haymarket was frequently clogged with waggons carrying the hay and straw essential for London's horses, including those housed in the Royal Mews which stood where Trafalgar Square is today.

At the bottom of Haymarket, in Cockspur Street, lived Patience Lovell Wright, the wax-modeller, sculptor and spy for Benjamin Franklin, whose studio became a rallying-point for Americans in London. Patience was 'tall and of sallow complexion, with high cheek bones, keen olive eyes and the glance of a maniac.' Abigail Adams described her as 'quite the slattern and queen of the sluts'. Although she was Franklin's main source of information on political 'atmosphere', the British government never suspected her spying role. In 1777 she wrote to Franklin: 'I meet with the greatest politeness from people in England. . . . I now believe that all my romantic education, joined with my father's courage, can be serviceable yet further to bring on the glorious civil cause of civil and religious liberty.' A letter written to her by George  Washington can be seen in the British Museum. Patience Lovell Wright modelled busts of King George III and Queen Charlotte, but fell from royal favour when she scolded them for making war on her country.[20]

There is an equestrian statue of George III dating from 1820 at the junction of Cockspur Street and Pall Mall. The horse's tail sticks out horizontally and this gave rise to the popular ditty:

Here stands a statue which critics rail
To point a moral and a tale.

Pall Mall leads into Trafalgar Square, one side of which is occupied by the National Gallery. In front of the gallery – looking towards Admiral Lord Nelson's column in the middle of Trafalgar Square – stands a statue of George Washington, a replica of the one in the Capitol of the State of Virginia, which was carved by the

French sculptor Houdon in 1785. Thomas Jefferson, James Monroe, Benjamin Franklin and others who knew Washington all declared Houdon's statue a remarkable likeness. 'It is a facsimile of Washington's person,' said Lafayette, and, according to Chief Justice Marshall, 'Nothing in bronze or stone could be a more perfect image than this statue of the living Washington.'[21] He is shown with his left hand on his cloak, which is thrown over thirteen upright rods, one for each of the original states. From his cloak hangs his sword, honourably laid aside after winning independence. The rods are in a bundle or *fasces* – the Roman symbol of administrative power – and rest on a ploughshare, representing agriculture as the foundation of national strength. George Washington wears his military clothes but is bareheaded and using a cane; his pose as a whole demonstrates the subordination of military to civil power. The statue was presented to the people of Great Britain and Ireland by the Commonwealth of Virginia and was unveiled on 30 June 1921.

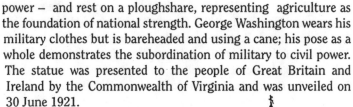

Close to Washington's statue is the 1724 church of St Martin-in-the-Fields, where Benjamin West was married in 1765. Buried in the church are Queen Kamamalu and King Kamehameha II of Hawaii, both of whom died during a visit to London in 1824. Hawaii was then known as the Sandwich Islands and was under British control. When George IV heard of the arrival in London of twenty-one-year-old Queen Kamamalu and her party, the British government assumed responsibility for their visit, paying their expenses and issuing them with warm clothing. The Hawaiian royals were housed in the luxurious Osbourne Caledonian Hotel overlooking the Thames near

Charing Cross, and plans were made to present them to the King. The Hawaiian visitors went to Westminster Abbey – where Queen Kamamalu leapt with fright when she first heard the organ – and sat in the royal boxes at the Theatre Royal Drury Lane and the Theatre Royal Covent Garden. Sadly, they all caught measles and Queen Kamamalu died on 8 July. She was buried in the vaults of St Martin-in-the-Fields, dressed in the traditional *pau* skirt, with flowers in her hair. Her husband was desolate and his condition worsened. He died on 14 July and was buried alongside his Queen.

Other members of the Hawaiian royal family to visit London, on later occasions, include Queen Emma, who travelled around England in 1865 raising money for the Anglican Mission in her country. Her programme included a journey to Paddington in the royal train, to be received by Queen Victoria at Windsor. In 1887 Queen Kapiolani of Hawaii, accompanied by her sister-in-law Princess Liliuokalani, was an official guest at Queen Victoria's jubilee celebrations. Queen Kapiolani demanded and was given a full sovereign's escort, as well as an invitation to dinner at Buckingham Palace. The *Illustrated London News* reported that

> The Queen of Hawaii has presented to the Queen a piece of work made entirely of the feathers of a very rare bird from the Sandwich Islands. It appears that there are only two of this particular feather on each bird, and it has taken some thousands of feathers to make the wreath which is the work of the Hawaiian Queen's own hands. It has been mounted on royal blue plush, set in a frame of gold with the Royal Arms and the arms of the Queen of Hawaii on either side, the whole being again surrounded by a border of royal blue set with golden stars with eight points, representing the eight islands in the Sandwich Group. Above is the royal crown and cushion set with diamonds.

In 1891, sixteen-year-old Princess Kaiulani of Hawaii was on holiday in London from her school near Bedford when she received news that the Hawaiian King had died and the new Hawaiian Queen had named her as the heir presumptive. Two years later, the Hawaiian monarchy was overthrown in a revolution led by nine American and four European businessmen. Princess Kaiulani left London for Washington to urge President Cleveland to save her throne. The President offered the Princess his sympathy, but in 1894 Hawaii became a republic. 'I shan't be much of a princess, shall I?' said Princess Kaiulani. 'They haven't left me much to live for. I think my heart is broken.' She died five years later, aged twenty-four. Hawaii was annexed by the USA in 1898, became a territory in 1900 and a state in 1959.[22]

At the corner of Trafalgar Square, off the Strand, is Craven Street, where Benjamin Franklin lived for fifteen years, thirteen of them at No. 7 – now No. 36 – which is still standing, preserved as his house and a museum. Franklin came to London as the representative of the Pennsylvania Assembly when he was fifty-one, in July 1757. His wife Deborah remained in Philadelphia, but he had with him two servants and his adult son-out-of-wedlock, William, who enrolled as a law student at the Middle Temple. Franklin's purpose in London was to secure taxes due on the estates of William Penn's descendants and, as he did not expect to

remain for more than a year, he rented four rooms in a house in Craven Street belonging to Margaret Stevenson, a thirty-eight-year-old widow.

As it turned out, Margaret Stevenson and her eighteen-year-old daughter Mary – whom Franklin called Polly – were to provide him with a happy and relaxed home life throughout his many years as an American representative in London. Margaret give him an ivory Chinese back-scratcher to ease his 'itching all over', aired his underwear and 'furnished him with long-sleeved nightgowns, flannel trousers and warm slippers, so that he could sleep snugly.' She arranged into neat piles the newspapers and documents which often littered his rooms. He valued, he said, her 'orderly attentions'.[23] Polly developed her reading with books provided by Franklin and made him garters in return for the poetry he wrote her. On her twenty-seventh birthday, after she had told him that she felt she was getting old, he presented her with the following specially penned lines:

> No hospitable man, possessed of generous wines,
> While they are in his vaults, repines
> That age impairs the casks; for he well knows
> The heavenly juice
> More fit for use
> Becomes, and still the older better grows.[24]

Unlike James Russell Lowell – who lived in London as the American Minister (Ambassador) more than a century later – Benjamin Franklin heartily disliked the city's notorious fog. 'The whole town is one great smoky house,' he complained, 'and every street a chimney; the air is full of

floating sea-coal soot, and you never get a sweet breath of what is pure without riding some miles for it in the country.' He proposed the introduction of
dustcarts and street-cleaning, but the idea was not taken up. He described in
his autobiography how he found at his door in Craven Street

> a poor woman sweeping my pavement with a birch broom; she
> appeared very pale and feeble, as just come out of a fit of sickness. I
> ask'd who employ'd her to sweep there. She said 'Nobody, but I am
> very poor and in distress, and I sweeps before gentlefolkses doors, and
> hopes they will give me somethings.' I bid her sweep the whole street
> clean, and I would give her a shilling: this was at nine o'clock; at 12
> she came for the shilling. I then judg'd that if that feeble woman could
> sweep a street in three hours, a strong active man might have done it
> in half the time.[25]

By 1770 Franklin was representing Georgia, New Jersey and
Massachusetts, as well as Pennsylvania. His pay of £1500 a year enabled him
to live like a gentleman and in the course of his life he amassed a fortune
worth $150,000. He was deeply involved in the political events unfolding in
Westminster and Whitehall, and tried until the last moment to prevent a
breach between the American colonists and the British government. On
Sunday 29 January 1775 the politics came to Franklin's home in Craven
Street when William Pitt, Earl of Chatham – a leading opponent of the government's American policies – arrived at his door with a proposed Act of
Parliament which he wanted Franklin to read. The Act, if passed, would have
meant that only Americans could tax Americans; the charters of the
colonies would have been inviolable and the Continental Congress would
have become official and permanent. The Earl of Chatham's impressive carriage waited outside Franklin's house for two hours, 'and being there while
people were at church, it was taken much notice of and talked of. . . . Such a
visit from so great a man, on so important a business flattered not a little my
vanity.'[26]

The Chatham–Franklin compromise proposals were roundly defeated in
Parliament, but Franklin still hoped Lord North's ministry would fall and
America could stay politically attached to Britain. He spent several hours
with Edmund Burke three days before Burke made his great speech on con-
ciliation. But that speech was to no avail and Franklin accepted that he had
to leave England. He spent his last day in Craven Street with Joseph
Priestley, a fellow scientist and philosopher, who saw that his American
friend was deeply upset by the prospect of an Anglo-American war.
Franklin's eyes filled with tears as he told Priestley that he believed if there
was war it would last for ten years. America would win, he predicted, but he
would not see the end of it. He sailed from Portsmouth on 21 March 1775,
accompanied by his grandson Temple – William's son-out-of-wedlock – and
on 5 May arrived in Philadelphia, where his wife had died the previous
winter.

Craven Street leads down to the Victoria Embankment, running along-side the Thames. Turning right, a stroll through the public gardens leads past statues of Samuel Plimsoll (1824–98), known as 'the sailors' friend' for his continuous efforts to improve their conditions; and William Tyndale (1484–1536), an English follower of Erasmus and Luther. Just beyond Tyndale, at the back of the Ministry of Defence, are Queen Mary's Steps, designed in 1691 by Sir Christopher Wren to give access from the old Palace of Whitehall to the royal barge moored on the river, which was then much wider than it is today. At the end of Victoria Embankment stands the modern Palace of Westminster.

SEVEN

Westminster and Whitehall

'Great poverty of ornament, the ball and crown repeated tediously all over the grand gate, near the Abbey, and *Vivat Regina* written incessantly all over the casements of the windows in the House of Lords. Houses of Parliament a magnificent document of English power and of their intention to make it last. The Irish harp and shamrock are carved with the rose and thistle over all the house. The Houses cover eight acres and are built of Bolsover stone. Fault, that there is no single view commanding great lines; only when it is finished the Speaker of the House of Commons will be able with a telescope to see the Lord Chancellor in the Lords. But mankind can so rarely build a house covering eight acres that 'tis a pity to deprive them of the joy of seeing a mass of grand and lofty lines.'

Ralph Waldo Emerson on the
Palace of Westminster under construction, 1848[1]

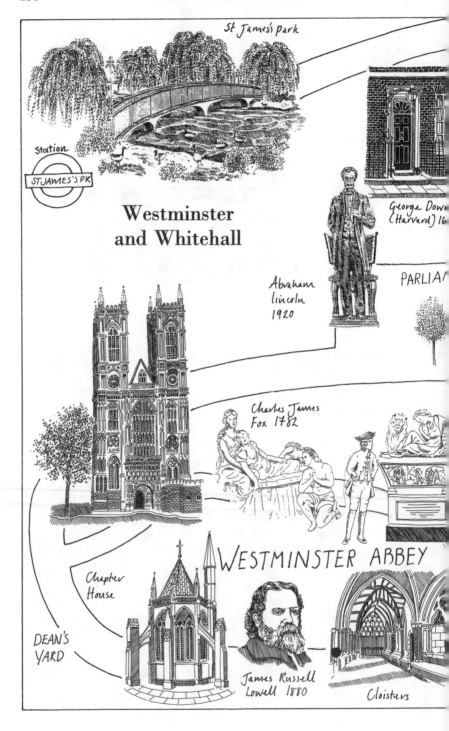

St James's park

Station
St JAMES'S PK

Westminster
and Whitehall

George Down
(Harvard) 16

Abraham
lincoln
1920

PARLIA'

Charles James
Fox 1782

Chapter
House

WESTMINSTER ABBEY

DEAN'S
YARD

James Russell
Lowell 1880

Cloisters

Banqueting House
1622

WHITEHALL

NG STREET

Princess
PocoHontas
1616

Sir
Walter
Ralegh

Station
WESTMINSTER

WESTMINSTER
BRIDGE

THAMES

Benjamin
Franklin
1774

Palace of
Westminster

St Margaret's:
Ralegh buried
1613

King
George III
1760

r John André
nedict and
ggy Arnold
80

King Henry VII
Bartholomew Columbus (1489)
and John Cabot (1496)

Newfoundland
Eskimos 1502

The modern Palace of Westminster – the Houses of Parliament – stands on what was once known as Thorney Isle, a chunk of marshy land in the delta of the River Tyburn, which flowed into the Thames. This inhospitable spot was first occupied thirteen centuries ago by a small community of monks. They inspired the deeply religious King Edward the Confessor to establish in 1065 a great Benedictine Abbey, which was called Westminster to distinguish it from the 'Eastminster' – St Paul's Cathedral. Edward the Confessor was buried in his abbey on the eve of the Norman Conquest in 1066. The building is depicted in the Bayeux Tapestry with the modest royal palace alongside it.

Edward the Confessor's palace was replaced by the much grander Westminster Hall, built for William the Conqueror's son, William Rufus, in 1099. Some 240 feet long and 67 feet wide, this was one of the largest halls in Europe and became the ceremonial centre of the kingdom as well as a principal royal residence. In 1236 it was flooded by the Thames and could be crossed only by rowing boat.

In 1265 Westminster Hall was the meeting place of the Parliament called by Simon de Montfort, to which knights from the shires and burgesses from the towns were invited for the first time. The knights and burgesses began to meet separately as the 'Commons', representing not the common people but the various rural and urban communities of the kingdom. The Commons gained the exclusive right to vote taxes and by 1377 it was said of the English king that 'the might of the Commons made him to reign.'

Westminster Hall was damaged by fire but restored in 1399, with the addition of a magnificent hammerbeam roof featuring the white hart badge of King Richard II. By now it had become the permanent home of the King's law courts, open to the public and with shops and market stalls lining the walls. Clustered around Westminster Hall itself were the other buildings which formed part of the Palace of Westminster, including royal domestic apartments and government offices such as the Exchequer.

It was in the Palace of Westminster that Henry VII, on 5 March 1496, signed the earliest surviving legal document referring to the project of establishing an English colony in the land that was soon to be named America. This was a royal charter by which the King gave to the Venetian mariner John Cabot and his sons Sebastian and Sanctus

> full and free authority, faculty and power of navigating to all parts, countries and seas of the east, west and north under our banners, flags and ensigns . . . to seek out, discover and find whatsoever islands, countries, regions or provinces of heathens or infidels, in whatever part of the world they be, which before this time were unknown to all Christians. . . . John and his sons . . . may occupy whatsoever towns, camps, cities or islands may be discovered by them, that they may be able to conquer, occupy and possess as our vassals and governors, lieutenants or deputies, acquiring for us the dominion, title and

jurisdiction over these towns, camps, cities, islands and mainlands so discovered. Providing that the said John and his sons . . . shall be bound and under obligation to us from all the fruits, profits, endowments, advantages, gains and incomes accruing from this voyage . . . to deduct a fifth part of the whole capital whether in goods or in money, for our use.[2]

The Cabots crossed the Atlantic under the English flag, reaching Newfoundland in barely four weeks. They sailed 870 miles along the coastline and returned to London in triumph, believing that they had reached the north-east shores of Asia. The sum of £10 was allocated from Henry VII's privy purse to 'to him that found the new isle'.

Lorenzo Pasquaglio, a Venetian living in London, wrote home to his brothers that

> our countryman who went with a ship . . . in quest of new islands is returned, and says that 700 leagues hence he discovered land, the territory of the Grand Cham . . . saw no human beings, but he has brought hither to the King certain snares which had been set to catch game, and a needle for making nets; he also found some felled trees, wherefore he supposed there were inhabitants, and returned to his ship in alarm. . . .
>
> The king has promised that in the spring our countrymen shall have ten ships, armed to his order, and at his request has conceded him all the prisoners, except such as are confined for high treason, to man his fleet.
>
> The king has given him money to amuse himself till then. . . . He is styled the great admiral. Vast honour is paid to him; he dresses in silk, and those English run after him like mad people, so that he can enlist as many of them as he pleases, and a number of our own rogues besides.
>
> The discoverer of these places planted on his newfoundland a large cross, with one flag of England and another of St Mark, by reason of his being a Venetian, so that our banner has floated very far afield.'[3]

The Milanese Ambassador in London, Soucino, wrote to the Duke of Milan describing the riches that Cabot had discovered in the New World:

> They say that the land is excellent and temperate, and they believe that Brazil wood and silk are native there. They assert that the sea there is swarming with fish, who can be taken not only with the net, but in baskets let down with a stone, so that it sinks in the water. I have heard this [Cabot] state so much. . . . His [English] companions say that they could bring so many fish that this kingdom would have no further need of Iceland. . . .
>
> But [Cabot] has his mind set upon even greater things, because he proposes to keep along the coast from the place at which he touched, more and more towards the east, until he reaches an island which he

calls Japan, situated in the equinoctial region, where he believes all the spices of the world have their origin, as well as the jewels.

He says that on previous occasions he has been to Mecca, to which all spices are borne by caravans from distant countries. When he asked those who brought them what was the place of origin of these spices, they answered that they did not know, but that other caravans came with the merchandise to their homes from distant countries, and these again said that the goods had been brought from other remote regions. He therefore reasons that if the easterns declare to the southerners that these things come from places far away from them, and so on from one to the other, always assuming that the earth is round, it follows as a matter of course that the last of all must take them in the north towards the west. . . .

By means of this they hope to make London a more important mart for spices than Alexandria . . . now they know where to go . . . the voyage will not take more than a fortnight, if they have good fortune, after leaving Ireland.

I have also spoken with a Burgandian, one of [Cabot's] companions, who corroborates everything. He wants to go back because the Admiral, which is the name given to [Cabot], has given him an island. He has given another to his barber, a Genoese by birth, and both consider themselves counts, while my lord the Admiral esteems himself at least a prince.

I also believe that some poor Italian friars will go on this voyage, who have the promise of bishoprics. As I have made friends with the Admiral, I might have an archbishopric if a chose to go there.[4]

When John Cabot's second transatlantic expedition set sail in 1498, his ship was 'manned and victualled at the King's cost' but 'divers merchants of London ventured in her small stocks. And in the company of the said ship sailed also . . . three or four small ships fraught with merchandise, as coarse cloth, caps, laces . . . and other trifles, and so departed at the beginning of May; of which . . . returned no tidings.'[5]

The Spanish Ambassador in London sent a coded letter to King Ferdinand and Queen Isabella of Spain, alerting them to the fact that the English King had sponsored John Cabot on a second transatlantic expedition. Having seen Cabot's map and the direction and distance of his journey, the Ambassador was convinced that he was heading for the land which belonged to the Spanish monarchs according to their convention with Portugal. Henry VII denied this.

The fate of this second Cabot expedition remains unknown, but over the next decade – according to royal accounts kept at Westminster – money was paid from the privy purse to sailors and merchants who brought from Newfoundland hawks, popinjays, wild mountain cats and 'other stuff' for King Henry VII. In 1502 three Eskimos 'taken in ye newfoundland' arrived in London.

They were, in the words of John Stow, writing three generations later,

> clothed in beasts' skins and eat raw flesh, but spoke such a language as no man could understand, of which three men, two of them were seen in the king's court at Westminster two years after. They were clothed like Englishmen, and could not be discerned from Englishmen.[6]

The Eskimos' land was called 'Prima Tierra Vista' by John Cabot's son Sebastian on the map he produced of the territory discovered on his father's voyage. Sebastian Cabot first came to London as a boy with his father and, although he lived, married and worked for most of his life in Spain, he returned to London in 1544, aged seventy-one. The commentary on his map described the new land as

> a large island which is near the land they gave the name of St John, because it was discovered the same day. The natives of it go about dressed in skins of animals; in their wars they use bows and arrows, lances and darts, and clubs of wood, and strings. The land is very sterile. There are in it many white bears, and very large stags, like horses, and many other animals. And in like manner there are immense quantities of fish – soles, salmon, very large cods and many other kinds of fish. They call the great multitude of them baccalaos; and there are also in this country dark-coloured falcons like crows, eagles, partridges, sandpipers and many other birds of different kinds.[7]

According to the great Elizabethan geographer Richard Hakluyt, copies of Sebastian Cabot's map were displayed 'in her Majesty's privy gallery at Westminster and in many ancient merchants' houses.'

By the reign of Elizabeth I (1558–1603), the Palace of Westminster had ceased to be a royal residence and when the monarchs were in London they lived at Whitehall Palace or St James's Palace. The clergy of St Stephen's Chapel in the Palace of Westminster had been dismissed in 1547 as part of Henry VIII's Dissolution of the Monasteries, and from the mid-sixteenth century St Stephen's Chapel became the permanent home of the House of Commons. (It measured only sixty feet by thirty feet, and for important debates MPs had to crowd into its galleries.) The White Chamber was the permanent home of the House of Lords, the cloisters and church crypt were parliamentary storehouses and the Jewel Tower was the Parliament Office. The judges continued to occupy Westminster Hall and departments of the Exchequer remained near it. The rest of the Palace of Westminster was used almost exclusively by Parliament.

In 1621 – the year the Virginia Company of London effectively granted independence to the Virginia colony – the Commons claimed the right to deal freely with all matters of grievance or policy and inscribed this Protestation in their Journal. King James I came to the House of Commons and with his own hands tore out the pages containing the Protestation. Relations between Crown and Commons continued to deteriorate until 1642, when James's son, King Charles I – who also believed in the Divine Right of Kings – came to the House of Commons to arrest five members, but 'the birds had flown'. Mr Speaker Lenthall refused to say where the MPs were, telling the King, 'I have neither eyes to see, nor tongue to speak in this place, but as this House is pleased to direct me.' The King left the House empty-handed and no monarch has entered it since then. The ensuing Civil War between Royalists ('Cavaliers') and Parliamentarians ('Roundheads') resulted in the trial of Charles I in Westminster Hall, and his execution in Whitehall on 30 January 1649. For eleven years Britain had no monarch but a Puritan Commonwealth ruled for most of the time by Oliver Cromwell.

A statue of Cromwell now stands on the sunken lawn in front of Westminster Hall, facing across St Margaret's Street towards a bust of Charles I in the wall of St Margaret's church. Cromwell was one of the regicides who signed Charles's death warrant, but he remained unpunished and when he died of natural causes in 1658 he was buried in Westminster Abbey. At the Restoration of the Monarchy in 1660 – when Charles's exiled son was crowned as King Charles II – Cromwell's body was dug up and hung, drawn and quartered with the rest of the regicides. His head was placed on the roof of Westminster Hall and rotted there for twenty-five years until it blew down.

In 1761 Westminster Hall was illumi-nated by a thousand lights for George III's Coronation banquet, which presented to the poet Thomas Gray

> the most magnificent spectacle I ever beheld. . . . The King bowing to the lords as he passed, with his crown on his head, and the sceptre and orb in his hand, took his place with great majesty and grace. So did the Queen with her crown, sceptre and rod. Then the supper was served on gold plates. Earl Talbot, the Duke of Bedford and the Earl of Effingham, in

their robes, all three on horseback, prancing and curveting, like the hobby horses in the rehearsal, ushered in the courses to the foot of the *haut-pas*.[8]

During the ceremonies a jewel fell out of the King's crown. Was this a symbolic warning, it was later asked, of what was to happen to the American colonies during his reign?

> When first portentous it was known
> Great George had jostled from his crown
> The brightest diamond there,
> The omen-mongers one and all
> Foretold some mischief must befall;
> Some loss beyond compare.[9]

Adjoining Westminster Hall, beyond the statue of Oliver Cromwell, is St Stephen's door – the public entrance to Parliament. It marks the site of St Stephen's Chapel, where the House of Commons sat at the time of the American Revolution.

The Members of Parliament were the law-makers for an empire fringed along the Atlantic coast of North America by thirteen colonies with a population of nearly two million. The American colonies reached south to the Spanish imperial outpost of St Augustine, Florida, and to the north and west were bordered by French possessions. Their territorial integrity was accepted by the French government in the Treaty of Paris, signed in 1763 at the end of the Seven Years' War (or French and Indian War). But with peace the grievances of the American colonial population against the British government became more keenly felt. American merchants were not allowed to trade in the non-British parts of the Caribbean. Their exports had to be transported in British ships and a standing army was introduced to prevent smuggling. Within the colonies British regulations prohibited the use of waterfalls, the erection of machinery and the building of iron-foundries. A ban on settlement beyond the Allegheny Mountains cut off the colonies from their hinterland.

The British government's annual military and civil expenditure in the American colonies had risen from £70,000 before the Seven Years' War to £350,000. A proposal to meet these costs by a tax on cider in Britain was so strongly opposed by MPs from the apple-growing counties that it had to be abandoned. Searching for an alternative source of revenue, the Chancellor of the Exchequer, George Grenville, on 10 March 1764 – late at night and to 'a thin House of Commons' – put forward his plan to impose stamp duties in the American colonies. One of the few MPs who opposed the plan was Colonel Barre, General Wolfe's comrade-in-arms at Quebec. When the Stamp Act was passed in February 1765, Barre told the House of Commons:

God knows I do not at this time speak from motives of party heat; what I deliver are the genuine sentiments of my heart. However superior to me in general knowledge and experience the reputable body of this house may be, yet I claim to know more of America than most of you, having seen and been conversant with that country.[10]

Chancellor Grenville consulted with the colonial agents in London and, according to Jared Ingersoll, the Connecticut agent, 'gave us a full hearing'. The Chancellor was not set upon the tax and said that 'if the Americans dislike it and prefer any other method I shall be content. Write therefore to your several Colonies, and if they choose any other mode, I shall be satisfied provided the money be raised.'[11]

When the Stamp Act was passed, William Pitt, the Earl of Chatham – who had resigned from the government in 1761 – was ill, but on his return to the House of Commons he vigorously attacked it. The Americans, he said, 'are the subjects of this kingdom, equally entitled with yourselves to all the natural rights of mankind, and the peculiar privileges of Englishmen; equally bound by its laws, and equally participating in the constitution of this free country.'[12] Benjamin Franklin, who had also been ill, was not greatly alarmed by the Act: the sum to be raised was only £100,000 and a Stamp Act was already in force in England. But he disliked the idea of introducing it into America, where many of his countrymen – particularly the pioneers on the frontier – were intolerant of interference. Faced with growing opposition both in America and at home, the government therefore considered repealing the Act whilst reasserting Parliamentary sovereignty over the colonies. A House of Commons Committee questioned Benjamin Franklin on this option for two hours. He pointed out that Americans already paid heavy taxes, the frontier counties – having been ravaged by war – paying little but the coastal cities more. Americans, he explained, would have to travel long distances to buy the required stamps, 'spending perhaps £3 or £4 in order that the Crown get sixpence.'

'Do you not think the people of America would submit to pay the stamp duty if it was moderated?'

'No, never, unless compelled by force of arms.'

'Can anything less than a military force carry the Stamp Act into execution?'

'I do not see how a military force can be applied to that purpose.'

'Why may it not be?'

'Suppose a military force be sent into America, they will find nobody in arms; what then are they to do? They cannot force a man to take stamps who chooses to do without them. They will not find a rebellion; they may indeed make one.'

Worried by the prospect of an American boycott of British goods, the Committee asked Franklin, 'What used to be the pride of the Americans?'

'To indulge in the fashions and manufactures of Great Britain.'

'What is now their pride?'

'To wear their old clothes over again until they can make new ones.'

On the question of Parliamentary sovereignty over the colonies, Franklin told MPs his belief that 'No ill consequences need be apprehended in America from an assertion of the abstract right on the part of the mother country.'[13] Eight days later the Stamp Act was repealed. A crowd was waiting outside the House of Commons and when Pitt appeared every man raised his hat and there was loud cheering. The most enthusiastic supporters went with him to his sedan chair and followed him to his house in Bond Street with shouts and blessings. Grenville, by contrast, was met with groans and hisses.

William Pitt's illness persisted, keeping him away from the House of Commons, and although he was elevated to the House of Lords his colleague the Duke of Grafton was later to write in his memoirs:

> I shall ever consider Lord Chatham's long illness, together with his resignation, as the most unhappy event that could have befallen our political state. Without entering into many other consequences at that time which called for his assistance I must think that the separation with America might have been avoided.[14]

After the death of George Grenville and William Pitt's resignation from the House of Commons in early 1767, Charles Townshend became Chancellor of the Exchequer and controlled government policy. On 13 May he put before the Commons his proposals for a tax on glass, red and white lead, painters' colours, paper and tea imported into the American colonies. This tax, he believed, could raise £40,000 a year without giving offence. Benjamin Franklin – who was consulted – considered such a taxation legitimate because it would not be imposed on the products of American labour on American soil, but the Chancellor's proposals aroused a storm of patriotic fury across the Atlantic. Non-importation associations were formed and rioting broke out. As the revolt gathered momentum a powerful minority in the House of Commons – led by John Wilkes – began to assert the right of Americans to determine their own destiny. Five seats in the House were occupied by Americans: the MP for Malden was John Huske of New Hampshire, the MP for Saltash was Paul Wentworth from New Hampshire, the MP for the City of London was Barlow Trecothic from Massachusetts, the MP for Bristol was Henry Cruger from New York and the MP for Elgin Burghs was Staats Long Morris from New York.

Franklin and Pitt continued to strive for reconciliation in the interests of the Anglo-American empire they both held dear. On 20 January 1775 they walked arm-in-arm through the lobby before Pitt went into the House of Lords. 'I must declare and avow,' he told their Lordships, 'that for solidity of reason, force of sagacity, and wisdom of conclusion, under such a complication of difficult circumstances, no nation or body of men can stand in preference to the general Congress at Philadelphia.'

As the War of Independence began, Franklin returned to America and Pitt was absent from the House of Lords for two years. He reappeared – his gouty limbs swathed in flannels – to move an appeal to George III to end the war. This could be done, he argued, by removing 'the accumulated grievances under which America was labouring . . . . The Americans are rebels but what are they rebels for? Surely not for defending their unquestionable rights.' In December 1777 he condemned the British use of Hessian mercenaries and Amerindians. 'Who is the man', he demanded to know, 'that has dared to authorise and associate to our arms the tomahawk and scalping knife of the savage?' When Pitt heard that the Duke of Richmond planned to appeal for withdrawal of British troops and amicable measures 'to recover the friend-ship of the revolted provinces', he rose from his sick-bed on 7 April to make a last speech in the House of Lords against dismemberment of the empire:

> Let us at least make one effort, and, if we must fall, let us fall like men! My Lords, ill as I am, yet as long as I can crawl to this House, and have strength to raise myself on my crutches, or lift my hand, I will vote against giving up the dependency of America on the sovereignty of Great Britain, and if no other Lord is of opinion with me, I will protest singly against the measure.[15]

He died a month later and his body lay in state for two days at Westminster.

On 12 June 1781, during the last debate in the House of Commons before news of the capture of Yorktown arrived, Charles James Fox – a consistent opponent of the government's American policy – appealed for peace and made a remarkable prediction:

> The only objection to my motion is that it must lead to American independence. But I venture to assert that within six months of the present day Ministers themselves will come forward to Parliament with some proposition of a similar nature.[16]

In the half-filled St Stephen's Chapel, only 99 members supported him against 172 for the government.

When peace terms were finally agreed, the United States obtained all the territory up to the Mississippi, the entire province of Maine and the right to fish off the Newfoundland Banks. Congress was not bound by the peace terms to do anything definite for the Loyalists other than advise the States to treat them humanely. William Wilberforce told the Commons that he hoped the Loyalists would receive redress from Congress; in Edmund Burke's view they 'had been deluded to it by England and had risked every-thing, and to such men the nation owed protection.'[17] Defending the Anglo-American peace terms, Lord Shelburne said

> I have but one answer to give to the House; it is an answer I gave my own bleeding heart. A part must be wounded that the whole of the Empire may not perish. If better terms could be had, think you . . . that I would not have embraced them? I had but the alternative either to accept the terms proposed, or to continue the War.[18]

On 5 December 1782, King George III came to the House of Lords to recognise formally the independence of the United States. The Americans Elkanah Watson, Benjamin West and John Singleton Copley went to hear him. Watson described the scene.

> After waiting nearly two hours the approach of the King was announced by a tremendous roar of artillery. He entered by a small door on the left of the throne, and immediately seated himself upon the Chair of State, in a graceful attitude, with his right foot resting upon a stool. He was clothed in royal robes. Apparently agitated, he drew from his pocket the scroll containing his speech. The Commons were summoned, and after the bustle of their entrance had subsided, he proceeded to read. . . . Every artery beat high and swelled with my proud American blood.[19]

George III, like many of his ministers, believed that the severing of the colonies from Britain would be the nation's undoing. From the throne he said:

> I make it my humble and earnest prayer to Almighty God that Great Britain may not feel the evils which might result from so great a dismemberment of the Empire, and that America may be free from those calamities which have formerly proved in the Mother Country how essential monarchy is to the enjoyment of constitutional liberty.[20]

These sentiments were ridiculed by Edmund Burke:

> The King is made by his ministers to fall upon his knees, and to deprecate the wrath of Heaven from the misguided American people, that they may not suffer from the want of Monarchy. A people who never were designed for Monarchy, who in their nature and character are adverse to Monarchy, and who never had any other than the smell of Monarchy from the distance of three thousand miles! They are now to be protected by the prayers of their former Sovereign from the consequences of its loss! Such whimpering and absurd piety has neither dignity, meaning nor common sense.[21]

Half a century later, in 1834, St Stephen's Chapel was burned to the ground in a fire that destroyed almost all the old Palace of Westminster, apart from Westminster Hall and the Jewel Tower. The fire began with the careless burning of ancient Exchequer tally-sticks in a stove beneath the House of Lords. 'The worn-out, worm-eaten, rotten old bits of wood were housed at Westminster,' Charles Dickens told an audience at Drury Lane,

> and it would naturally occur to any intelligent person that nothing could be easier than to allow them to be carried away for firewood by the miserable people who live in that neighbourhood. However, they never had been useful, and official routine required that they never should be, and so the order went forth that they should be privately and confidentially burned.[22]

With the old Palace of Westminster smouldering in ruins, King William IV offered the homeless Commons and Lords the use of Buckingham Palace. Green Park was considered as a site for their new home, but the Duke of Wellington insisted they remain alongside the Thames so that they could never be completely surrounded by demonstrators on all four sides of the building. Architects were invited to produce designs for a purpose-built House of Parliament 'in the Gothic or Elizabethan style'. Of the ninety-seven designs submitted, Charles Barry's was chosen.

From the St Stephen's door of Barry's splendid building, the path beside the House of Lords car park in Old Palace Yard leads to the Victoria Tower royal entrance. It has, as Ralph Waldo Emerson observed, 'the ball and crown repeated tediously all over the grand gate'. In the Victoria Tower Gardens a colourful Gothic drinking fountain commemorates the emancipation of slaves in 1834, and the British anti-slavery leaders Buxton, Wilberforce, Clarkson, Macaulay, Brougham and Lushington. On the far side of the Thames, to the left of Lambeth Palace there is a small white church spire with the red-and-blue stars and stripes etched around. This is the Lincoln Tower of Christ Church in Westminster Bridge Road. It was erected to commemorate the abolition of slavery in the USA in 1865, and 'as a token of international brotherhood'. The £71,000 which the tower cost was raised by English and American donations, the foundation stone was laid by the American Minister (Ambassador) on 9 July 1874 and it was inaugurated by Sir Thomas Buxton on 4 July 1876.

In 1618 a Thames rowing boat brought Sir Walter Ralegh on his final journey from the Tower to the Palace of Westminster, to be executed in Old Palace Yard. After the execution, his headless body was buried 'within ye chancel' of St Margaret's church. A brass plaque close to the altar now marks the burial place. Its inscription reads:

Should you reflect on his errors
Remember his many virtues
And that he was a mortal.

St Margaret's — built in 1523 and the parish church of the House of Commons since 1614 — contains a large stained-glass window commemorating Ralegh. It was presented by a group of American citizens in 1888 and the poem which accompanies the

window was written by the American
Minister in London at the time,
James Russell Lowell:

> The New World's sons from
>   England's breasts we drew
> Such milk as bids remember
>   whence we came;
> Proud of her Past wherefrom
>   our Present grew
> This window we inscribe with
>   Ralegh's name.

The exit from St Margaret's, under
the Ralegh window, leads to the patch
of ground where it is believed the
remains of Charles I's regicides,
including Oliver Cromwell, were
finally laid to rest. To the left is
Westminster Abbey, rebuilt in the thirteenth century for King Henry III to
replace the original Norman abbey built here in the eleventh century for
Edward the Confessor. Every Coronation of a British monarch has taken
place at Westminster Abbey and the corpses of many kings and queens lie
among the four thousand buried beneath the abbey floor.

> Think how many royal bones
> Sleep within these heaps of stones:
> Here they lie, had realms and lands,
> Who now want strength to stir their hands:
> Where from their pulpits seal'd with dust
> They preach, 'In greatness is no trust.'
> Here's an acre, sown indeed
> With the richest, royall'st seed
> That the earth did e'er suck in,
> Since the first man died for sin.[23]

These thoughts of the early seventeenth-century English poet Francis
Beaumont were echoed by Oliver Wendell Holmes, the Massachusetts-born
physician and author of *Our Hundred Days in Europe*, after he visited
Westminster Abbey in 1886. 'On the whole,' he wrote,

> the Abbey produces a distinct sense of being overcrowded. . . . Look up
> at the lofty roof, which we willingly pardon for shutting out the
> heaven above us – at least in an average London day; look down at the
> floor, and think of what precious relics it covers but do not look
> around you with the hope of getting any clear, concentrated, satisfying
> effect from this great museum of gigantic funereal bric-a-brac.[24]

Immediately inside the great west door of the abbey is a tablet on a wall to the right surmounted by the American eagle. It commemorates Franklin D. Roosevelt and the inscription was written jointly by the British Prime Minister Clement Attlee and Winston Churchill, MP: 'To the honoured memory of Franklin Delano Roosevelt, 1882–1945. A faithful friend of freedom and of Britain, four times president of the United States. Erected by the Government of the United Kingdom'. At the unveiling of the tablet in 1948 Attlee said:

It is fitting we should commemorate here the man whose high courage, foresight, wisdom and broad humanity contributed so

Westminster Abbey

greatly to preserve the ideals of Christian freedom and democracy which are the common heritage of the English-speaking peoples.

Churchill recalled that Westminster Abbey had been described by the English historian, Lord Macaulay, as

> that temple of silence and reconciliation where the enmities of twenty generations lie buried. But now, today, it is not the ending of enmities we celebrate. This tablet to Franklin Delano Roosevelt proclaims the growth of enduring friendship and the rebirth of brotherhood between two great nations on whose wisdom, valour and virtue the future of humanity in no small degree depends. Long may it testify from these old walls![25]

Winston Churchill – whose New York-born mother 'Jennie' Jerome was one-quarter Iroquois – is himself commemorated by a large tablet in the floor near the Roosevelt plaque.

Beyond Churchill's tablet is the grave of the Unknown Soldier, the only one in Westminster Abbey which may not be walked over. On 17 October 1921, General Pershing – in the presence of the British Prime Minister Lloyd George, Earl Haig, Winston Churchill, the American Ambassador and American soldiers and sailors – placed above the breast of the Unknown Soldier the American Congressional Medal of Honour. At the same time the British Victoria Cross was awarded to the Unknown Soldier in the United States. The Congressional Medal is now in a small glass case on a nearby pillar.

In the nave a stained-glass window above the abbot's pew commemorates the officers and men of the British Flying Corps who fell in the First World War. The window was presented by Mrs Louise Bennet of West Virginia, whose son was killed in France. In the north choir aisle another stained-glass window, showing the American arms and eagle, is a tribute to 'British prisoners who died in Germany 1914–18' from a former American Ambassador in Berlin, J. W. Gerard.

At the west end of the north aisle is a monument to Charles James Fox which includes the figure of a black American. Tucked behind it is a memorial to Lord Howe, Brigadier-General of British forces in America at the time of the Seven Years' War. When Howe was killed on 6 July 1758, aged thirty-four, 'the province of Massachusetts Bay in New England by an order of the Great and General Court . . . caused this monument to be erected . . . in testimony of the

sense they had of his services and military virtues and of the affection their officers and soldiers bore to his command.'

Over the west door is a statue of William Pitt, the Earl of Chatham, and close by a tablet in the floor marks the spot where George Peabody was briefly buried at the abbey. 'Here were deposited', the inscription reads, 'from November 12 to December 11 1869 the remains of George Peabody, then removed to his native country and buried at Danvers, now Peabody, Mass.'

In the south aisle stand the stone figures of two Amerindians with beaded hair. They are holding up the monument to Lieutenant-Colonel Robert Townshend who was killed, aged twenty-eight, by a cannon ball during the Seven Years' War (French and Indian War) 'as he was reconnoitring the French lines at Triconderagoe in North America.' He was the brother of Charles Townshend, whose tax proposals as Chancellor were later to precipitate the Boston Tea Party. Though his death was premature, 'his life was glorious, enrolling him with . . . those immortal statesmen and commanders whose wisdom and intrepidity . . . extended the commerce, enlarged the dominion and upheld the majesty of these kingdoms beyond the idea of any former age.'

A little further along the south aisle is the monument to Major John André, a Londoner of Franco-Swiss parentage who during the American War of Independence joined the British Army in Canada. He became aide-de-camp to the British Commander Sir Henry Clinton and then, as Adjutant-General, was intermediary in negotiations with General Benedict Arnold. Arnold's wife Peggy, from Philadelphia, was a reigning beauty in London and a friend of John André. Through Peggy, Benedict Arnold provided André with papers which enabled him to penetrate George Washington's lines on the Hudson River. Major André undertook a secret mission to Arnold with proposals for the betrayal of West Point to British forces. When he was captured by the Americans, compromising documents were found hidden in his stockings and a court martial condemned him to death as a spy. Although, in George Washington's words, Major André was 'more unfortunate than criminal', he was hanged at Tappan, New York, on 2 October 1780. The whole British Army went into mourning and King George III ordered this monument to be erected in Westminster Abbey, topped by figures of a weeping Britannia and a lion. The monument depicts Major André on his way to be executed with a petition to George Washington pleading unsuccessfully for a soldier's death by firing squad rather than hanging. The inscription on the monument says that André, 'when employed in an important but hazardous enterprise fell a sacrifice to his zeal for king and country . . . aged 29, universally beloved and esteemed by the army which he served, and lamented even by his foes.'

Sir Henry Clinton had made every effort to save Major André other than giving up Benedict Arnold. When news came of the British surrender at

Yorktown, George III refused at first to accept that he had lost the war. Fearing the effect on his personal and political prestige if he did not get the colonies back, the King commissioned Benedict Arnold to draw up his *Thoughts on the American War*. Most Americans, Arnold argued, could not express their dissatisfaction with the United States because they were excluded from elections. With farmers groaning under the weight of taxation, Congress bankrupt, the American currency worthless, the Continental Army rife with desertion and French troops going home, there was still a possibility of reunion with Britain. Benedict Arnold claimed that he had been offered £10,000 by Major André to change sides. He received £6000 and a permanent commission as a British Army colonel, with an annual salary of £450 until the end of the war and thereafter half pay for the rest of his life. Peggy Arnold – much admired by King George III and Queen Charlotte – received £500 a year and the Arnold children were also granted British government pensions. It is known that Benedict and Peggy Arnold came to have a look at the Major André monument in Westminster Abbey, but not what their thoughts were as they stood in front of it.

Major André's body remained buried at Tappan for forty years before being dug up and brought back to England. The flesh and clothes – apart from a leather thong – had disintegrated, but the skeleton was intact. The roots of a peach tree had reached the coffin, pierced the lid and twisted themselves around André's skull. The tree was carefully removed and in due course planted in King George IV's garden at Carlton House in London. Major André's skeleton was placed in a mahogany chest and 'The courtesy and good feeling of the Americans was remarkable. The bier was decorated with garlands and flowers as it was transported to the ship.'[26] In London the skeleton was buried at Westminster Abbey, nine feet from the monument. Those present included Major André's sisters – who were given the few surviving locks of his hair – and the Dean of Westminster Abbey – who kept the string tied around the hair. Soon after the burial, the heads of both George Washington and Major André were chipped off the monument and taken to America.

In 1805 Benjamin Silliman, the Yale Natural History professor, visited the Major André monument.

> Although a small one [he wrote], it naturally attracted the attention of an American. I was gratified to see that the inscription contained no reflection on General Washington, notwithstanding the injurious aspersions which were so liberally thrown on his character at the time. Now, I believe, he is universally allowed to have done only his duty. The monument, which is of white marble, exhibits an historical sketch of the last scene of André's life. They are leading him to execution, and General Washington is represented as refusing to receive a message which is at that moment brought to him by a flag of truce from the English general. The countenances of the surrounding

American officers are expressive of the deepest sympathy in the sufferings of the gallant victim; but it is well known that General Washington was not present at the execution. The mob have knocked off the heads of André, Washington and another American officer, which gives the monument a deformed appearance.[27]

In 1823 Charles Lamb, the English writer, published a long letter in the *London Magazine* in the form of an essay under his pseudonym, Elia. Addressed to Robert Southey Esq., who had said Lamb's writing needed 'sounder religious feeling', it complained about a fee being imposed for entrance to Westminster Abbey:

> For forty years that I have known the fabric, the only well-attested charge of violation . . . has been a ridiculous dismemberment committed upon the effigy of that amiable spy, Major André. And it is for this – the wanton mischief of some schoolboy, fired perhaps with raw notions of Transatlantic Freedom . . . that the people of England are made to pay a new Peter's Pence . . . or must content themselves with contemplating the ragged exterior of their Cathedral. The mischief was done about the time that you were a scholar there. Do you know anything about the unfortunate relic? Can you help in this emergency to find the nose? Or can you give . . . a notion (from memory) of its pristine life and vigour? I am willing for peace's sake to subscribe my guinea towards the restoration of the lamented feature.[28]

After Dean Stanley went to America in 1879 to visit Cyrus W. Field at Irvington, a monument was erected on the site of Major André's execution at Tappan. The inscription on the monument read:

> Here died, October 2, 1780, Major John André, of the British Army who, entering the American lines on a secret mission to Benedict Arnold for the surrender of West Point, was taken prisoner, tried and condemned as a spy. His death, though according to the stern code of war, moved even his enemies to pity; and both armies mourned the fate of one so young and so brave. In 1821 his remains were removed to Westminster Abbey. A hundred years after the execution this stone was placed above the spot where he lay, by a citizen of the United States against which he fought, not to perpetuate the record of strife, but in token of those better feelings which have since united two nations, one in race, in language and in religion, with the hope that this friendly union will never be broken.

This monument, however, offended some Americans and was dynamited, as was the one that replaced it. Another monument was eventually put up where Major André had been captured at Tarrytown, New York.

Further along the south aisle of Westminster Abbey, on the wall to the right, is a tablet commemorating Colonel Joseph Lemuel Chester, who was born in Norwich, Connecticut, but lived in London for many years and was the editor of the Westminster Abbey Register. The tablet was installed after his death in 1882, 'in grateful memory of the disinterested labour of an American master of genealogical learning . . . by the Dean and Chapter of Westminster.'

Beyond Chester's memorial is one to William Wragg Esq., of South Carolina, 'who, when the American colonies revolted from Great Britain, inflexibly maintained his loyalty to the person and government of his sovereign and was therefore compell'd to leave his distrest family and ample fortune . . . those who have survived him . . . deplore the loss of a most tender husband, an affectionate parent, a good master and a warm friend.' Wragg left for England as the War of Independence began, but was shipwrecked and drowned off the coast of Holland on 3 September 1777. The carving on his monument shows the wrecked ship and Wragg sinking beneath the waves within sight of land.

The south aisle leads to Poets' Corner, alongside the high altar where British monarchs have been crowned for nine centuries. Behind the bookstall in Poets' Corner is the bearded head of Henry Wadsworth Longfellow, placed 'amongst the memorials of the poets of England by the English admirers of an American poet'. It was unveiled in 1884 with a speech by James Russell Lowell.

Probably buried somewhere in Poets' Corner – exactly where remains unknown – is the geographer Richard Hakluyt (1552–1616). Hakluyt played a leading role in the Elizabethan colonisation of North America, from the voyages of exploration – embarked upon with the hope of commercial advantage and discovery of a direct passage to the Indies – up to the establishment of a permanent colony in Virginia. In 1584 he wrote *The Discourse of Western Planting*, which logically and forcefully presented the arguments for English colonisation of America and the necessity of state support for it. As well as providing economic gains, colonisation would 'bridle' the King of Spain and be of great political benefit to England. The *Discourse* was presented to Elizabeth I as a secret report and not made public until 1877.

The economic attractions of colonisation were, however, made public in 1585 by Hakluyt's cousin and mentor, the lawyer Richard Hakluyt the Elder, in a pamphlet addressed to London merchants and entitled *Inducements to the liking of the voyage intended towards Virginia*. The aims of the intended voyage were, he wrote, 'To plant Christian religion, to traffic [trade] and to conquer. To plant Christian religion without conquest, will be hard. Traffic easily followeth conquest: conquest is not easy. Traffic without conquest seemeth possible, and not uneasy. What is to be done, is the question?'

Virginia would be a source of agricultural products and raw materials but it could also become a market for 'hats, bonnets, knives, fishhooks, copper kettles, beads, looking glasses, bugles and a thousand kinds of other wrought wares'. This would help solve the unemployment problem in England.

If the people of Virginia were 'content to live naked' there would be no trade possibilities unless their culture could be changed. Neither would there be trade if they wanted to 'live in abundance' but had all they needed. If there was demand for English goods but no precious metals or goods to pay for them the local economy could be developed.

The natural and human resources should be assessed from the point of view of what they could produce 'that England doth want or doth desire', care being taken that the people 'were drawn by all courtesy into love with our nation; that we become not hateful to them.' Avoiding bloodshed would make the English colony stable, profitable and better able to resist other colonising powers. In addition 'some ancient captains of mild disposition and great judgement' should seize, man and fortify the mouths and banks of rivers. Harbours should be built for the Navy 'that we may be lords of the gates and entries, to go and come in at pleasure, and to lie in safety, and be able to command and to control all within.'

Hog-rearing would be a good economic activity for the colony because hogs could be fed on roots and acorns without 'spoiling your corn'. They would be the food for 'the multitude continually employed in labour' and some could also be salted, barrelled and exported to England, the barrels then being sold to the English herring trade.

A textile industry could be developed by 'receiving the savage women and their children of both sexes by courtesy into your protection and employing the English women and the others. ' Textiles could be exported to England and the business could be expanded into the West Indies, 'victual and labour being cheap there.'

The sorts of men suitable for the voyage to Virginia were those with mining , construction, farming, shipbuilding and weapon-making skills. 'A skilful painter is also to be carried with you . . . to bring the descriptions of all the beasts, birds, fishes, trees, towns etc.'[29]

Close to Poets' Corner, an exit from the church leads to the Westminster Abbey cloisters, where long ago the monks used to exercise and take fresh air. On the floor of the north cloister – which houses the abbey's brass-rubbing centre – is a small slab marked simply 'John Burgoyne 1723–1792'. John Burgoyne – nicknamed 'Jack Bragg' – first went to America to  accompany General Gage at the Battle of Bunker Hill, the first major battle of the War of Independence, fought on 17 June 1775. After some time in Canada, with Sir Guy Carleton, Burgoyne planned the disastrous expedition which led to the surrender of his five thousand British troops at Saratoga in 1777. This proved to be a turning-point in George Washington's campaign and secured the French alliance with the Americans. When Washington allowed Burgoyne to return to England he was warmly welcomed by Charles

James Fox but vigorously blamed by others. He retired from military life and pursued a literary career. His comedy *The Heiress* was successfully produced by David Garrick at the Theatre Royal Drury Lane.

In the east cloister is the entrance to the Chapter House. This is where the Commons met from 1352 to 1395, much to the annoyance of the monks, who complained that their shuffling and stamping wore out the expensive tiled floor. None the less, the floor is still in good condition, although the medieval wall-painting of a crowd of middle-aged male individuals may well be the monks' unflattering portraits of the knights and burgesses they managed to turf out.

Beside the stairs leading up to the Chapter House a stained-glass window depicts the Pilgrim Fathers landing in America with Bibles in hand; and slaves harnessed together by neck-halters, then freed by St Ambrose breaking their manacles. The window also features the heraldic devices of the USA, Harvard, the UK and Westminster. It was installed 'in memory of James Russell Lowell United States Minister at the Court of St James from 1880–1885 by his English friends'. Lowell's stone head appears below it . Alongside Lowell's memorial tablet is one to Walter Hines Page, American Ambassador 1913–18 – 'the friend of Britain in her sorest hour'.

In the south cloister, on the wall to the left, is a colourful glazed map showing the routes of three great circumnavigators of the globe – Sir Francis Drake, Captain James Cook and Sir Francis Chichester – with their ships of the sixteenth, eighteenth and twentieth centuries. Drake's route, in red, shows where he landed on the west coast of North America in 1579. Cook is best known for his discovery of Australia, but he also led a British exploration of Hawaii. On his last scientific mission there in 1777, American and French ships were instructed by Thomas Jefferson to allow him safe passage.

At the end of the south cloister is the gate into Dean's Yard and the playing fields of Westminster School. From Dean's Yard the public path leads out to Broad Sanctuary, so called because of the ancient right of sanctuary within the abbey. Across the road, in front of the Middlesex Court House, stands a bronze statue of Abraham Lincoln, which is a copy of the famous marble one in Lincoln Park, Chicago. It was unveiled on 28 July 1920 by the

Duke of Connaught. 'We commemorate him', said Lord Bryce at the unveiling,

> as a hero who belongs to the whole world, because he showed what fame may be won, and what services rendered by a plain son of the people unaided by any gifts of fortune. His life and character stand like a beacon light of hope to us in all these dark days of strife and confusion.[30]

To Lincoln's right, the tower of St Margaret's displays a modern, bright-blue sun-dial, installed to commemorate the ecumenical service held in the church on 16 November 1974, for the Twentieth Session of the North Atlantic Assembly. The service was conducted by the Chaplain to the Speaker of the House of Commons with the assistance of clergy from NATO countries represented by their MPs.

Straight ahead of Abraham Lincoln – on the far side of Parliament Square – is the House of Commons building, designed by Charles Barry but rebuilt after the Second World War. It is dominated by the clock-tower popularly known as 'Big Ben'. In fact it was not the clock-tower itself but the largest bell inside it which MPs named Big Ben in 1859. They were inspired either by Sir Benjamin Hall – the large Welshman who was Commissioner of Works – or by seventeen-stone Benjamin Caunt, London's champion prizefighter. Adjoining the first floor of the Big Ben tower is a room designed to confine rebellious MPs; it was last used for that purpose in 1880 when Charles Bradlaugh, MP, was sent to it.

There are 635 members of the House of Commons and over 1100 members of the House of Lords. The Lords Spiritual consist of twenty-four bishops and the two archbishops of the Church of England; the Lords Temporal are dukes, marquesses, earls, viscounts and barons, whose titles are mainly hereditary but some of whom are life peers. The Houses of Parliament contain over a thousand rooms, a hundred staircases and two miles of corridors.

There are more corridors of power off Parliament Square to the left, in Whitehall, the home of the British civil service. The civil servants who work here are recruited through examinations, which stem from the Northcote–Trevelyan report of 1854. This concluded that

> admission to the civil service is . . . for the unambitious and the indolent or incapable. . . . We recommend that a central Board should be constituted for conducting the examination of all candidates for the public service. . . . No other means can be devised of avoiding the evils of patronage.

Queen Victoria opposed the introduction of an examination system on the grounds that it would open high office to 'low people without breeding or feelings of gentlemen'.

The vast Old Home Office building at the Parliament Square end of Whitehall, which now houses the Foreign Office, was completed in the 1870s. It is decorated with buxom female figures symbolising different parts of the world, including America. Opposite, a statue of Sir Walter Ralegh stands in front of the Ministry of Defence building – the largest office block in London when it was completed in the 1950s.

Beyond the Foreign Office is Downing Street, which gets its name from George Downing, a graduate of Harvard University who began his career as the humble instructor of New England seamen. He was described by Samuel

Pepys as 'a stingy fellow' and 'a perfidious rogue'. Downing was born in Dublin in 1623 but his father, a London solicitor, took him to Salem, Massachusetts, when he was in his teens. He lived in America for seven years and sailed to the West Indies as a spiritual instructor before returning to England to serve as a chaplain in the Parliamentary Army during the English Civil War. In 1655 he was part of the group who wanted Oliver Cromwell to become king. After the Restoration of the Monarchy in 1660 he was appointed – despite his Commonwealth background – as one of the four Tellers of the Receipt of the Exchequer. His excuse for his previous allegiance to Cromwell was that he had been brought up in New England 'and had sucked in principles that, since, his reason had made him see were erroneous.'

In 1681 George Downing acquired a ninety-nine year lease for land between the Cockpit and St James's Park, for which he paid £20 per year to the Crown and £4 per year to the Keeper of Whitehall. The houses he built there, in what became known as Downing Street, had aristocratic tenants but reverted to the Crown when the lease expired. In 1731 George II offered No. 10 Downing Street to Sir Robert Walpole, who was Britain's first Prime Minister although he never took that title. Walpole declined to accept 10

Downing Street as a personal gift, but he agreed with the King that the house should become the official residence of the First Lord of the Treasury, and it is as First Lord of the Treasury that the Prime Minister occupies the premises today.[31]

Beyond Downing Street is the office of the Privy Council, the body composed of top politicians, law lords, archbishops and others who serve the monarch as private advisors. Benjamin Franklin was called before the Privy Council on 29 January 1774 after admitting in print that he had sent to the Committee of Correspondence in Boston confidential letters written by Thomas Hutchinson, Governor of Massachusetts, to Thomas Whateley, the former private secretary to George Grenville.

The Hutchinson letters sought to prejudice the cause of the patriots, who considered them treasonable. Franklin had acquired the letters from a relative of George Grenville, John Temple, who claimed descent from Lady Godiva, had been born in Boston, educated in England and had become close to the American patriot leaders – with whom he had always sympathised – through his marriage to the daughter of James Bowdoin. After the War of Independence – when he was appointed as the first British Consul to the USA – Temple took with him to America, for his father-in-law, a writing table used by William Pitt, the Earl of Chatham. Temple had given Franklin the Hutchinson letters to send to the Committee of Correspondence on condition that they not be copied and that their source be kept secret. They were published in Boston, however, and Temple was suspected of stealing them. This led to a Hyde Park duel in which the lanky, stone-deaf Temple wounded the pot-bellied brother of Thomas Whateley. When Benjamin Franklin heard about the duel he wrote to the *Public Advertiser* explaining his role in the publication of the letters.

Franklin still hoped that an irrevocable breach between the American patriots and the British government could be prevented and he would have served as one of the sponsors of a great Anglo-American Atlantic empire.

These hopes were severely shaken by the response he received when he tried to justify his actions over the Hutchinson letters to thirty-five hostile members of the Privy Council in full regalia, laden with decorations. For the occasion he carried his magic staff, donned a large wig and wore his 'fine suit of spotted Manchester velvet'. The Solicitor-General, representing Thomas Hutchinson – who considered Franklin 'a low and middle-class politician, a revolutionist and a none too scrupulous journalist' – gave him such a dressing-down that he decided not to use the suit again until he had been vindicated. His friends Edmund Burke, Jeremy Bentham and Joseph Priestley shook his hand as he departed from the Privy Council in disgrace. 'I was never before so sensible of the power of a good conscience,' he said to Priestley over breakfast next morning.[32] Two days later King George III sacked him as Postmaster in the Colonies. John Temple was also dismissed from British government service. When Franklin returned to Europe as Minister Plenipotentiary from the American Congress in 1777, Lord Rockingham remarked: 'I cannot refrain from paying my tribute of admiration to the vigour, magnanimity and determined resolution of the old man. The horrid scene at the Privy Council is still in my memory.'[33]

Almost opposite the Privy Council – which in Franklin's day was housed in a building called the Cockpit – stands the early seventeenth-century Banqueting House, which is all that remains of Whitehall Palace. In the early sixteenth century young King Henry VIII lived at the Palace of Westminster and this site was occupied by York Place, the London residence of the Archbishops of York. When Cardinal Wolsey — the most powerful man in the kingdom next to the King – was Archbishop of York, the hospitality at York Place was legendary. In 1518, a guest wrote of 'a most sumptuous supper, the like of which was never given either by Cleopatra or Caligula'. Despite his power and splendour, Wolsey was unable to persuade the Pope to grant Henry VIII a divorce from his first wife, Catherine of Aragon, so that he could marry Anne Boleyn and try to produce a male heir. Wolsey fell from power and was condemned to death in 1530, but he died on the way to his execution. One of the charges against him was 'that he, knowing himself to have the foul and contagious disease of the great pox had, with his perilous infected breath, come daily to the King blowing on him.'

Henry VIII took over York Place and a new White Hall was built for royal feasting and merry-making. As a gentleman explains in Shakespeare's *Famous History of the Life of King Henry VIII*:

You must no more call it York Place, that's past,
For since the Cardinal fell that title's lost.
'Tis now the King's and called Whitehall.

A tilt-yard was laid out for the open-air royal entertainments which
Queen Elizabeth I enjoyed until the end of her days. In 1601, when she was
sixty-eight, the Queen personally ordered the tilt-yard to be prepared for
'bearbaiting at Shrovetide. Her Majesty says she is very well and hath commanded the bears, the bull and the ape to be baited. Upon Wednesday she
will have solemn dancing.' Ceremonial tournaments and jousting staged in
the tilt-yard enabled fancifully attired courtiers to pay elaborate tribute to
their royal mistress, as did the theatrical 'masques and mummeries' performed indoors at the Banqueting House in Whitehall.

In 1619 King James I commissioned Inigo Jones to design a new
Banqueting House as the centre of the conglomeration of Tudor royal buildings known as Whitehall Palace. Inigo Jones had studied Italian architecture
and his Banqueting House was the first Renaissance building in England. Its
single great room is a double cube 55 feet high and wide and 110 feet long,
with a 'Great Neech' at the south end for the monarch. James I's son, King
Charles I, commissioned the Flemish artist Peter Paul Rubens to paint a
series of pictures for the ceiling which would glorify James I and the Divine
Right of Kings. The canvases were finished by 1634, but trouble over export

Banqueting House

and import duties delayed despatch for a year, during which they remained rolled. Rubens touched up the paintings before they left Belgium for London but excused himself, on grounds of ill-health, from personally supervising their installation at the Banqueting House. The allegorical paintings show *The Apotheosis of James I*, *The Union of England and Scotland* and *The Benefits of the Government of James I*. To protect the paintings, King Charles banned any future staging in the Banqueting House of masques, because they required smoke-producing lights. He stood beneath the paintings in 1649 before stepping out of a window on to the scaffold especially erected in Whitehall for his execution.

Charles's last moments on the scaffold were recorded by John Rushworth in his *Historical Collections*, published between 1659 and 1701. The King told the executioner 'I shall say but short prayers, and then thrust out my hands.' He asked Dr Juxon, Bishop of London, for his nightcap, put it on and then said to the executioner, 'Does my hair trouble you?' The executioner asked the King to put all his hair under the cap. Charles turned to Dr Juxon and said, 'I have a good cause and a gracious God on my side,' to which Juxon replied, 'There is but one stage more. This stage is turbulent and troublesome: it is a short one. . . . You haste to a crown of glory.' The King answered, 'I go from a corruptible to an incorruptible Crown, where no disturbance can be.' Juxon responded, 'You are exchanged from a temporal to an eternal Crown, a good exchange.' Charles took off his cloak and badge of the Order of the Garter, handed them to Juxon, then 'laid his head upon the block. And after a little pause, stretching forth his hands, the executioner at one blow severed his head from his body.'[34]

After the execution of King Charles, for a while Whitehall Palace was deserted. It became, in the words of a contemporary pamphlet,

a palace without a presence. You may walk without rub into the hall. There are not strong smells out of the kitchen to delight your nostrils withal. Nor the greasy scullions to be seen over head and ears in a kettle of kidneys. Nor anything else to stop your progress into the house. You may walk into the presence chamber with your hat, spurs and sword on. And if you will presume to be so unmannerly you may sit down in the chair of state.

In 1654 Oliver Cromwell moved into Whitehall Palace and his wife began keeping an open table for officers of the New Model Army. She also engaged 'a surveyor to make in her room some little labyrinths and trap-stairs by which she might at all times unseen pass to and fro, and come unawares upon her servants at their duties and keep them vigilant and honest in the discharge thereof.' Cromwell's regime became a military dictatorship totally dependent on a large standing army, which national finances were inadequate to support. When he died, his son Richard – 'Tumbledown Dick' – was declared Protector. The generals, however, refused to recognise Richard and the Commonwealth began to disintegrate into conflicting army factions. In 1660 General Monk marched south from Scotland, joined General Fairfax at York and proceeded to London, where they persuaded the Rump Parliament to dissolve itself after making arrangements for a new election. General Monk negotiated with the exiled Prince Charles, son of Charles I, that he should return as King on certain conditions: only those directly responsible for his father's regicide were to be punished; there was to be religious tolerance; and existing property rights were to be respected.

The Lords and Commons – now predominantly Royalist and Presbyterian – assembled in the Banqueting House to welcome King Charles II and 'in two shining speeches testified their vows of affection and fidelity to the utmost degree of loyalty.' The French Ambassador wrote to King Louis XIV: 'This government has a monarchical appearance because there is a King, but at bottom it is very far from being a monarchy.'

The permissiveness of court life at Whitehall Palace in the reign of Charles II ensured his place in popular history as England's 'Merry Monarch'. Any well-dressed person could go into the great stone gallery and watch him pass to and from the state apartments. When underwear belonging to a royal mistress was hung out in the Privy Garden to dry, Samuel Pepys recorded with glee that he had seen 'the finest smocks and linen petticoats of my Lady Castlemaine – it did me good to look upon them.'

In 1681 Charles II made a secret alliance with Louis XIV of France guaranteeing him sufficient subsidy to be financially independent of the British Parliament. For the last four years of his reign he had more absolute power than either his father or his grandfather, James I, had had. But in the long run – unless it were to be dependent on the King of France – an absolutist regime in Britain was bound to turn to the Whig merchants of the City of London for the cash needed to maintain a standing army. It also required the support of the Tories, who had been appointed by the Crown as Justices of the Peace in the countryside and on to Common Councils in the towns and cities, including London. That support was lost when Charles II's successor – his brother, King James II, formerly James, Duke of York – in 1688 ordered the Church of England clergy to proclaim from their pulpits the end of bans against Catholics holding military and civil office. Catholicism – 'Popery and wooden shoes' – was identified in England with foreign domination and poverty. The Whigs, who had been ousted from central and local government, now found that the Tories, who had been appointed to positions of power by the Crown, were willing to ally with them in dethroning the Catholic James II in favour of his daughter Mary and her husband, William of Orange, both of whom were Protestants.

A convention of Whigs and Tories offered William and Mary the Crown as dual monarchs on condition that they would have no control over the army or judiciary and would respect Parliament's exclusive right to pass laws and raise taxes. As William of Orange prepared to cross from Holland to England with his army, James II watched the weathervane (which is still on the roof of the Banqueting House) for signs of 'the Protestant wind'. When William landed, James went from the Banqueting House to a boat on the Thames and thence to Ireland, where, in 1690, he was killed and William's forces were victorious at the Battle of the Boyne.

The Crown was formally offered to William and Mary at the Banqueting House on 13 February 1689 and they were proclaimed King William III and Queen Mary II. William's asthma was adversely affected by the damp atmosphere in Whitehall Palace, so he and Mary preferred to live at Kensington Palace. In 1698 a fire – supposedly started when clothes put in front of a hearth to dry went up in flames – blazed for fifteen hours, destroying all the buildings of Whitehall Palace apart from the Banqueting House. John Evelyn wrote in his diary, 'Whitehall utterly burnt to the ground, nothing but the walls and ruins left.' The court moved to the Palace of St James.

In 1750 work began on the building known as Horse Guards, which is situated immediately opposite the Banqueting House, on the spot where the guard house of the Palace of Whitehall used to stand. Horse Guards – with its distinctive cupola – was designed by William Kent and is one of the finest Georgian buildings in London. In the days before Big Ben, the Horse Guards clock, it was said, 'directs the dinner of each careful dame'. Nowadays, mounted soldiers from the Household Cavalry – the Life Guards, and the Blues and Royals – change guard on the Whitehall side of Horse Guards every day, at 11 a.m. Monday–Saturday and 10 a.m. on Sundays. On the far side of Horse Guards, through the arch under its clock, is Horse Guards Parade, on the site of the Whitehall Palace tilt-yard. Here each year on the monarch's official birthday (10 June) the Trooping of the Colour takes place. One of the regiments of the Brigade of Guards 'troops' its colours before the monarch; there is then a combined march-past and the monarch leads the

Guards from the parade ground. For most of the year Horse Guards Parade serves as a civil service car park adjoining the back garden of 10 Downing Street.

At the end of Horse Guards Parade lies St James's Park, the prettiest of London's royal parks and famous for its exotic birds, which were introduced here three centuries ago. John Evelyn described in his diary going

> to St James's where I saw the pelicans – a fowl between a stork and a swan brought from Astrachan by the Russian Ambassador. I also saw two Balearian cranes, one of which having had one of his legs broken and cut off above the knee, had a wooden leg and thigh with a joint so accurately made that the creature could walk and use it as well as if it had been natural. It has been made by a soldier.

From the footbridge over the lake in the park there is a fine view of the six-hundred-room Buckingham Palace, which has been the monarch's official London residence since Queen Victoria came to the throne in 1837. Buckingham Palace was first acquired by the royal family in 1764, when George III bought it as Buckingham House from the Duke of Buckingham to use as a private residence.

In 1768 Benjamin West made his way to Buckingham House, through St James's Park, clutching his painting *The Landing of Agrippina at Brundisium with the Ashes of Germanicus*. The painting had been well received and George III had summoned the young American artist to bring it to Buckingham House for a private viewing. It was carried from room to room until suitable light was found. The King liked the painting and brought Queen Charlotte to see it, explaining the subject matter to her. He then showed Benjamin West an empty panel measuring seven feet by ten feet in what was called the Warm Room. A valet was sent to fetch volume seventeen of Livy's *History of Rome* and West left Buckingham House with

Buckingham Palace

a royal commission for a painting of the final departure of Regulus from Rome. His model for the Roman general in the painting was to be his American assistant, Charles Peale.

George III took an interest in science as well as art, to the extent of trying to tell the Royal Society what to do. When a five-man committee was set up by the Royal Society to make a public recommendation on the design of lightning-conductors, one committee member thought that the instruments should have blunt ends, while the other four agreed that they should end in sharp points spread out like a fan – the design devised by Benjamin Franklin, who had been awarded a medal by the Royal Society, and elected a member, after the success of his 'experiment for drawing lightning from clouds'. The King, however, put his weight behind the blunt-ended design and said that the President of the Royal Society should change the committee's recommendation. 'Sire,' he was told, 'I cannot reverse the laws and operations of nature.' To this the monarch replied: 'Then you are not fit to be President of the Royal Society!' and went off to order blunt-ended lightning-conductors for Buckingham House.[35] The affair was summed up in rhyme by one of Benjamin Franklin's supporters:

> While you, great George, for knowledge hunt,
> And sharp conductors change for blunt,
> The nation's out of joint;
> Franklin a wiser course pursues,
> And all your thunder useless views,
> By keeping to the point.[36]

In 1783 – after George III had formally accepted the independence of the United States but before he had received its diplomatic representatives – Benjamin West was given permission to take John Adams and John Jay on a guided tour of Buckingham House while the royal family was away at Windsor Palace. Adams noted that the King's library contained 'every book that a king ought to have . . . maps, charts etc. of all his dominions in the four quarters of the world, and models of every fortress.'[37]

In 1918 President Woodrow Wilson became the first non-royal head of state to stay at Buckingham Palace when he and his second wife were guests of King George V and Queen Mary. The King and Queen met the Americans at Charing Cross Station, accompanied them to the palace in royal coaches, with outriders and footmen dressed in crimson liveries, and escorted them to the Belgian Suite overlooking the forty-five-acre garden at the back of the palace. Their large living room had windows reaching to the floor and was full of fresh flowers. Edith Bolling Wilson recalled in her memoirs that

My husband's bedroom had a large alcove cut off by heavy red curtains. His Majesty lifted one of these to disclose a well-equipped bath and a small electric heater. My room was enormous, with the largest bed I ever saw. It contained no heat at all. . . . My bath, at the end of our hall, had a marble tub, beside which stood a high-backed chair as big as a throne.[38]

The guests were invited on to the palace balcony and waved small Union Jacks for the benefit of the crowd below, while their Majesties waved small Stars and Stripes flags. The visit was judged a success, despite Edith's refusal to curtsy to the Queen and the President's use of 'Sir' rather than 'your Majesty'.

In 1919 the American saxophonist Sidney Bechet and his quartet gave a performance at a royal garden party at Buckingham Palace. George V told the musicians the piece he had most enjoyed was 'Characteristic Blues'. In his autobiography Bechet recalled, 'It was just like Grand Central Station with a lot of carpets and things on the walls. By the time we got to play I was thinking I'd gone through enough doors to do me for a month.'[39]

The path from the St James's Park footbridge, to the right, leads into the Mall, on the far side of which is the red-brick Marlborough House, designed by Sir Christopher Wren for the Duchess of Marlborough and completed in 1711. It was in Marlborough House that King Edward VIII – later the Duke of Windsor – told his recently widowed mother Queen Mary that he was going to give up the throne to marry twice-divorced Wallis Simpson, an American citizen.

As Prince of Wales, Edward – known within his family as David – had cut quite a dash in the USA. After he visited New York in 1924, grey flannel trousers and blue shirts with soft collars became all the rage. He liked things American, particularly jazz.

In 1930 Wallis Simpson and her businessman husband Ernest took a three-bedroom flat, with adjacent servants' rooms, at Bryanston Court, near the Edgware Road between Marylebone Road and Oxford Street. Their routine included weekly monitoring of the household accounts, which Ernest kept in a ledger, meticulously recording in his tiny handwriting the purchase of every pound of sugar and every bottle of vinegar. Wallis numbered among her American acquaintants the twin sister of Gloria Vanderbilt, who had become Lady Thelma Furness after marrying a British shipping magnate. Lady Thelma was a close friend of the Prince of Wales – who was smitten by her charms – and it was through her that Wallis Simpson was introduced to him.

From 1933 the Prince began to drop into the Simpsons' flat for a quiet drink at about 5 p.m., sometimes staying for dinner when Mr Simpson came home from the City. The Simpsons were occasionally invited for weekends at Fort Belvedere, the Prince's mock-Gothic hideaway in Windsor Park. Before a year was out it was common knowledge – in Mayfair – that Wallis Simpson had replaced Lady Thelma Furness as the object of the Prince's affections. Ernest Simpson quietly disappeared from the scene. The Prince decided he was going to marry Wallis and in 1935 she finally separated from her husband. 'David' wished to tell his father what was going on, but George V was ill and died in January 1936. His son was now the uncrowned King Edward VIII.

Most British subjects knew nothing of the royal romance because of a total press black-out on the story in the UK. Prime Minister Stanley Baldwin had personally obtained the silence of *The Times*. But there was nothing to stop the American press covering the romance, and this was done to the tune of half a million news items, making it one of the top stories of the 1930s. In the summer of 1936 the European and American press were full of reports and pictures of the new King and Wallis Simpson cruising in the Mediterranean, but all such coverage was removed from foreign publications before they reached the UK. Ellen Wilkinson, a Labour MP, asked in Parliament why magazines imported from the USA were arriving with pages missing.

In September Edward VIII invited Wallis to Balmoral Castle, where she introduced 'the three-decker toasted sandwich as a late supper item'. He had excused himself from the official opening of the Aberdeen Infirmary on the grounds that he was mourning his father, but that day he was seen meeting Wallis Simpson at the railway station; this soon became known as 'the Balmoral episode'. The British public began to get an inkling that something was afoot when pictures of Wallis started to appear in newspapers. On her return to London from Balmoral, she spent a week at Claridge's Hotel before moving into a four-storey house in Cumberland Terrace, near Regent's Park.

When David's brother 'Bertie' – the future King George VI – heard that Wallis Simpson had acted as hostess at Balmoral Castle and slept in Queen Mary's old room he wrote to his mother, telling her he feared that the royal way of life was being interfered with. Queen Mary was in the process of moving from Buckingham Palace to Marlborough House and it was here that she handed the problem over to the Prime Minister Stanley Baldwin. It was, she told him, 'a pretty kettle of fish.'[40]

Meanwhile, Wallis Simpson was proceeding with her divorce. Baldwin asked the King to persuade her to drop the proceedings but was told that he had no right to interfere in other people's private affairs. Wallis's lawyer had arranged for her divorce case to be heard in the Suffolk town of Ipswich, to avoid publicity, but twenty journalists found the court room and did not miss the fact that Ipswich was the birthplace of Cardinal Wolsey, the great churchman who had failed to obtain a divorce from Catherine of Aragon for Henry VIII. 'King's Moll Reno'd in Wolsey's Home Town' ran the headline of a US news report that Wallis Simpson had received her decree *nisi*. The way now seemed clear for a royal wedding, just before the Coronation: 'King Will Wed Wally', one of William Randolph Hearst's newspapers announced. Edward VIII believed, it claimed, that the most important thing for the peace and welfare of the world is an intimate understanding and relationship between England and America, and that his marriage with this very gifted lady may help to bring about that beneficial co-operation between English-speaking nations.[41]

Such American press speculation was felt by the British government to be seriously damaging to Britain's image abroad, particularly in the British Dominions, where the Crown, as Stanley Baldwin put it, was the 'last link of Empire that is left'.[42] The British press remained silent, but the King's private secretary warned him that the silence was about to be broken and that there was a danger the government might resign. 'If your Majesty will permit me to say so,' he wrote 'there is only one step which holds out any prospect of avoiding this dangerous situation and that is for Mrs Simpson to go abroad *without delay*.'[43]

The King was furious. On 16 November he saw Baldwin and told him that he intended to marry Wallis Simpson and if necessary would renounce the throne. That evening he dined with his mother and sister at Marlborough House. In Queen Mary's boudoir, after dinner, he broached the subject of Wallis – the love of his life. Their sympathy turned to astonishment when he told them that he was prepared to abdicate in order to marry her. Queen Mary implored her son to do no such thing – for the sake of the family and the country he must make a personal sacrifice. Her son pleaded with her to meet Wallis Simpson.

'Why will you not receive her?' he asked.

'Because she is an adventuress,' replied the Queen.[44]

When David informed his brother of his intention to abdicate if necessary, Bertie hurried to see their mother at Marlborough House. He did not want to succeed to the throne, he told her. If the job were thrust upon him he would do his best, but he feared that the whole fabric of royalty might collapse. 'He sobbed on my shoulder', Queen Mary later recalled, 'for a whole hour – on a sofa.'

On 3 December the British press broke its silence. *The Times* observed that 'there are many daughters of America whom the King might have married with the approval and rejoicing of his people,' but not one who 'had already two former husbands living from whom in succession she had obtained a divorce.' Not a single kind word was said about Wallis Simpson. Hostile crowds gathered outside her house, she received sackloads of abusive and threatening letters, a brick was thrown through her window. She told David she would leave him to save the situation, but that was the last thing he wanted. Escorted by Lord Brownlow and a detective, Wallis was driven down to Newhaven by the King's chauffeur and took the night ferry to France.

Queen Mary had picked up the papers breaking the news over breakfast at

Marlborough House. 'Really!' she is said to have exclaimed. 'This might be Roumania!' When David came to dine he told her that he had no desire to involve her or the royal family: this was something he must handle alone. He repeated that he could not bring himself to live as King without Wallis. Queen Mary listened with revulsion and incredulity as he read to her the Instrument of Abdication that he would deliver to Parliament. He would also make a broadcast to the nation from Windsor Palace.

Just before the broadcast, Wallis Simpson telephoned the King from abroad. He had taken it for granted that some of his staff would attend to arrangements for him to join her, but none of them did a thing; as he later said, they seemed to evaporate. Even his valet refused to go with him. It was left to Wallis to arrange for him to stay at the Rothschild home near Vienna.

Queen Mary was at Windsor Palace with Edward VIII when he broadcast his abdication speech on 10 December. He paid tribute to the comfort he had received from his mother 'during these hard days'. It had been settled that he would receive the title of Duke of Windsor and be granted an allowance of £25,000 a year. But he was never again to set foot in Britain without the permission of his brother, 'Bertie', who was now the uncrowned King George VI. By 11 p.m. the Duke of Windsor had boarded HMS *Fury* at Southampton and was on his way to a lifetime in exile. Queen Mary was by then back home in Marlborough House, sitting down to the warmth and quiet attention of her staff. 'All *this*', she said, 'thrown away for *that*.'[45]

George VI's daughters, the young Princesses Elizabeth and Margaret Rose, were understandably curious about all the fuss. According to a royal servant, when Margaret asked her sister if she knew what was going on, the future Queen Elizabeth II replied: 'I think Uncle David would like to marry Mrs Baldwin but Mr Baldwin does not like him to.'[46]

Queen Mary was the last member of the royal family to live in Marlborough House, which in 1959 became the administrative headquarters of the Commonwealth. There is a plaque with a carved frieze of Queen Mary's head on the corner of Marlborough House, in the Mall, and Marlborough Road.

EIGHT

Little America

'Grosvenor Square . . . is one of the finest squares in London. The air is as pure as it can be so near a great city. It is but a small distance from Hyde Park, round which I sometimes walk but oftener ride. It resembles Boston Common, much larger, and more beautiful with trees.'

Abigail Adams, letter to her sister, *1785*

Station
MARBLE ARCH

Gordon Selfridge
opens Selfridge's
Department Store
1906

OXFORD ST

PARK LANE

NORTH AUDLEY St

Abigail
Adams
1785

Eisenhower

U.S.
Embassy

GROSVENOR

SQUARE

PARK LANE

HYDE PARK

Franklin D
Roosevelt

Apsley House
The American Graces
Charm London
Society 1816

CURZON STREET

Henry
James
1869

John
Steinbeck
1943

PICCADILLY.

Theodore Roosevelt's Wedding 1888

ST GEORGE ST

CONDUIT STREET

STREET

NEW BOND STREET

Little America

STREET

OLD BOND STREET

Ritz Hotel
Mary Pickford and Douglas Fairbanks abandon their honeymoon 1920

GRAFTON ST

HAY HILL

BERKELEY STREET

DOVER ST

Mark Twain Complains about Brown's Hotel 1907

t Hotel:
Zelda
eat giant
ies

1844– Texan
1845 Legation

PICKERING PL

ST JAMES'S ST

PALL MALL

THE RITZ

PICCADILLY

St James Palace

Queen Mary (Wallis Simpson's Mother-in-law 1936)

MARLBOROUGH RD

s Hotel

REEN PARK

am

John Adams 1755

Benjamin West 1768

THE MALL

Station

ST JAMES'S PK

At the top of Marlborough Road, turning to the left, is the gatehouse of St James's Palace, a London landmark for more than four and a half centuries. St James's – built in 1533 for King Henry VIII on the site of a women's leprosy hospital – was a principal London residence of the Kings and Queens of England until 1809, when it was damaged by fire. Although now received at Buckingham Palace, foreign Ambassadors are still formally accredited to the Court of St James.

The first American Minister Plenipotentiary to Britain, John Adams, was received by George III at St James's Palace on 1 June 1785. He had hurried from Paris on the advice of the British Ambassador to be in time for the celebrations for the King's birthday on 4 June. 'The appointment of a minister from the United States to your Majesty's Court', he said to the King, 'will form an epoch in the history of England and of America. . . . restoring . . . the old good  nature and the old good humour.' Adams was visibly agitated while speaking, 'for I felt more than I did or could express'. Replying, with a tremor in his voice, King George said 'I have done nothing in the late contest but what I thought myself indispensably bound to do. . . . I was the last to consent to the separation; but the separation having been made, and having become inevitable, I have always said, as I say now, that I would be the first to meet the friendship of the United States as an independent power.'[1] Adams hoped to deal with British evacuation of western outposts in America, American debts to British creditors and a treaty of commerce between Britain and America, but none of these issues was quickly resolved.

John Trumbull, the American soldier–artist who was working on his painting of *The Declaration of Independence* in Paris, brought it to London at that time and met Adams. 'Mr Adams was taking leave of the Court of St James,' he wrote, 'and preparatory to the voyage to America, had the powder combed out of his hair. Its colour and natural curl were beautiful, and I took that opportunity to paint his portrait in the small Declaration of Independence.'[2]

The road leading from the St James's Palace gatehouse is St James's Street, where twenty-nine Americans, many of them lawyers, met at the Thatched House Tavern on 26 March 1774 to draw up petitions to the House of Commons, the House of Lords and King George III protesting against the closure of the port of Boston. Next morning Henry Laurens wrote to his son that the British Prime Minister, Lord North, 'may possibly fix the Badge of Slavery upon the Sea Coast, but this will hasten the beginning of Independence.'[3]

Off St James's Street, to the right, is a little alleyway called Pickering

Place. From 1842 to 1845, when the Republic of Texas had diplomatic ministers at the Court of St James, the Texan Legation was housed here. Opposite is St James's Place, where James Fenimore Cooper, author of *The Last of the Mohicans*, lived in 1828 while finishing *Notions of the Americans*, an attack on British prejudices against the USA. Cooper once waited more than an hour to catch a glimpse of King William IV coming out in his carriage through the St James's Palace gatehouse. 'I never',he noted, 'saw less apparent communion between a Sovereign and his people.'[4]

St James's Street leads to Piccadilly, which gets its odd name from the 'piccadill' or stiff frill worn in the reign of James I by young men as a ruff around their necks, or sewn to the cuffs and hems of their coats. In 1623 a tailor's house, near the windmill where Great Windmill Street is today, became known as 'Piccadilly Hall' – either because the owner's fortune came from making and selling piccadills or because it was on the very outskirts of town, as piccadills were attached to the edge of garments.

In the eighteenth century the road which took the name Piccadilly became lined with aristocratic mansions. As Horace Walpole wrote to a friend in 1759, 'When do you come? If it is not soon you will find a new town. I stared today at Piccadilly like a country squire! There are twenty new stone houses. At first I concluded that all the grooms that used to live there had got estates and built palaces.'

In modern Piccadilly, to the left off St James's Street, stands the Ritz Hotel – London's first major steel-framed building – opened in 1906. Douglas Fairbanks and Mary Pickford planned to spend their honeymoon here in 1920, but hundreds of English fans swarmed into the hotel dining room looking for them and they had to be spirited away to the country estate of the Duke and Duchess of Sutherland.

Almost opposite the Ritz, at 74–5 Piccadilly, an imposing 1920s building, with up-market car showrooms on the ground floor, is known as Devonshire House. It replaced the eighteenth-century Devonshire House which was the London home of the Dukes of Devonshire. At the time of the fifth Duke and his lively, enchanting, extravagant wife Georgiana, Devonshire House was the social centre of Whig opposition to the Tory government of George III. In its historic salons, which had long echoed with political gossip, every phase of the American colonists' struggle was fervently discussed. Those invited to the discussions in Devonshire House included Charles James Fox, Dr Johnson, Horace Walpole, Richard Brinsley Sheridan and Benjamin Franklin.

The original gates of Devonshire House are now at the edge of Green Park, overlooking Piccadilly. Green Park is said to be so called because the lepers from St James's hospital were buried here, so trees and grass were planted but no flowers. A small reservoir in the park was one of the places where Benjamin Franklin conducted experiments to discover the soothing effects of oil on choppy water.

Opposite the Devonshire House gates is Half Moon Street, where the American novelist and critic Henry James stayed at Fleming's Hotel in 1869, when he was twenty-six and visiting Europe for the first time. While he was away from America, his beloved cousin Minny Temple died of tuberculosis; her death, he later observed, marked the end of his youth. One of the greatest and most influential figures in American literature, in his most characteristic work James explored the conflict between the culture of the New World and the Old. Describing his first impression of London, he wrote:

> The uproar of Piccadilly hummed away at the end of the street, and the rattle of a heartless hansom passed close to my ears. A sudden horror of the whole place came over me, like a tiger-pounce of homesickness which had been watching its moment. London was hideous, vicious, cruel, and above all over-whelming. . . . I should have to go

out for my dinner ... and that effort assumed the form of a desperate and dangerous quest. It appeared to me that I would rather remain dinnerless, would rather even starve, than sally forth into that infernal town, where the natural fate of an obscure stranger would be trampled to death in Piccadilly and his carcass thrown into the Thames. I did not starve, however, and I eventually attached myself by a hundred human links to the dreadful, delightful city. That momentary vision of its smeared face and stony heart has remained memorable to me, but I am happy to say that I can easily summon up others.[5]

Another American who lodged in Half Moon Street was Edmund Wilson, author of *To the Finland Station* (1940), *The Scrolls from the Dead Sea* (1955) and *Patriotic Gore* (1962). He spent July 1945 in London, as a journalist for the *New Yorker*, covering the British post-war General Election which brought a landslide victory for the Labour Party. 'There is about London today,' he observed,

a certain flavour of Soviet Moscow. It surprises the Londoners if you remark on this and does not particularly please them. But people told me at the American Embassy that several other visitors who had been in Russia had said the same sort of thing. The regimentation and the tension imposed by the resistance to Germany have produced certain results very similar to those of the effort, during the twenties and thirties, to make the Soviet Union self-dependent.

The people look rather shabby, but almost everybody looks equally shabby. A great number are working for the government, and everyone has a definite task. There is the atmosphere of emergency and transition to which everybody has settled down; many things are left undone or unfinished – in London the repair of buildings, in Moscow the carrying out of civic projects – leaving what would in normal times be regarded as intolerable eyesores.

There is a great deal of getting oneself registered and of having to have passes in order to do things, and people are always lining up and waiting for hours in queues. There is also the relative democracy of manners – one of the striking changes in London – of people in the same boat who cannot afford to be too rude to one another, all threatened by a common danger and obliged to work together.[6]

While working in London, Wilson stayed at the Green Park Hotel in Half Moon Street. This seemed to be 'a condemned brothel,' he noted, 'with its lift that accommodated only two and that with the greatest difficulty.' The 'curious little nexus of streets' around the hotel was a 'whore district' where he met a girl called Odette, from Montmartre in Paris. In London since 1939, Odette worked during the day for the French Red Cross wrapping parcels and was knitting the director a sweater. In her green room, used 'purely for professional purposes', Odette became restless when Wilson 'simply wanted to lie and talk, even though I paid her for an hour and a half. She finally got out her knitting.' A small blonde English woman 'after I had been with Odette showed me my way back to Half Moon Street and was very nice about it – though I had to decline her invitation, telling her I had just been to see a friend. "You've had it? Charming," she said."[7]

Beyond Half Moon Street, the marked dip in the road is the natural valley of the River Tyburn, which used to cross Piccadilly before flowing through Green Park towards Buckingham Palace and into the Thames at Westminster. On the far side of the Tyburn valley is the Athenaeum Hotel, where John Steinbeck stayed when he came to London in June 1943 as a correspondent for the *Herald Tribune*. Looking out of his window, he discovered 'all of London I have ever read about is there.' He could see St Paul's, Whitehall, St James's Palace and 'a little further right is Big Ben, so close that I can set my watch by it.'[8] Steinbeck was famous in England,  particularly for *The Grapes of Wrath* (1939) – for which he had won America's Pulitzer Prize – and even though he was fairly new to newspaper journalism, his columns were carried in Britain in the mass-circulation *Daily Express*.

At the end of Piccadilly is Hyde Park Corner – not to be confused with Speakers' Corner, which is the corner of Hyde Park close to Marble Arch. To the left of the vast Hyde Park Corner traffic island is the back of the Buckingham Palace garden, and on the far side is the building that used to be St George's Hospital, where the American surgeon Philip Physick worked from 1789. Born in Philadelphia, Physick graduated from the University of Pennsylvania in 1785 and travelled to London to study under John Hunter, one of the foremost surgeons of the day and a noted experimenter. In 1792 Physick was elected a member of the Royal College of Surgeons in London. He later returned to work in the Pennsylvania Hospital and became Professor of Surgery at the University of Pennsylvania. The surgical technology which he originated or improved included needle forceps to tie deep vessels and a guillotine for performing tonsillectomies. Physick was the first American to use a stomach tube for gastric lavage and to employ animal ligatures, notably catgut, in surgery. He specialised in procedures involving the urinary tract and gall bladder.

The large, dark-yellow building at Hyde Park Corner, overlooking Hyde Park, is Apsley House, the home from 1816 of the Duke of Wellington and known as No. 1 London. It was one of those houses which were not for domestic but for public life – a life of continual entertaining in drawing rooms, ante-rooms and dining rooms. Here a sentence might be delivered which would echo around political England. An introduction could mean the beginning of a career, a deft criticism the dethronement of a policy.

Among the many guests entertained by 'The Iron Duke' at No. 1 London

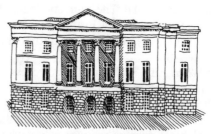

were three attractive young Baltimore sisters, Mary, Louisa and Elizabeth Caton, who were known in London Society as 'the American Graces'. They were the granddaughters of Charles Carroll, the longest-surviving signatory of the Declaration of Independence, and in Washington the sisters were the stars of the new Republican Court, where their good looks, their wealth and patrician connections had carried everything before them. Mary Caton was married to William Patterson, whose sister Elizabeth married the brother of the Emperor Napoleon, Jerome Bonaparte, later King of Westphalia. When Mary and her two unmarried sisters arrived in London, the sensation they made at the court of the Prince Regent was 'phenomenal'. After her husband died, Mary Patterson married the Duke of Wellington's brother, the Marquis of Wellesley, Lord Lieutenant of Ireland, and went on to reign supreme at the vice-regal court in Dublin. Louisa Caton married Colonel Sir Felton Hervey, then, as the widowed Lady Hervey, married the Marquis of Carmarthen, in due course becoming Duchess of Leeds. Elizabeth Caton married Lord Stafford and lived until 1862.

These inspiring examples encouraged a tidal wave of high-society transatlantic romances and marriages, against which one titled mother sounded a note of caution. 'Pray, don't marry an American,' wrote Lady Elizabeth Foster to her son Augustus when he was the British Minister (Ambassador) in Washington, 'or, if you must, let her be rich, for really the more I see of poverty the more detestable it appears to me.'[9] At the Coronation in 1901 of Queen Victoria's son, King Edward VII, twenty-four of the peeresses were of American birth.

From Apsley House, the six-laned Park Lane runs north towards Marble Arch alongside Hyde Park, the largest of London's parks, extending over 340 acres. The land which now forms the park was bequeathed to the monks of Westminster Abbey by Geoffrey de Mandeville soon after the Norman Conquest of 1066. A habitat for wild deer, bulls and boars, it was taken over as a royal hunting ground by King Henry VIII after the Dissolution of the Monasteries in 1536. His daughter, the future Elizabeth I, loved hunting here on horseback, using crossbows and handguns, with her girlhood sports companions Kate Ashley and Blanche Parry in attendance.

Hyde Park was opened to the public at the beginning of the seventeenth century, but when it was sold by a decree of Parliament in 1652, one of the new owners imposed an entrance fee of a shilling for each carriage and sixpence for each horse. In the reign of Charles II, Hyde Park was reclaimed as a royal park and a brick wall was built around it. An enclosure within the park – called first 'The Tour' and then 'The Ring' – became 'the rendez-vous of fashion and beauty. Everyone who had either sparkling eyes or a splendid equipage constantly repaired thither and the King seemed pleased with the place.'

When King William III went to live at Kensington Palace, he had three hundred lamps hung from trees along the road through Hyde Park to St James's Palace. This *'route du roi'*, known today as 'Rotten Row', was the first road in England to be lit at night. The lights did not deter the Hyde Park highwaymen, however, one of whom was hanged in 1687 for killing a woman who swallowed her wedding ring rather than give it up.

In the eighteenth century Hyde Park was used as a duelling ground and those who fought duels here included John Wilkes, John Temple, Richard Brinsley Sheridan and Charles James Fox. Hyde Park was also a place where families went to 'take the air' – although not very effectively, as Benjamin Franklin observed:

> Many families go out once a day to take the air; three or four persons in a coach, one perhaps sick; these go three or four miles or as many turns in Hyde Park with the glasses both up and closed, all breathing over and over again the same air they brought out of the town with them in the coach with the least change possible and rendering worse and worse every minute, and this they call taking the air.[10]

The Serpentine Lake in Hyde Park was created in 1730 for George II's Queen Caroline, who was a keen landscape gardener. In the exceptionally cold winter of 1763–4, the frozen Serpentine was used as a skating rink. Twenty-six-year-old Benjamin West, newly arrived in London, was applauded for demonstrating the Quaker Salute, as performed in Philadelphia. 'There never was a more brilliant exhibition than Hyde Park afforded on Sunday,' reported the *Morning Herald*, 'Ministers, Lords, Commons, all on the ice. . . . Mr West the celebrated painter, and Dr Hewitt were the best. They danced a minuet on their skates, to the admiration of the spectators.'[11]

Off Park Lane, to the right beyond the Hilton Hotel, is Curzon Street, on the left side of which, standing detached and well back from the street, is a Georgian stucco-fronted mansion with columns, pediment and bow-fronted wings. This is Crewe House, where the American Ambassador Frank B. Kellog lived in 1924–5. Before becoming Ambassador, Kellog served as special counsel for the United States government in cases against the Standard Oil Company and the Union Pacific,

Southern Pacific and Harriman railroads. He was elected President of the American Bar Association and a member of the Senate. After his ambassadorship in London, he served as Secretary of State from 1925 to 1929 in President Calvin Coolidge's Cabinet, and under him the Tacna-Arica dispute between Chile and Peru was settled. In response to a suggestion from the French Foreign Minister, Aristide Briand, for a treaty of perpetual friendship between France and the United States, Kellog proposed inviting the nations of the world to sign an agreement outlawing war. Sixty-three nations joined the Briand–Kellog Pact, and in 1929 Kellog was awarded the Nobel Peace Prize. From 1930 to 1935 he was a member of the Permanent Court of International Justice at The Hague.

Opposite Crewe House is Shepherd Market, a network of narrow streets and alleys designed in 1735 by Edward Shepherd, the architect of much of Mayfair. It was built on the site of a saturnalian fifteen-day annual May Fair (which gave its name to the whole district), held for the previous fifty years.

At the end of Curzon Street is Lansdowne Row, which gets its name from Lord Shelburne, Marquess of Lansdowne, who supported William Pitt, the Earl of Chatham's motion for the withdrawal of British troops from Boston. In the words of the official record, the Marquess of Lansdowne 'condemned the madness, injustice and infatuation of coercing the Americans into a blind and servile submission.' King George III called him 'the Jesuit of Berkeley Square'.[12] His house in Berkeley Square was often visited by Benjamin Franklin and later became the home of Wisconsin-born Gordon Selfridge, founder of Selfridge's department store in Oxford Street. He entertained members of the royal family there when it was his home from 1921 to 1929, The drawing room of Lansdowne House is now in the Museum of Arts, Philadelphia, and the dining room is in the Metropolitan Museum, New York.

Lansdowne Row leads to Berkeley Street. No. 17 Berkeley Street was the office of Miss Rosalind Wheeler, an American who was one of the first women to operate an estate agent's (real-estate) business in London. It failed, and in the early 1930s her body was found floating in the Thames near London Bridge.

On the far side of Berkeley Street, Hay Hill leads up to Dover Street. Brown's Hotel in Dover Street, was where Theodore Roosevelt began his honeymoon with Edith Kermit Carow, in 1886, and where Franklin and Eleanor Roosevelt spent part of their honeymoon in 1905. During his last visit to London in 1907, when he was seventy-two, Mark Twain stayed at Brown's and found it typical of the 'family hotels' which were

Mark Twain

a London speciality. God has not permitted them to exist elsewhere.
... All modern inconveniences are furnished, and some that have been
obsolete for a century. . . . They exist upon tradition. . . . Some quite
respectable Englishmen still frequent them through inherited habit
and arrested development; and many Americans also, through igno-
rance and superstition. The rooms are as interesting as the Tower of
London, but older I think. Older and dearer. The lift was a gift from
William the Conqueror, some of the beds are prehistoric. They repre-
sent geological periods. Mine is the oldest.[13]

At the top of Dover Street is Grafton Street, where Benjamin Franklin held
clandestine conversations with Lord Howe and his sister, who were related by
marriage – through the out-of-wedlock daughter of King George I – to the
royal family. When Lord Howe and his sister asked Franklin what were the
grounds of the quarrel between Great Britain and the colonies, he said it was
'a matter of punctilio which two or three sensible people might settle in an
hour.' In 1844, Phineas T. Barnum, creator of 'the Greatest Show on Earth',
stayed in Grafton Street, when he brought the tiny, seven-year-old Charles
Stratton to London from New England as 'Tom Thumb'. Barnum's young
singing-and-dancing star became the darling of the British aristocracy and
received an invitation to Buckingham Palace, where he performed a horn-
pipe for Queen Victoria and gave his impression of Napoleon.

At the end of Grafton Street is New Bond Street. Turning left into it, the
second street on the right is Conduit Street. Living here in the late seventeenth century was William Law, the Scottish financier who invented the
term 'millionaire' and founded the ill-fated Mississippi Company. Obliged to
leave London after a duel, Law persuaded the French regent, the Duc
d'Orléans, to allow him to set up in Paris a private bank modelled on the
Bank of England, and a company with a monopoly of commerce in
Louisiana. As reports spread of gold and silver discovered on the banks of
the Mississippi, the price of the Mississippi Company's shares rose fortyfold.
The increase was fuelled by the unrestrained issue of paper money from
Law's bank. In 1719 the 'Mississippi Bubble' burst when prudent speculators
began to sell their shares for government *billets d'état*, which they used to
buy precious metal, diamonds or land. As the value of these *billets d'état*
depreciated rapidly, people desperately exchanged them for household items
such as wax and soap, paying astronomical prices. At the end of 1720 Law
was forced to flee France. The French government wound up the Mississippi
Company and accepted responsibility for its $340 million debts.

To the left from Conduit Street is St George's Street, taking its name from
St George's church, Hanover Square. In 1880 the British novelist George
Eliot, then aged sixty-one, was married in this church to the American
banker John Walter Cross, an old family friend who was twenty years her
junior. The man she had lived with for the previous twenty-six years, George
Henry Lewes, had recently died, and George Eliot herself died within a few

months of her marriage. As Mary Ann Evans, her translations of Spinoza's *Tractatus Theologico-Politicus* and Feuerbach's *Essence of Christianity* had brought her into contact with the philosopher Herbert Spencer, who became a close friend, and it was through Spencer that she met Lewes, who suggested that she try writing fiction. She created her pseudonym by combining his first name with Eliot, which she chose because it was 'a good mouth-filling, easily pronounced word'. *Adam Bede, The Mill on the Floss, Silas Marner, Middlemarch* and *Daniel Deronda* made George Eliot one of the foremost novelists of her time.

In 1852, while working as assistant editor of the *Westminster Review*, George Eliot recorded, in a letter to her friend Sarah Hennel, an anecdote about Ralph Waldo Emerson, the American author of *English Traits*. Emerson had angered the Scottish political philosopher Thomas Carlyle by saying that he did not believe in the Devil. Carlyle, 'to convert him took him amongst all the horrors of London – gin shops etc – and finally to the House of Commons plying him at every turn with the question "Do you believe in the Devil noo?" '[14] In 1877, Henry James met Herbert Spencer while visiting George Eliot. When

George Henry Lewes introduced me to him as an American [James wrote] it seemed to me that at this fact, coupled with my name, his attention was aroused. . . . But something instantly happened to separate me from him, and soon after he went away. The Lewes were very urbane and friendly. . . . The great George Eliot herself is both sweet and superior, and has a delightful expression in her large, long, pale, equine face. I had my turn at sitting beside her and being conversed with in a low, but most harmonious tone.

Also married in St George's church, in 1888, were Theodore Roosevelt and Edith Kermit Carow. Their best man was Sir Cecil Spring, who was later appointed British Ambassador in Washington. 'Characteristically,' Roosevelt wrote of Spring, 'he had me married in bright orange gloves which I accepted with a calm wholly unwarranted.' 'Dear Springy', wrote the bride's sister, 'was so delightful and like himself when I went to put on Edith's veil. I warned Theodore to  start immediately for the church as it was a foggy day and they were intensely occupied in a discussion over the population of an island in the southern Pacific.' Roosevelt was described in the church register as '28, widower, ranchman'.[15]

Facing St George's church from Hanover Square is the 1831 bronze statue of William Pitt the Younger, the son of William Pitt, Earl of Chatham. Pitt the Younger became Prime Minister of Great Britain in 1783, when he was only twenty-four, and went on to lead the new Toryism then emerging. While this statue was being placed on its pedestal one morning, the workmen went off to have their breakfasts; during their absence a rope was thrown around the neck of the figure of Pitt and 'a vigorous attempt was made by several sturdy reformers to pull it down'. Someone rushed to tell the sculptor's secretary what was happening, but he said with a smile, 'The clamps are leaded and they may pull till doomsday.'[16]

No. 25 Hanover Square was where Nathaniel Hawthorne lived with his family in 1855 while exploring London and recording his impressions for his *English Notebooks*. He was appalled by what he saw of the life of London's poor. Because their housing was so bad, the East Enders conducted much of their social life outdoors, making their streets a 'sky-roofed saloon, so regally hung with its sombre canopy of coal-smoke.' When lumps of coal fell from an overloaded cart into the muddy road, Hawthorne saw half a dozen women and children rush to retrieve them, 'like a flock of hens and chickens gobbling up some spilt corn.' In contrast to the fattened carcasses '[which] Englishmen loved to gaze at in the market . . . stupendous halves of mighty beefs, or muttons ornamented with carved bas-reliefs of fat on their ribs and shoulders', the shops for the poor sold only 'bits and gobbets of lean meat, selvages snipt off the steaks, tough and stringy morsels, bare bones smitten away from joints by the cleaver; tripe, liver, bullocks' feet, or whatever else was cheapest and divisible into the smallest lots.' On every street corner there was a spirit vault – known colloqially as the gin shop – set off with 'the magnificence of gilded door-posts'. Ragged children came with 'old shaving-mugs or broken-nosed teapots' to get 'a little poison' for their parents. 'Inconceivably sluttish women' chatted at the counter from noontime, 'quaffing off the mixture with a relish', and men drank there all day as long as they had 'a halfpenny left.'[17]

Left from Hanover Square is Brook Street, towards the end of which, on the left, is London's most exclusive hotel, Claridge's. Zelda and Scott Fitzgerald stayed here in June 1921, when twenty-one-year-old Zelda was four months pregnant. They were entertained by Lady Randolph Churchill – 'Jennie' Jerome – and ate 'strawberries as big as tomatoes'. Now twenty-five years old, Scott Fitzgerald, from St Paul, Minnesota, had been educated in private schools and encouraged by his parents, who were not affluent, to dream of material and social success. He dropped out of Princeton College to accept an army commission and met Zelda Sayre, when she was seventeen, at a country-club dance in Montgomery, Alabama, where her father was the local judge. Zelda was a beautiful, self-willed Southern belle and Scott determined to earn enough money to marry her. They became engaged, but when Scott went to work for a New York advertising agency

Claridge's

Zelda broke it off. Scott then returned to St Paul to revise a novel he had written earlier, but which had been rejected. When the novel was published as *This Side of Paradise* in March 1920, it was an instant success and the following month the couple were married.

Their extended honeymoon in New York was the start of what Fitzgerald called 'the greatest, gaudiest spree in history' – a succession of all-night parties and drunken escapades that made Scott and Zelda the focus of scandalised attention wherever they went. The hero of *This Side of Paradise* found inner peace only when he lost his fortune and came to realise that his greatest asset was the unselfishness buried deep in his nature. Despite this implied moral warning, the novel was to influence a generation of young people to seek escape from disillusionment through pleasure in fleeting affairs and temporary loyalties.

After the birth of their daughter, 'Scottie', Zelda and Scott began to fear the pressures of their fame and popularity. Scott's *The Beautiful and the Damned* (1922) told the story of a wealthy young artist and his wife destroyed by their extravagance and dissipation. In 1924 Scott and Zelda retreated to live in the south of France with the American expatriate community, which was celebrated by Ernest Hemingway and others as the 'lost generation'. Scott's *The Great Gatsby*, published in 1925, was to prove his most balanced and artistically successful treatment of the American Dream ultimately corrupted.

In the late 1920s Scott began to drink heavily and Zelda became obsessed with the idea of a career in ballet, practising in her room night and day. She was offered the chance of joining the San Carlo Opera Ballet in Naples but turned it down. During the winter of 1928–9 she wrote a series of six sketches about the lives of isolated young heiresses and ballerinas, five of which were published as co-authored by herself and Scott, and one under Scott's name only. In 1930 Zelda suffered a severe mental breakdown, followed by another in 1932, the year in which her novel *Save Me the Waltz* was published. An exhibition of her paintings and drawings was held in New York the following year, but she was diagnosed schizophrenic and spent most of the rest of her life in Highland Hospital, Asheville, where she died in a fire with nine other women patients in 1948.

Scott Fitzgerald's novel *Tender is the Night* (1934), about a young psychiatrist married to a schizophrenic, was not well received. His attempt to establish a script-writing career in Hollywood failed, but he found emotional stability living there quietly with the British gossip columnist Sheilah Graham until his death from a heart attack in 1940.

William 'Wild Bill' Donovan, the wartime director of the Office of Strategic Services (OSS) – forerunner of the CIA – stayed at Claridge's in 1940 while on a special mission for President Roosevelt to assess British ability and will to continue fighting Germany. Harry Hopkins – also a Roosevelt personal representative – stayed at the hotel in 1941. He used to leave highly classified documents scattered about his room and once sent a suit to the hotel dry-cleaners with top-secret cables in the pocket. General Eisenhower was assigned a suite of rooms at Claridge's in 1942, after he had been named Commander-in-Chief of the American Forces in Europe and was spending a month meeting British leaders. He disliked the hotel because the black-and-gold décor resembled a Hollywood set, and his bedroom was painted 'whorehouse pink'. He moved to the Dorchester Hotel before going to North Africa in November. Arthur Goldberg, an OSS official, invited Samuel Zygelbojm, the representative of the Jewish Board in the Polish government-in-exile, to dinner at Claridge's in 1943, when he had to tell him that President Roosevelt had refused his request to bomb the railroads leading to Nazi concentration camps. Zygelbojm committed suicide the next day.

Beyond Claridge's, 75 Brook Street is the American Chamber of Commerce. Opposite, on the corner, is 9 Grosvenor Square. An inscription on its wall reads:

> In this house lived John Adams, Minister of Great Britain, May 1785 to March 1788, afterwards second President of the United States. From here his daughter Abigail was married to Colonel William Stephens Smith, first secretary to the Legation and an officer in the revolutionary army on Washington's staff. John Adams and Abigail, his wife, through character and personality, did much to create understanding between the two English-speaking nations. In memory this tablet is placed by Colonial Dames of America. 1933.

This house was discovered in 1785 by Abigail Adams. While her husband spent a week preparing the speech he would deliver to King George III at the Court of St James, she went house-hunting and 'my good genius carried me to one in Grosvenor Square.' The house was smaller than their home in Paris, but Abigail liked the location and her husband signed a twenty-one-month lease at a rent of £160 per year. On the ground floor were two dining rooms – one for the family and one 'which will hold fifteen persons with ease' – plus a 'long room', which John Adams turned into 'an office for doing Publick business'. On the first floor were the main drawing room, a sitting room, a small breakfast room and a 'long room' where, wrote nineteen-year-old Nabby Adams, 'Pappa has put his Library'. Nabbey's bedroom was on the third floor and from her window she could see 'the tops of all the Houses which surround us – and I can count a hundred Chimneys.' The eight servants lived in rooms on the fourth floor. At the Adamses' first major dinner party, on 1 October 1785,

> the whole diplomatic corps dined here; that is, his Lordship the Marquis of Carmarthen, and all the foreign ministers, fifteen in all. . . . As good luck would have it, Captain Hay returned from the West Indies, and presented us with a noble turtle, weighing a hundred and fourteen pounds, which was dressed upon this occasion. [18]

No women were invited to the dinner and Abigail Adams herself had to eat elsewhere.

Among those who came to 9 Grosvenor Square to see John Adams on official business were American sea-captains angry at the seizure of American seamen by British Navy press-gangs in the Port of London. Two of the men so seized – whose cases Adams put before the British Foreign Secretary, the Marquis of Carmarthen – were 'John Cowley, a native of the City of New York' and 'a negro man, called Primus'. According to Captain John Douglass, the press-gang seized the men, forced them 'on board his Majesty's brig'. They then came on board his vessel and tried to search it but his chief mate stopped them and told them in no uncertain terms that the men were American citizens.

John Adams was the first of five United States Ministers to the Court of St James who became President. He served as Minister 1785–8 and as President 1797–1801; James Monroe was Minister 1803–7 and President 1817–25; John Quincy Adams was Minister 1815–17 and President 1825–9; Martin Van Buren was Minister 1831–2 and President 1835–40; James Buchanan was Minister 1853–6 and President 1857–61. No Ambassadors have become President. The title changed from Minister to Ambassador in 1893. The full title is 'Ambassador Extraordinary and Plenipotentiary', 'Extraordinary' meaning that the Ambassador is the personal representative of the President to Her Majesty the Queen, and 'Plenipotentiary' indicating full power to negotiate. The Ambassador is responsible not only for the work of the various sections of the Embassy, but also for the activities of all US executive departments and agencies with representatives in Britain, apart from US military commands.

The Embassy is divided into six main sections: Political; Economic and Commercial; Consular; Public Affairs; Administrative; and Defense. The Defense Section (Department of Defense) is headed by the Defense Attaché and – with representatives from the Air Force, Army and Navy – is responsible for liaison with British defence and military leaders and with the US military commands in the United Kingom. It acts as advisor to the Ambassador on all military matters. The Embassy offices – known as 'the Chancery' – were first located in Great Cumberland Place and later in Piccadilly, Portland Place and Grosvenor Gardens. In 1938 they were moved to No. 1 Grosvenor Square. During the Second World War, when the Chancery was on one side and General Eisenhower's headquarters on the other, Grosvenor Square was nicknamed 'Eisenhowerplatz' and 'Little America'.

In 1947 the Duke of Westminster donated land in the centre of Grosvenor Square for a memorial to President Roosevelt. The bronze statue by Sir William Reid Dick was paid for by donations of not more than five shillings per person from two hundred thousand British subscribers. Thousands of people gathered in Grosvenor Square on 12 April 1948 – the third anniversary of Roosevelt's death – for its ceremonial unveiling by his widow, Eleanor Roosevelt. In the words of one of those present, 'The whole Square, newly turfed, looked like a perfect green carpet patterned with beds of hyacinths, narcissi and wall-flowers.' Members of the royal family in attendance included the King George VI and Queen Elizabeth, Princess Elizabeth and the Duke of Edinburgh, Princess Margaret, the Duke and Duchess of Gloucester, the

Franklin D. Roosevelt

Duchess of Kent and her three children, and Princess Alice, Countess of Athlone, and the Earl of Athlone. Also present were Prime Minister Clement Attlee with members of his government, and Winston Churchill, the Leader of the Opposition.

When the King, Mrs Roosevelt and the Chairman of the Memorial Committee of Pilgrims, Viscount Greenwood, were assembled on the dais, the Archbishop of Canterbury opened the proceedings and the boys' choir of St Paul's Cathedral sang the 23rd Psalm. Then followed the King's speech, in which he welcomed Mrs Roosevelt 'with pleasure and yet with sadness'. He went on to say that her husband was

> one of the outstanding men of our time and it was she who supported him through all the trials which he had to face. She shared to the full with him the heavy burden of his public career, and as a delegate to the United Nations she is now carrying on his work by championing the principles of freedom and humanity which inspired him throughout his life.

When his speech was over, the King accompanied Mrs Roosevelt along the wide stone path towards the statue, wrapped in two large Union Jacks which fell away when she pulled the white cord. In the quietness that immediately ensued only the gentle splashing of the fountains on either side of the memorial could be heard, until, with startling suddenness, the Band of the Royal Marines played the first chords of 'The Star-Spangled Banner', with the King standing at the salute. Wreaths were laid at the foot of the memorial, the US Ambassador made a speech and the ceremony closed with the singing of 'The Battle Hymn of the Republic', a short prayer and blessing by the Archbishop, and the sounding of reveille by fifteen trumpeters.[19]

Grosvenor Square now has along the entire length of its west side the modern offices of the American Embassy, completed in 1960. The US Department of State competition for the design of a new Chancery for London was won by the American architect Eero Saarenin, who also designed the Gateway Arch in St Louis, Missouri, and the US Air Force Academy Chapel in Colorado Springs. The architect's brief called for a building to house all the major sections of the Embassy under one roof, in a style to blend with the exist-

ing architecture of the square. It has over six hundred rooms on nine floors, providing 225,000 square feet of working space for more than seven hundred employees, less than half of whom are Americans. Only six floors, including a 'penthouse' set back from the façade, are above ground level, to conform in height with the surrounding buildings; the remaining three floors are below ground. The building is made of pre-cast reinforced concrete, faced with Portland stone and decorated with gold anodised aluminium. The gilded eagle has a thirty-five-foot wing-span and its design was inspired by a wooden eagle carved before Independence and now housed in a New England museum.

North Audley Street leads from the statue of President Eisenhower, in front of the Chancery, to Oxford Street and Selfridge's. Gordon Selfridge began working in Marshall Field, Chicago, in 1877, and soon became a junior partner. In 1902 he bought his own Chicago store but did not like competing with his old firm, so he sold out and left for Europe. In 1906 he decided to build a store in Oxford Street. Sam Waring of Waring and Gillow, the furniture makers, agreed to back him on condition that he did not sell furniture – a condition that Selfridge always honoured.

The Selfridge's building was conceived in a giant Ionic order by Chicago architect Daniel Burnham, in consultation with Frank Swales. Executed by the English architect R. F. Atkinson, and completed in 1928 by Sir John Burnet, the building was originally intended to have a huge tower. There were 130 departments on eight floors, covering six acres, with goods displayed as if in an exhibition, at eye-level, on counters where they could be handled by customers. The cosmetics and perfumery departments were put immediately inside the main entrance to entice passers-by, and women, alone or together, were made particularly welcome in the spacious restaurant.

Selfridge's

Gordon Selfridge invented 'spending a day at Selfridge's', the 'bargain basement' and 'only so many shopping days to Christmas'. He brought a window-dresser from Chicago and kept the attractive displays floodlit when the store was closed. In his seventies, lonely after the death of his wife, Selfridge began to shower gifts on young actresses. Living above his substantial income, he ran up debts of more than £250,000 to the Inland Revenue and £120,000 to the store. In 1939 his fellow directors voted him off the board and gave him an annual pension of £2000. He died in 1947, aged ninety. In 1952 Selfridge's was bought by Lewis's Investment Trust and Charles Clore of the British Shoe Corporation.

Shoppers turning right out of Selfridge's and continuing up Oxford Street towards Marble Arch follow the fatal route of past Londoners who were said to have 'gone west' – not to great open spaces at a western frontier, but from Newgate Prison, in the City of London, on the three-mile three-hour journey in a cart called 'the lurch', to be hanged in public at Tyburn.

'I have walked the streets a great deal . . . and always take a certain pleasure in being in the midst of human life. . . . These broad, thronged streets are so evidently the veins and arteries of an enormous city. London is . . . in every one of them.'

Nathaniel Hawthorne,
The English Notebooks, *6 December 1857*

Sources

Introduction

1 A. F. Pollard (ed.), *The Reign of Henry VII from Contemporary Sources*, 1913, Vol 2, pp. 326–7.
2 Captain Gonzalo Fernandez de Oviedo, *General and Natural History of the Indies*, 1547, ch. 4; see J.M. Cohen (ed.), *The Four Voyages of Christopher Columbus*, 1969, p. 33.
3 Ben Jonson, George Chapman and John Marston, *Eastward Hoe*, 1605, act III, scene ii.

Chapter 1: The Tower of London

1 William Kent, *London for Americans*, 1950, pp. 161–2.
2 Robert Latham and William Matthews (eds.), *The Diary of Samuel Pepys*, 1970–83, Vol. 7, p. 30; 30 January 1666.
3 Ibid., Vol. 8, p. 595; 29 December 1667.
4 Ibid., Vol. 9, p. 446; 12 February 1669.
5 Ibid., Vol. 9, p. 337; 25 October 1668.
6 William Kent, *London for the Literary Pilgrim*, 1949, p. 158.
7 Latham and Matthews, *The Diary of Samuel Pepys*, Vol. 5, p. 283; 29 September 1664.
8 Ibid., Vol. 3, p. 1; 1 January 1662.
9 Ibid., Vol. 2, p. 115; 5 June 1661.
10 Ibid., Vol. 7, p. 113; 30 April 1666.
11 Ibid., Vol. 3, p. 4; 6 January 1662.
12 Ibid., Vol. 8, p. 164; 12 April 1667.
13 Ibid., Vol. 7, pp. 289–94; 2–5 September 1666.
14 Governor Winthrop, in J. E. Wrench, *Transatlantic London*, 1949, p. 79.
15 Oliver Cromwell, ibid., p. 80.
16 Latham and Matthews, *The Diary of Samuel Pepys*, Vol. 3, pp. 108–9; 14 June 1662.
17 Benjamin Silliman, *A Journal of Travels in England, Holland and Scotland*, 1820, Vol. 1, pp. 187–8.
18 Kent, *London for Americans*, p. 143.
19 Nathaniel Hawthorne, *Complete Works*, ed. George Parsons Lathrope, 1883, Vol. 8, p. 106.

20 Wrench, *Transatlantic London*, p. 34.
21 David Duncan Wallace, *The Life of Henry Laurens*, 1915, p. 388.
22 John Quincy Adams, *The Diary of John Quincy Adams 1794–1845*, 1928, p. 16.
23 Dexter Perkins, *The Monroe Doctrine, 1823–1826*, 1927, p. 91.
24 Ernest R. May, *The Making of the Monroe Doctrine*, 1975, p. 199.

Chapter 2: The City

1 Ben Jonson, George Chapman and John Marston, *Eastward Hoe*, 1605, act III, scene ii.
2 William Penn, letter to Robert Turner, 5 March 1681, in Catherine Owens Peare, *William Penn*, 1966, p. 215.
3 Peare, *William Penn*, p. 225.
4 Christopher Hill, *Reformation to Industrial Revolution*, 1980, p. 200.
5 J. E. Wrench, *Transatlantic London*, 1949, p. 91.
6 Ibid., pp. 94–5.
7 John G. Whittier (ed.), *The Journal of John Woolman*, 1882, p. 261.
8 Howard Zinn, *A People's History of the United States*, 1980, p. 24.
9 John Stow, *The Survey of London*, ed. H.B. Wheatley, 1912, p. 131.
10 Geoffrey Chaucer, *Troilus and Criseyde*, Book 5, verse 169.
11 Quotations relating to Thomas Weston and the Pilgrim Fathers from George F. Willison, *Saints and Strangers*, 1966, pp. 50–130.
12 Stow, *The Survey of London*, p. 130.
13 Ibid., pp. 130–1.
14 Quotations relating to Thomas Morton and Merry Mount from Willison, *Saints and Strangers*, pp. 163–8.
15 Quotations relating to coffee houses from Felix Barker and Peter Jackson, *London: 2000 Years of a City and Its People*, 1974, p. 173.
16 William Kent, *London for Americans*, 1950, p. 45.
17 Rev. John Newton, *The Journal of a Slave Trader*, ed. Bernard Martin and Mark Spurrell, 1962, pp. 98, 103.
18 Hill, *Reformation to Industrial Revolution*, p. 227.
19 Peter Fryer, *Staying Power: the History of Black People in Britain*, 1984, p. 17.
20 Michael Craton, *Sinews of Empire*, 1974, p. 119.
21 Fryer, *Staying Power*, p. 17.
22 Zinn, *A People's History of the United States*, pp. 35 and 36.
23 Ibid., p. 88.
24 Nathaniel Hawthorne, *Complete Works*, ed. George Parsons Lathrope, 1883, Vol. 7, pp. 363–403.
25 Kent, *London for Americans*, p. 68.
26 S. Bannister, *William Paterson, the Merchant Statesman and Founder of the Bank of England*, 1857, p. 49.
27 Hill, *Reformation to Industrial Revolution*, p. 184.
28 Dillon, Lloyd George, Baldwin, Swing and Hemingway quotations from David Dimbleby and David Reynolds, *An Ocean Apart*, 1988, pp. 25, 93, 94, 95.

29 Quotations relating to George Peabody and the Peabody Trust from Peabody Trust, *125 Years of Caring for Londoners – Peabody Trust 1862–1987*, 1987; and Kent, *London for Americans*, pp. 151–5.

30 Samuel Curwen, *Journal and Letters of an American Refugee in England 1775–1784*, 1842, pp. 4 and 38.

31 Wrench, *Transatlantic London*, p. 54.

32 Brian N. Morton, *Americans in London*, 1988, pp. 1, 2, 255–6.

33 London Corporation, Common Council, *Addresses presented from the Court of Common Council to the King . . . between 23rd October 1760 and 12th October 1770*, Guildhall Library, 1778, pp. 39, 41, 42, 43.

34 Zinn, *A People's History of the United States*, p. 65.

35 Guildhall quotations from London Corporation, Common Council, *Addresses, Remonstrances and Petitions commencing 24th June 1769*, Guildhall Library, 1778, pp. 52, 64, 73, 84, 85–6, 93, 114–15, 116–17, 147–9.

36 Sir Edwin Sandys is characterised as 'the founder-in-chief of representative government in America' in the dedication of Matthew Page Andrews, *The Soul of the Nation*, 1943.

37 'The Three Charters of the Virginia Company of London with seven related documents', in *Jamestown 350th Anniversary Historical Booklets Nos 1–5*, ed. E. G. Swem, pp. 45 and 47.

38 Gondomar, letter to King Philip III of Spain, in Alexander Brown, *The Genesis of the United States*, 1897, Vol. 1, p. 246.

39 'The Three Charters of the Virginia Company of London with seven related documents', in *Jamestown 350th Anniversary Historical Booklets Nos 1–5*, ed. E. G. Swem, p. 62.

40 Wesley Frank Craven, 'The Virginia Company of London', in *Jamestown 350th Anniversary Historical Booklets Nos 1–5*, ed. E. G. Swem, p. 23.

41 Wrench, *Transatlantic London*, p. 51.

42 Susan Myra Kingsbury (ed.), *Records of the Virginia Company*, 1906–35, Vol. 1, p. 51.

43 Ibid., Vol. 1, p. 566.

44 Wrench, *Transatlantic London*, p. 51.

45 Kingsbury, *Records of the Virginia Company*, Vol. 3, p. 484.

46 Wrench, *Transatlantic London*, p. 52.

47 Ibid., p. 52.

48 Kingsbury, *Records of the Virginia Company*, Vol. 1, p. 5.

49 John Wesley, *An Extract of the Rev. Mr. John Wesley's Journal from his Embarking for Georgia to his Return to London*, 1743, pp. 49–50.

50 Benjamin Franklin, *Autobiography*, 1948 edn, pp. 34–41.

51 Daniel Defoe, *Moll Flanders*, 1981 edn, pp. 8, 327, 331, 341.

52 Quotations relating to Captain John Smith from Captain John Smith, *A True Relation of Virginia*, ed. C. Deane, 1866, pp. 66, 12, 14, 15, 33, 34, 37, 43, 49, 53, 59, 69, 74, 75, 77.

53 London Corporation, Common Council, *Addresses, Remonstrances and Petitions . . . commencing 24th June 1769*, Guildhall Library, 1778, pp. 118–26.

Chapter 3: St Paul's Cathedral

1 Thomas Paine, *Common Sense*, 1859 edn, p. 37.
2 Alfred Own Aldridge, *Man of Reason – the Life of Thomas Paine*, 1959, p. 109.
3 Thomas Paine, *The Rights of Man*, ed. H. Collins, 1969, p. 232.
4 William Kent, *London for Americans*, 1950, p. 76.
5 Ibid., p. 76.
6 Nathaniel Hawthorne, *Complete Works*, ed. George Parsons Lathrope, 1883, Vol. 8, p. 91.
7 Benjamin Silliman, *A Journal of Travels in England, Holland and Scotland*, 1820, Vol. 1, pp. 199–200.
8 Kent, *London for Americans*, p. 135.
9 Ibid., p. 87.
10 Ibid., p. 122.
11 Ibid., p. 194.
12 J. E. Wrench, *Transatlantic London*, 1949, p. 54.

Chapter 4: Fleet Street

1 John White, letter to Richard Hakluyt, in Nigel Hamilton, *America Began at Greenwich*, 1976, p. 20.
2 Walter G. Bell, *More About Unknown London*, 1921, p. 18.
3 Samuel Johnson, *Taxation no Tyranny*, 1775, pp. 6, 7, 38, 63, 64, 89.
4 John Wilkes, *Essay on Woman*, 1871 edn, p. 14.
5 Brian N. Morton, *Americans in London*, 1988, p. 109.

Chapter 5: Inns of Court and Law Courts

1 Lord Diplock, *Links Between the Middle Temple and the United States of America*, 1971.
2 John Betjeman, *2 Temple Place*, n.d., p. 1.
3 The analysis of Judge Blackstone's influence on American law is from notes supplied to the author in June 1985 by Professor W. A. Carroll.
4 Thomas More, *Utopia*, ed. Paul Turner, 1965, p. 119.
5 John Rastell, *An Interlude of the Four Elements*, 1519, pp. 33, 34, 35, 37.
6 Rt Hon. Sir Robert Megarry, *An Introduction to Lincoln's Inn*, 1980.
7 S. Graveson (ed.), *The History of the Life of Thomas Ellwood written by his own hand*, 1906 edn, p. 4.
8 Benjamin Franklin, *Autobiography*, 1948 edn, pp. 41–2.
9 William Kent, *London for Americans*, 1950, pp. 126–7.

Chapter 6: Theatreland

1 Latham and Matthews, *The Diary of Samuel Pepys*, 1970–83, Vol. 6, p. 120; 7 June 1665.
2 Recollections by Ellen Hill, in Gavin Weightman and Steve Humphries, *The Making of Modern London 1815–1914*, 1983, p. 167.
3 James Boswell, *London Journal 1762–1763*, ed. Frederick A. Pottle, 1950, p. 264.
4 Brian N. Morton, *Americans in London*, 1988, p. 48.
5 Ibid., p. 49.
6 Ibid., pp. 50–1.
7 Ibid., p. 274.
8 Ibid., p. 275.
9 William Saroyan, *The Adventures of Wesley Jackson*, 1957, pp. 167, 174, 175, 206, 207.
10 J. M.Barrie, *Charles Frohman: A Tribute*, 1915, p. 6.
11 John Gay, *The Beggar's Opera*, 1728, act I, scene vii.
12 Charles Dickens Jnr, *Dickens's Dictionary of London*, 1885, p. 92.
13 Morton, *Americans in London*, p. 120.
14 Bradley Smith, *The American Way of Sex*, 1978, p. 53.
15 Ben Weinreb and Christopher Hibbert, *The London Encyclopaedia*, 1983, p. 451.
16 Elkanah Watson, *Men and Times of the Revolution: Memoirs of Elkanah Watson*, 1856, p. 175.
17 Weinreb and Hibbert, *The London Encyclopaedia*, p. 452.
18 Henry Mayhew, *London's Underworld*, ed. Peter Quennell, 1983, p. 39.
19 Morton, *Americans in London*, p. 247.
20 Quotations relating to Patience Lovell Wright from an unpublished essay by Jo Anne Balderson, 1988; and J. E. Wrench, *Transatlantic London*, 1949, pp. 159–62.
21 William Kent, *London for Americans*, 1950, p. 191.
22 Quotations relating to Hawaiian royalty in London from an unpublished essay by Peg Foster, 1988.
23 Wrench, *Transatlantic London*, p. 137.
24 Smith, *The American Way of Sex*, p. 62.
25 Benjamin Franklin, *Autobiography*, 1948 edn, pp. 120–1.
26 Kent, *London for Americans*, p. 58.

Chapter 7: Westminster and Whitehall

1 William Kent, *London for Americans*, 1950, p. 126.
2 Clements R. Markham (ed.), *The Journal of Christopher Columbus and documents of John Cabot and Corte Real*, 1893, pp. 197–9.
3 Lorenzo Pasqualigo, letter to his brothers Alvise and Francesco Pasqualigo, 23 August 1497, in Markham, *The Journal of Christopher Columbus*, pp. 201–2.
4 Soucino, letter to Sforza, Duke of Milan, 18 December 1497, in Markham, *The Journal of Christopher Columbus*, pp. 202–3.

5 A. F. Pollard (ed.), *The Reign of Henry VII from Contemporary Sources*, 1913, Vol. 2, p. 343.

6 John Stow, *Chronicle*, ed. Howe, 1631, p. 483.

7 Richard Hakluyt, *The Principal Navigations, Voyages, Trafiques and Discoveries of the English Nation*, 1904 edn, Vol. 7, p. 146.

8 J. Heneage Jesse, *George III*, 1867, Vol. 1, p. 102.

9 J. E. Wrench, *Transatlantic London*, 1949, p. 129.

10 Ibid., p. 131.

11 Ibid., p. 131.

12 Ibid., p. 132.

13 Brian N. Morton, *Americans in London*, 1988, p. 280.

14 Wrench, *Transatlantic London*, p. 135.

15 Quotations from speeches of the Earl of Chatham to the House of Lords from Wrench, *Transatlantic London*, pp. 157, 221, 222, 223.

16 Ibid., p. 223.

17 Ibid., p. 227.

18 Ibid., p. 227.

19 Elkanah Watson, *Men and Times of the Revolution: the Memoirs of Elkanah Watson*, 1856, pp. 177–8.

20 Jesse, *George III*, Vol. 2, p. 399.

21 Ibid., p. 403.

22 William Kent, *Encyclopaedia of London*, 1970, p. 582.

23 Francis Beaumont, 'On the Tombs in Westminster', in *The Works of the English Poets from Chaucer to Cowper*, ed. Alexander Chalmers, 1810, p. 204.

24 Oliver Wendell Holmes, *Our Hundred Days in Europe*, 1886, p. 91.

25 Kent, *London for Americans*, p. 205.

26 Quotations relating to Major André from Kent, *London for Americans*, pp. 198–202.

27 Benjamin Silliman, *A Journal of Travels in England, Holland and Scotland*, 1820, Vol. 1, p. 152.

28 Charles Lamb, 'The Tombs of the Abbey', *The Works of Charles Lamb*, ed. Charles Kent, 1889, p. 147.

29 Richard Hakluyt the Elder, *Inducements to the liking of the voyage intended towards Virginia*, 1585, pp. 30, 33, 36.

30 Kent, *London for Americans*, p. 184.

31 John Beresford, *The Godfather of Downing Street: Sir George Downing 1623–84*, 1925, p. 29.

32 Wrench, *Transatlantic London*, p. 156.

33 Ibid., p. 159.

34 Roger Lockyer (ed.), *The Trial of Charles I: A Contemporary Account taken from the memoirs of Sir Thomas Herbert and John Rushworth*, 1959, pp. 136–7.

35 Kent, *London for Americans*, p. 60.

36 Jared Sparks, *Franklin Works*, 1844, Vol. 1, p. 342.

37 Morton, *Americans in London*, p. 36.

38 Edith Bolling Wilson, *Memoirs of Mrs Woodrow Wilson*, 1939, p. 230.

39 Sidney Bechet, *Treat It Gentle*, 1960, p. 128.

40 David Duff, *Queen Mary*, 1985, p. 209.

41 David Dimbleby and David Reynolds, *An Ocean Apart*, 1988, p. 114.

42 Ibid., p. 114.
43 Duff, *Queen Mary*, p. 207.
44 Ibid., p. 208.
45 Ibid., pp. 209, 213.
46 Ibid., p. 211.

Chapter 8: Little America

1 John Adams, letter to John Jay, 2 June 1785, in *Works*, Vol. 8, pp. 255–9.
2 Brian N. Morton, *Americans in London*, 1988, p. 126.
3 Henry Laurens, letter to his son, 26 March 1774, in Morton, *Americans in London*, pp. 232–3.
4 Morton, *Americans in London*, p. 219.
5 Henry James, *The Art of Travel*, 1958 edn.
6 Edmund Wilson, *Europe Without Baedecker*, 1947, pp. 4–5.
7 Edmund Wilson, *The Forties*, ed. Leon Edel, 1983, pp. 107–9.
8 Morton, *Americans in London*, p. 198.
9 Thomas Hunt Martin, *The Americans' London*, 1926, p. 79.
10 William Kent, *London for Americans*, 1950, p. 57.
11 Morton, *Americans in London*, p. 144.
12 Martin, *The Americans' London*, p. 82.
13 Morton, *Americans in London*, pp. 93–4.
14 Kent, *London for Americans*, p. 125.
15 Ibid., p. 218.
16 Ben Weinreb and Christopher Hibbert, *The London Encyclopaedia*, 1983, p. 821.
17 Morton, *Americans in London*, pp. 224–5.
18 Ibid., pp. 123–6.
19 Kent, *London for Americans*, pp. 187–90.

Index